The Dancer's Gift

The Dancer's Gift

SOCIOLOGY IN LIFE

Second Edition

Meredith Kennedy, Marty Zusman,
Tracie Gardner, and David Knox

East Carolina University

SAN DIEGO

Bassim Hamadeh, CEO and Publisher
Laura Pasquale, Acquisitions Editor
Amy Smith, Project Editor
Berenice Quirino, Associate Production Editor
Jess Estrella, Senior Graphic Designer
Stephanie Kohl, Licensing Associate
Natalie Piccotti, Director of Marketing
Kassie Graves, Vice President of Editorial
Jamie Giganti, Director of Academic Publishing

3970 Sorrento Valley Blvd., Ste. 500, San Diego, CA 92121

Meredith Kennedy dedicates this book to Owen and Sullivan, who live, love, and learn every day of their lives.

Marty Zusman dedicates *The Dancer's Gift* to his wife, Karen, the love of his life.

Tracie Gardner dedicates *The Dancer's Gift* to her parents, Carlyn and Larry Brown, who gave her the most precious gifts of all—their unconditional love and friendship.

David Knox dedicates this book to his wife, Dd, with whom the dance of life continues.

Contents

PROLOGUE

THE MUSIC PICKED up. Tambourines, sticks, and coconut shells joined the drums, and female voices flowed through the rhythms like honey and jasmine. A deep, throaty voice rose above the rest, filling the night air with a mournful glow, the sorrow of parting always on the other side of being together. The husky, beautiful voice rose and fell, riding the melody of the pulsing female chorus like a dolphin in the ocean swells, telling of love and luck and life and a thousand other things that blossomed in the hearts of those who listened.

Marcel began to move, his limbs loose and flowing in the firelight. He felt good, he felt strong, and the worries of the past few days fell away quickly. How had he thought that it wouldn't be like old times? This was fine, and he felt the goodwill of everyone as they encouraged him with their clapping and swaying. He danced and whirled, filled with Grand-mère's singing, and felt the joy rise in him, pulsing and beating and bringing life to his moves. In retrospect, Marcel would have given anything to prevent what happened next.

INTRODUCTION

S OCIOLOGY STUDENTS SOMETIMES ask, "What does sociology have to do with me?" Our answer is "everything," and this novel—a love story—is a unique way of bringing the sociological concepts and perspective into awareness. Storytelling is an age-old setting for making sense of the world and provides a way of reminding all of us that we are not alone. Storytelling is also, in every culture, a major venue for the passing on of knowledge, ideas, and values from one generation to the next. In the modern world, the transmission of knowledge has become institutionalized, and much of our learning occurs in classrooms and from textbooks. *The Dancer's Gift: Sociology in Life* combines the best of both worlds. By using fiction to illustrate the basic perspectives and concepts of sociology, we reunite the transmission of knowledge with the joy and familiarity of storytelling.

What happens when a dance major from a Caribbean island falls in love with the WASP daughter of a prominent attorney? Set in an East Coast liberal arts college, Marcel and Samantha's story crosses social, cultural, and geographical boundaries as they find their way in a confusing world. Everyone can relate to love, life, friendship, and career choices as a young adult out on their own for the first time, and Marcel and Samantha find this especially challenging coming from very different backgrounds. Leaving their respective comfort zones, they each venture into the other's world, finding adventure, delight, surprise, and finally, an unexpected trauma that uncovers difficult truths.

The basic concepts of sociology are defined and explained as the tale unfolds. The novel, with its characters, relationships, dialogue and subplots, bring these sociological concepts to life. This love-story-through-a-sociological-lens not only provides a foundation for understanding social systems but reveals our common humanity though the characters of Samantha and Marcel. Readers will learn over 200 embedded sociology terms as the story unfolds, giving depth and context as students build their own foundations in sociology.

This book is for anyone who's ever been in love, anyone who's ever felt lost and confused, anyone who has endured a crisis, and anyone who's ever wondered about the great cosmic joke of making us social creatures and then not finding an owner's manual. We think we live our lives with no script, no study guides, and no Disney endings, and the exams are on a daily basis. By studying sociology we attempt to make some sense of this, and by using stories in the learning of it, we may enrich our paths to understanding. Getting there is as important as the final destination, so read on for a journey into the sociology of life. Your destination is your own, and we hope this read helps you find your own way there.

While each of the 12 chapters of *The Dancer's Gift* reveals a new phase in the relationship between Samantha and Marcel, a specific area of sociology is introduced as a backdrop. The areas are the sociological perspective (1); socialization (2); culture (3); sex and gender (4); research methods (5); organizations (6); population and social change (7); religion (8); family (9); race and ethnicity (10); deviance (11); and stratification, social class, and economy (12).

—Meredith Kennedy, Marty E. Zusman, Tracie Gardner, and David Knox

People Like Us

The Sociological Perspective

THE CLEAR SEPTEMBER air filled Samantha's head as she breathed in, standing on the curb outside Emerson Hall. Her gaze swept the majestic brick building, wondering where the window of number 306 would be. Most of the west-facing windows of the old residence hall looked much like the others, but she knew it was there, somewhere on the third floor. Soon she would be looking out that particular window, standing in her room, a newly purchased stack of textbooks on her desk. And when she was finally there, looking out at this scene from her dorm room window, things would be different. Very different. She was considering a major in sociology, the first step in her law career, and she'd be 200 miles away from her parents. **Sociology** is the scientific study of individuals in groups, organizations, cultures and societies; and of the interrelationships of individuals, groups, organizations, cultures and societies. Samantha wants to go to law school, and plans to major in sociology in order to build a foundation of understanding how people behave in social contexts.

Back when Samantha had studied sociology in high school, she'd been surprised at how much sense it made. She had always believed as her parents had socialized her to believe, that individuals were responsible for their own destinies. Individuals who succeeded were those who had a healthy life, were motivated, had a high IQ, and worked hard. In her sociology class in high school, Samantha began to question the belief that individuals determine their life experiences and circumstances; she began to develop sociological imagination. This is the ability and willingness to see the connections between our personal lives and the social world in which we live. The term *sociological imagination* was coined by the sociologist C. Wright Mills.

Samantha learned that it was the social context—not the individual—that largely determined whether a person was educated, achieved occupational success, or lived a long life. The social context includes groups, families, and societies. Individuals, according to the sociological perspective, are shaped by the type of group or family or community or society they were born into or lived within. To help explain patterns and social outcomes, sociologists use the perspectives of functionalism, conflict, and symbolic interactionism, which Samantha found interesting.

Functionalism (also called structural-functionalism) is a theoretical perspective that views society as a system of interconnected parts that work together in harmony to maintain a state of balance and social equilibrium. Functionalism emphasizes the interconnectedness of society by focusing on how each part of society affects and is affected by other parts. When an aspect of a society or social system contributes to the stability of that social system, we say that it is functional; when some aspect of a society or social system disrupts a social system, we say that it is dysfunctional. Attending college, as Samantha is doing, is functional for the economic institution as college education prepares young adults to be productive members of the labor force. However, when young adults leave home to go to college, their families' normal patterns of interaction are disrupted; hence, going away to college may be dysfunctional for families.

Conflict perspective views society as comprised of different groups that compete for power, prestige (or social respect), and wealth. The conflict perspective explains social patterns and events by identifying which groups have power and benefit from a particular social pattern or event. For example, although the US educational system is supposed to provide all Americans with the means to achieve success, in reality, educational opportunities and the quality of education are not distributed equally. Samantha grew up in a wealthy community that provided ample funds for its public schools to provide the best educational facilities, books, materials, equipment, and personnel. According to the conflict perspective, students who live and go to school in poorer school districts are unfairly disadvantaged in their opportunities to receive a quality education.

Symbolic interactionism suggests that human behavior and emotions are influenced by meanings, labels and definitions that are learned through interaction with others. Samantha's long-term goal in college is to obtain a law degree, as she has learned from her father that the practice of law is an honorable and important role. However, sometimes Samantha questions her career goal because her friends sometimes tell lawyer jokes that portray lawyers as ruthless and greedy "sharks" that take advantage of people who have legal problems. Whether or not Samantha maintains her career goal of becoming a lawyer may depend in part on which meanings, labels, and definitions of lawyer she adopts.

Samantha always remembered her instructor's opening words: "While psychology focuses on the individual, sociology focuses on the context in which the individual is molded." She felt strongly that this knowledge would help her become a good lawyer. She couldn't wait to get started.

She looked back up at the residence hall, her home for the next year. If her new roommate happened to be looking out of 306 at the street in front of Emerson Hall, she would see Samantha Cahill and her mother getting out of a BMW and her father parking a white Lexus behind it. The Lexus had been Samantha's 18th birthday present, and she wished for the hundredth time that she'd been able to drive it herself for the four-hour trip to school. But her father had wanted to test it out, make sure the front end was aligned, the brakes working, everything shipshape before he left his youngest daughter on her own with it.

"Dad, it's a brand-new car," Samantha had pointed out. Of course he was ready for this, with his talk about wind shear, timing chains, and high-speed stress. And of course she'd been a member of the Cahill family long enough (18 and a half years, in fact) to be able to translate: I'm not spending a total of eight hours in one day in the car with your mother. You can do half of it. It won't kill you.

The four-hour ride with her mother hadn't killed her, but she'd lost a few zillion more lung cells in the thick, secondhand carbon-monoxide atmosphere, compliments of Carlton cigarettes. Her mother's **individualism** (a philosophy in which an individual's decisions and actions are based on his or her own wants and needs rather than on the wants and needs of the group) bothered her; the windows had to stay rolled up because her mother liked air conditioning. Her mother had chattered on and on about all the friends Samantha would be making at school and stories about her own year of college.

"You know, not many of us girls back then went for more than a year or two. As a **group** (two or more people who share a common identity and interact on a regular basis), we used to say if it took you more than two years at college to find a husband, you might as well give it up!" Samantha's mother tittered. "Can you imagine, Sammy? We were worried about being old maids at age 20. And now you're on your way to a law career. I never would have thought of that at your age! Just don't forget about getting married, honey, I do expect grandchildren someday."

At that point Samantha had put on her iPod headphones and cranked the music up as far as it would go. In fact, her mother's freshman—and only—year of college had been quite successful. She had met Winston Edward Cahill, a pre-law junior, and they had married after Ed graduated.

Three years of law school later he had joined his father's law firm in northern New Hampshire, and their first daughter, Audrey, had been born soon after. Samantha had come along two years after that, and the Cahill family was complete. Now her father's law firm was the second largest in the state, and W. Edward Cahill looked forward to having his younger daughter carry on the tradition and eventually become a partner. Samantha suspected her father had really wanted a son to carry on the family law tradition, which just meant she would have to be better and smarter than any son would have been. Audrey, the firstborn, was firmly entrenched in a graphic arts career and wanted nothing to do with law.

Samantha wondered if she'd have to come up with an extraneous first initial when she finished law school. Everyone at her father's firm was W. Edward or L. Talbott or P. Fitzsimmons ("Fitz" to his friends and colleagues) something-or-other. Nobody in the law world went by his or her first name. She could be "S. Burns Cahill"; Burns was her middle name as well as her mother's maiden name, but she wasn't crazy about being known as "Burns." Maybe she could add an initial to the front: M. Samantha Cahill (and just leave everyone wondering what the M stood for).

"Samantha, honey," called her father, W. Edward, "is this box on top fragile?" He had the trunk of the BMW open and was pulling out a cardboard box. Her mother, who wouldn't be handling anything heavier than a cigarette, stood on the sidewalk tying a scarf over her hair and putting on large square sunglasses. They had little flaps, which extended back to her temples and were supposed to protect the skin around her eyes from sunlight. The surgical alterations to the skin around her eyes had taken years off her appearance but wouldn't stand up to natural sunlight. The special glasses had cost $650.

"Look, Sammy," said her mother as Samantha set the box down on the sidewalk. She followed her mother's gaze to the residence hall next to Emerson. A young Black man was carrying a battered duffel bag up the steps. He was tall and slender and had a magnificent head of dreadlocks.

"Hmmm," mused her mother, and Samantha felt herself going tense. *Don't, Mom! Whatever you're going to say*—"Well, I think that's just fine," said Mrs. Cahill. "I think it's *wonderful* that the school gives opportunities to people like that."

"Mom," hissed Samantha.

"*What*, Sammy."

"'People like that?'" Come *on*, Mom! That's so snobby."

"Oh, relax, Samantha. Just look at him, with his duffel bag and his dreadlocks. I'm just saying that he doesn't *look* like he can afford the $25,000 tuition for a semester here, and I think it's great that he's gotten some help. In this day and age, colleges need to diversify, that's all. Or am I not allowed to express my opinion?" Samantha could hear an abrasive edge to her mother's voice, which could easily escalate into shrill accusations. Familiar territory, parry and defense, and Samantha didn't want to go there. Not today, not now. This was the first day of her real life, and she wouldn't let her mother spoil it with her harping on **stereotypes**. This is an oversimplified or exaggerated generalization about the characteristics and behaviors of a category of individuals.

Stereotypes are either untrue or gross distortions of reality. Mrs. Cahill is stereotyping the young man she sees on the basis of his race and appearance; she assumes that lower-class Blacks have low levels of intelligence and are not well suited for the academic rigors of the university. Mrs. Cahill assumes that the young Black man she observed must have been accepted into the university because of affirmative action, rather than on his own merit.

Gritting her teeth, Samantha replied, "Do you have the dorm list, Mom? Let's go in and find my room." She picked up the moving box and headed up the steps. Glancing over at the hall next door, the guy with the duffel bag was already gone.

***

When they found 306, Samantha's mother was the first one into the room. She promptly planted herself in front of a young woman lounging on one of the beds and extended a well-manicured hand.

"Hello, I'm Leslie Burns Cahill."

Why does she do that? thought Samantha, embarrassed by her mother's snobbish formality. Does she really expect her to fall in smoothly with *"Oh, the Cape Cod Burnses? We usually summer on Cape Cod."* This would then be Leslie Burns Cahill's cue to smile graciously (only now it's become a slightly robotic smirk since her plastic surgery) and say "No, the Gerald Burnses of New Bedford," and this would raise the gate on her mother's favorite game of **status** (a social position within a group or society), a litany of names and places that could go on *ad nauseam*.

It bugged Samantha to no end that her mother had not achieved her own status (**achieved status** is a social position gained through personal effort or choice) but bragged anyway. An accident of birth had given Leslie Burns Cahill an **ascribed status** she would otherwise never have achieved. Ascribed status is a social position that society assigns to an individual on the basis of factors over which the individual has no control. Statuses such as "male," "female," "Black," "White," "Hispanic," and "senior citizen" are ascribed statuses because individuals do not choose their sex, race, ethnicity, or age. When we are young, our social class status is ascribed because we do not choose or control it; our social class is determined by that of our family. In our adulthood, we can influence our social class by the choices we make in education, employment, and/or marriage. Thus, in adulthood, our social class status is achieved. Mrs. Cahill was born into an upper-class family, so her upper-class status growing up was an ascribed status. However, she chose to marry a successful attorney; consequently, her social class status as an adult is an achieved status.

Seeming unimpressed by Mrs. Cahill's social graces, Samantha's roommate casually shook Leslie Burns Cahill's hand and replied, "Hi. Dash Goldman." Samantha wondered if her roommate realized how close she'd come to a verbal marathon of senators, board members, benefactors, and brittle ex-wives and if she would have been suitably impressed. Dash Goldman, with her buzzed, spiked, blond hair, the ring in her eyebrow, orange lipstick, and blue nail polish, presented a striking contrast to the conservatively groomed Mrs. Cahill. Samantha liked her already and looked forward to hanging out with her and other residents of the dorm. Although she knew she'd be beginning anew without emotional ties as a secondary group, she hoped that before long she would be able to develop some primary group relationships at school. **Primary groups** are small and characterized by personal and informal interaction that is personal and informal (a family, for example). Like many first-semester college students, Samantha hopes to form primary group relationships with her dorm roommates. A **secondary group** may be large or small and is characterized by interaction that is impersonal and formal. Until Samantha develops close, personal relationships with other students, most of her social interactions at school will be in secondary groups.

Mrs. Cahill blinked, the handshake frozen in space between them, and then glanced at a piece of paper in her left hand. "Oh!" She chirped, the prefabricated smile still perfectly in place, the eyes expressionless as they glanced back up and settled on the young woman's pierced eyebrow. "It says "Eleanor Goldman" on the dorm assignment list."

The roommate withdrew her hand and regarded Mrs. Cahill calmly. "It used to be "Eleanor-Elaine." My mother took a pretentious pill when I was born, thought I needed a hyphenated name. I didn't. So I dropped everything but the dash."

Samantha stepped in front of her mother and shook her roommate's hand before Mrs. Cahill could get her voice back. Samantha smiled broadly and said, "Hi Dash. I'm Samantha." *Can you tell my mother takes a pretentious pill daily? Along with her scotch and Perrier with a twist of lemon?* She would have sold her soul at that moment to have her parents beamed to a distant planet.

***

Samantha picked at her prime rib and folded and refolded the linen napkin in her lap. She had wanted to eat at the cafeteria, but her mother wouldn't have it. This was it, the big send-off, and they had to do it right (translated: her way). Nothing but a $200 dinner at a fancy downtown restaurant would do, even if Samantha knew it would take forever and she didn't think she could bear much more of her mother's sniping at her father. She glanced over at her dad, who was getting progressively drunk, his usual way of coping. Thank God Dash Goldman had declined Leslie Burns Cahill's offer to join them for dinner. Samantha was very uncomfortable with her parents' personalities and her own self-concept.

In psychology, **personality** refers to a relatively enduring set of qualities and traits that characterize an individual. From a sociological perspective, personality may be viewed as being influenced by social contexts. For example, Samantha displays an outgoing, gregarious personality when she is with her friends but a withdrawn and subdued personality when she is with her parents.

Self-concept is the image an individual has of him- or herself. Sociologists emphasize that we develop our self-concepts through interaction with others. According to sociologist C. H. Cooley (1864–1929), during social interaction we note how others view us by how they respond and what they say to us. This image of ourselves that is conveyed by how others interact with us is called the "looking-glass self." Samantha's self-concept has been shaped in part by what her parents have said to her and the ways in which they have responded to her over the years. For example, Samantha's parents have consistently praised her for her academic accomplishments, which has contributed to Samantha's being self-confident and ambitious. However, her parents have also responded to Samantha as if she were better than other kids because of her privileged upbringing and family background. Samantha is beginning to feel uncomfortable with this self-concept of superiority.

Mrs. Cahill had already sent her poached salmon back to the kitchen twice.

"You can always tell when there's Oriental staff in the kitchen," said Mrs. Cahill, to no one in particular. "They never cook the fish well enough."

Slouching in her chair, Samantha mumbled, "*Asian*, Mom." Her mother looked at her archly, and Samantha knew she had overstepped her **role** (a set of behaviors associated with a particular status or social position). Samantha sighed; this kind of role conflict and role strain plagued her relationships with her parents.

Role conflict is a situation in which an individual occupying two different social statuses or positions is confronted with conflicting role expectations. As a student, if Samantha lets a racial slur slide by she feels she is perpetuating negative stereotypes. As a daughter, she should keep her mouth shut and not react to her mother's comment. In one case she disrespects Asian people, in the other she disrespects her mother—she can't respect both at the same time in this situation. **Role strain,** on the other hand, is a situation in which one status involves conflicting expectations. Samantha finds it difficult to know what constitutes being a good daughter; her father wants her to finish college and law school in order to become a lawyer, while her mother wants her to get married and raise a family.

Ed Cahill ordered another martini.

Samantha watched her mother out of the corner of her eye as Mrs. Cahill fussed over the meal and picked the croutons off her salad. Hadn't her mother once been beautiful? What had happened? *Maybe it was the surgery*, thought Samantha. Her smile had changed; she looked different now. In an attempt to keep the now-smooth skin around her eyes quiescent, she seemed to be cultivating a smile that only used the lower half of her face. It was a little disconcerting, even after a year. Samantha glanced away; it seemed to her that her mother's new face, now free of crow's feet, had disguised her natural beauty, replacing her smile with some kind of infomercial. This embarrassed Samantha, who sometimes felt an attack of lame excuses about to burst from her mouth. She could practically see the dialogue bubbles floating around the room: *Sorry, she's missing her flower arranging class and that makes her nervous ... She means well, she just has to boost her self-esteem with a little name-dropping ...* Samantha's thoughts threatened to spiral out of control, scattering like leaves in a dust storm.

Samantha's mother was talking about school again.

"Samantha, this seems to be a very progressive school. I think it will be so good for you to be exposed to these people. A Jewish roommate! And that Black boy next door, he looked like one of those Rastas or something. All that hair. I wonder if there are even Iranians on campus. Ed, didn't Mary Ellen Whittaker say her son is going to school with an Iranian boy?"

Ignoring his wife, Ed Cahill turned to Samantha and smiled. Or tried to. "You know, honey, all those people—whatever, diversity—this will be great preparation for your law career. You never know who you'll have to defend."

"'Those people' are just going to school here, like everyone else!" Samantha exclaimed, exasperated. "They're not here to help me with my law career!" For God's sake, did they have to be so narrow-minded? The manifest function of school was to educate; the latent function was to find friends, get married, and escape parents! She made a conscious decision to stay away from the stereotypes her parents seemed to embrace. She didn't like the belief that people of other races, religions, and nationalities were inferior. **Manifest function** is a consequence or outcome that is intended and commonly recognized. Most people recognize that the intended consequence or outcome of college is to provide education that is needed to prepare individuals for the workforce. **Latent function** is a consequence or outcome that is unintended and not commonly recognized. Latent functions of a college education include providing opportunities to make friends and to find a life partner. College also helps young adults like Samantha become independent from their parents.

"Ed, maybe you can get away with ignoring a question in the courtroom, but I certainly don't appreciate it," said Mrs. Cahill icily. She was adept at making an issue out of anything; Samantha often thought her mother should have become a lawyer.

Samantha looked at her parents and wondered which to do first: laugh like a hyena or run naked through the potted ferns. Maybe both. In desperation she asked her father about his work.

"What's going on with the Carson Corporation case? Are they still trying to put Mrs. Wheeler out on the street?"

"Mrs. Wheeler will be well taken care of. She's the only remaining holdout of the 38 houses they're buying up," her father replied.

"Don't you mean 'taking over?' So the corporation can tear all the houses down, raze the forest, and put up another factory nobody needs?"

"Sammy, Carson will be providing over a thousand new jobs once the factory is up and running, and once we get Mrs. Wheeler to cooperate, that shouldn't take more than 18 months or so. They'll be building new roads, new sewer systems, and helping the economy. Everyone will benefit."

"Except the families forced out of their homes, except everyone else in the community who will now have higher taxes to pay, except the piping plover whose habitat will be destroyed. If I were an attorney, I'd be defending the neighborhood association fighting this factory project, not helping the Carson Corporation," Samantha declared, her prime rib forgotten.

"Come on, Sammy," replied her father. "You won't make any money doing that, and the factory's got to be built *somewhere*. Once the neighborhood association sees the benefits that will eventually come from the project, they'll change their tune. There's always conflict between the tree-huggers and the corporations."

"Samantha," interjected her mother, "They shouldn't have to hold up an important project like this on account of some tree frog."

Both Samantha and Ed Cahill looked at her mother.

"It's a bird, Mom. The piping plover is a bird, and it's endangered ."

***

Finally, Samantha found herself in her dorm room after her parents had left for the drive home. She flopped back on her bed, her hands behind her head, exhausted but too excited to sleep. At last, at last, she's here and her parents are not. *Thank God.*

***

Marcel Devereaux dropped the duffel bag on the bed and stretched his arms up over his head. Carrying it from the bus station had made his shoulders ache, and his finely tuned dancer's body felt every little pull and strain. If he didn't straighten his neck and spine now, the ache in his muscles would work its way deeper, seeping like a damp fog into his bones. It would slow his reflexes and give an edge to his movements, which normally flowed like cream from an overturned bucket. But now, after 16 hours in transit, some of those hours in a cramped aircraft seat and many wandering through airport terminals, he didn't feel very smooth and flowing. With a sigh, he sat down next to the old duffel bag and surveyed his room.

It was a nice room, spacious and light with a dormer window, a couple of small desks, and two closets. It wasn't big enough to do any real stretching or dance. He would have to spend a lot of time in the studios and practice rooms for that. But Marcel was looking forward to sharing a room with only one other person, a change from sleeping with three brothers at home, two in each bed. What luxury—a bed all to himself, his own closet, and never having to wait for the bathroom! This was unheard-of in his society on the Caribbean island of Martinique; having a mama, grandma, and three sisters meant that the one bathroom was usually occupied, and the five men of the family had to wait. It did have running water, but his father usually just gave up and used the outhouse by the garden. Not Marcel; he hated the dirty, fly-infested wooden box. He always waited for the real toilet. **Society** is the people, institutions, and culture of a defined territory. The society into which you are born shapes your thoughts and actions. Marcel is who he is (in part) because he comes from the culture of Martinique.

Another twin bed in the dorm room faced his, already made up with a plain bedspread, with a garment bag draped across it. Matching suitcases stood outside the closet at the end of the bed, the property of his as-yet-unseen roommate. The luggage set looked brand new and very expensive, perhaps a graduation gift from a relative? Marcel opened up a crumpled piece of paper from his jacket pocket, the dorm list. "Kyle Parker" occupied the other bed. He hadn't been here when Marcel first arrived; maybe he was at the cafeteria.

Marcel regarded the old duffel bag on the bed next to him; it looked battered and deflated. He thought about the folk society in which he was reared and where the bag was made; a lady who went to his family's church had given it to him. **Folk society** is a traditional society that emphasizes personal interactions, religious morals, family importance, and personal ties. The interaction in Marcel's folk society is characterized by long-standing good manners, shared beliefs, sharing of belongings, and the providing of comfort, which seems to have been passed unchanged from generation to generation.

"Marcel, you go on and take it," Mrs. Matthias had said, handing him the bag with a catch in her voice. "Clement would be proud to know it's going to America, you going to college and all. The good Lord knows Clement don't need it no more."

"Yes, ma'am. Thank you, ma'am," Marcel had said, accepting the bag graciously. She had dabbed at her eyes and blown her nose loudly into a lace hanker chef. Clement Matthias, her son, had died in a fall from a cliff last year. Marcel's mother, Thielda Devereaux, had sat Mrs. Matthias down with a glass of lemonade and patted her hand, and the two women had an interaction in which they had mourned long and loud about beloved sons who died and who went away to school.

Clement's duffel bag now contained all of Marcel's worldly possessions, including his clothes, a pair of sneakers, a rosary given to him by his mother, and a dog-eared copy of Pride and Prejudice, his favorite book. His youngest brother, Lyon, had given him a broken Pez dispenser (after eating up all the Pez candies first). Marcel smiled and put it away in a desk drawer, reminding himself to buy Lyon a new one and send it to him—with the candy.

It took only a few minutes to unpack the duffel bag and get everything put away. The bag itself he stuffed into the back of the closet, feeling vaguely disloyal for not wanting to leave it out in the open, next to Kyle Parker's new matching luggage.

Marcel got undressed, wanting to shower first before going to the cafeteria, and put on a cotton bathrobe, made for him by his oldest sister, Daria. Sitting on his bed, Marcel rubbed his aching feet. The new shiny shoes purchased by his mother for the big trip had chafed and pinched his feet mercilessly.

"*Maman*," he had moaned, "I'm a *dancer*. I *need* my feet. What good will they do if these shoes make to blister me and drop them off my own legs! Won't I lose my scholarship then?"

"No sassin', Mister Man," his mother had retorted. "Nobody say that Thielda Devereaux babies walkin' round barefoot. Come you here, tuck you shirt in." And she proceeded to do it for him. After eight babies, she was the adored matriarch of her seven living children, and she took no nonsense from any of them. Resistance was hopeless.

Marcel's father, Desmond Devereaux, had been in similar pain at the airport on Martinique, his normally unclad feet stuffed into pointed wingtips. Marcel smiled as he remembered the cluster of Devereaux boys at the terminal: his brothers, every single one of them uncomfortable and chafing in hand-me-down shoes, buttoned-up collars, and on best behavior under threat of doom from *Maman*. Only Marcel and his father had had to suffer the real torture of brand-new shoes; there hadn't been enough money for new ones all around, a saving grace for which his brothers were very grateful.

Desmond Devereaux had gruffly hugged his son before he got on the plane, and Marcel had been surprised to see the old man's eyes glisten. He felt the depth of love often experienced in primary groups.

"Damn shoes," Desmond had muttered, wiping his eyes with a crumpled-up old hankie. "You take the be-sainted t'ings off after you get on the plane, you hear?"

And his mother. How beautiful she was, resplendent in her Sunday dress, yards and yards of magenta taffeta straining to contain an ample body created by the natural fallout of eight babies. A fake-fur hat rode majestically on her head, a prized accessory usually only seen at weddings and funerals. His sister Mariette had once snuck it out of its box in the closet and paraded around outside wearing it and hadn't been able to sit down for the rest of the day after *Maman* caught her. Mariette, Daria, and his younger sister Daphne looked lovely in brightly flowered dresses and big hats. They reminded him of some wild and overgrown garden, blooming with bright cotton and babies. Both Mariette and Daria had young ones, and Daria was pregnant again.

Marcel had nearly suffocated in his mother's engulfing embrace. "My boy, my Mister Man," she had moaned, "leavin' so far away." It had been hard for Marcel to keep from getting choked up himself; they all knew there wouldn't be enough money for visits back home. Unless money grew on trees in America (and many on Martinique thought it did), he would be away for the whole four years of his scholarship. But now it was time to go. His future was calling him, and he didn't think he could stand another minute on this stifling, tiny island.

"*Maman*, I got to get on the plane now. I'll call you when I get there." He extracted himself from her sobbing embrace as she had pressed the rosary into his hand. She'd had it for years; he'd never seen her without it. It was symbolic of her faith.

"We'll pray for you, Marcel!" She had called out to him, and he had waved as he walked away without turning around, already missing her and the rest of his family by the gate. He didn't want anyone to see the tears in his eyes, which he couldn't blame on the shoes. He wondered how his new American peers would think of him breaking down at his departure.

***

Marcel paused, his hand on the doorknob of the dorm room door, suddenly nervous about walking down the hall to the bathroom. Was he supposed to change his clothes when he got there? He knew that the toilet facilities were unisex, but he experienced anomie with respect to the **norms** (socially defined rules of behavior). **Anomie** is a state of normlessness; a situation in which norms are conflicting or unclear, leaving individuals uncertain about how they should behave. In Marcel's case, his anomie stems from unfamiliarity with his new context. Did people walk down the hall in their bathrobes and bare feet? He would just have to go for it. What the heck, just act like you do this all the time, Marcel. Head high, he sauntered down the hallway to the unisex bathroom, swinging his toilet kit. He didn't run into anyone and heaved a sigh of relief.

After showering in the unisex bathroom (and hiding in the shower stall when two girls came in, talking loudly), Marcel returned to his room to find his new roommate in residence. Kyle Parker was a small, sallow-faced youth with glasses and a bad complexion. He was sitting at his desk, which he pulled around so that the back of it was now between himself and Marcel's bed, like a shield.

"Good evening," said Marcel politely. "I am Marcel Devereaux. You must be Kyle."

Kyle looked up from his desk, staring at Marcel as if he'd just dropped down from a spaceship. He ignored Marcel's outstretched hand, and Marcel gracefully withdrew it.

"You from Jamaica?" asked Kyle.

"No, I am from Martinique."

"Oh. ... Is that near Jamaica?"

Marcel shook his head. "No, it's farther south in the Caribbean. It's near Barbados, about 400 miles from Venezuela."

Pausing on his way to his closet, it occurred to Marcel that perhaps being barefoot in a bathrobe wasn't the best situation for meeting people for the first time. Maybe it threw them off guard. Was it his imagination, or was his roommate a little weird? Taking a deep breath and finding a deep well of good manners pounded into him by Thielda Devereaux, he turned back to Kyle and asked, "Where are you from?"

Kyle scrunched down farther in his chair, apparently engrossed by some papers on his desk. "Connecticut," he mumbled. "New Haven."

"Oh. Near New York? I am hoping to go to the Juilliard School of Dance some-day. Maybe we will be neighbors."

His roommate grunted, not looking up.

Marcel dressed quickly and put the *be-sainted* shoes back on. He tried again:

"I'm going to the cafeteria for some dinner. Do you want to come?"

There was no answer. Marcel said good-bye and headed out of the residence hall, wondering what kind of place this was where new roommates were treated so rudely, or if maybe Kyle just didn't like him.

***

The cafeteria was weird. At first Marcel wasn't sure where he was supposed to start or what he could order at the grill. A large, glass-covered island in the middle turned out to be a salad bar, and he was amazed at the variety of food it offered. At home, if they ever had a salad, it consisted of shredded cabbage with a few onions and chili sauce, but this ... this was incredible. Different kinds of lettuce (endive? baby greens? radicchio? Wasn't it all just lettuce?), vegetables, eggs, ham, crabmeat, all kinds of things. His plate finally ended up looking like a kaleidoscope, with a little of everything, even the greenish wiggling stuff. He had no idea what it was but piled it on the plate anyway, where it sagged and ran and turned the fake crabmeat green.

The girl at the cash register who checked his meal card wanted to know if he was from Jamaica.

By the time he sat down to eat, having added a plate of greasy fried chicken and a cup of tomato soup, he wasn't very hungry anymore. He sat by himself, nibbling at a drumstick, thinking of his mother's chicken and dumplings, cooked outside over an open fire in a big cast-iron pot.

How many scrumptious dinners had magically come out of that cooking pot over the years, as Marcel and his brothers and sisters had collected firewood and tended the fire? How many nights had they cleared away the cooking utensils after dinner and sat around the fire, his grandma and sisters singing, his brothers drum-ming and Marcel's feet flying across the earth, dancing his heart out under the wide Caribbean sky? The moonlit evenings and the wind sighing in the papaya trees had filled him up and made his body lighter than air. What would fill him now? Fluo-rescent lights on an unforgiving dance floor?

Stop it, Marcel. You're acting like a baby. Your future is here, not on some little island no one's ever heard of, Marcel berated himself. *Yes, my future is here, but my past is there. You can't have one without the other.*

Pushing his tray away, he left the cafeteria to find a telephone.

***

"Mr. Thibodeaux?" He could hardly hear; the connection wasn't very good. It had taken Marcel 20 minutes to get through to his neighbors, the Thibodeaux family down the road, who had a telephone. "Mr. Thibodeaux, it's Marcel! Marcel Devereaux. I'm calling from America." He didn't bother to get more specific; he'd tried to explain before he left where his school was located, but to no avail. As far as everyone there was concerned, he'd simply gone to America.

"Ah? Devereaux?" There was a commotion in the background. The phone was being handed around. A new voice came on, a schoolgirl speaking very formal English. "Yes, please? May I know who is calling, please?" Speaking with someone in America was a good chance to practice English instead of the native French.

"Hey, Francine, it's Marcel. I'm in America. Can you hear me? I'm in America!"

"Marcel! Marcel Devereaux!" More commotion as the phone was handed around again. Giggling, laughter, and exclamations piped through the line at 50 cents a minute.

"Marcel!" A new voice, female and giggling. "Hallo, Marcel! Have you seen Snoop Dogg?"

Marcel grinned into the phone. "No, Marie, I haven't seen Snoop Dogg. I'm going to his house next week, though." Marie, the oldest Thibodeaux girl, passed this tidbit on and he could hear riotous laughter in the background.

"Marie? Marie! Can you please—" More giggling and exclamations. The phone was passed around again. *For God's sake, are they playing football with it?*

"Marie, I want to speak to my—"

"Hallo, is that Marcel?" Yet a new voice. *Maman* Thibodeaux.

"Yes, ma'am. Good evening, ma'am. How are you?"

"I am just fine, Marcel. Are you in America? Are you well?"

"Yes, ma'am. I'm in America. I'm fine. And the family? Is everyone there well?"

"Oh, yes, Marcel! Everyone is fine! How is it in America?"

"Well, it's fine, everything is—Mrs. Thibodeaux, can I speak to my mother, please?"

"She is coming, Marcel! I sent my son to get your brother, he says she's in the pumpkin patch."

There was another interminable round of pass-the-phone, and finally a beloved voice sailed through the line, from 2000 miles away.

"Wah! Wah!" Thielda Devereaux was reduced to incoherent joyful noises.

"Hallo, *Maman*! I'm in America!"

"My boy! My boy!" He could feel her face smiling as if it would split.

"*Maman*, what time is it there? It's 7:30 here."

"What? No, Marcel, it's 5:30! You watch is wrong!"

Marcel laughed. "No, Maman, it's the time change, it's 7:30 here."

"What? Say you what, my boy? You don't be changin' the time, you better change you clock. It's 5:30! Are you eating? What they feedin' you there?"

"Yes, Maman, there's plenty to eat. I went to the cafeteria."

"The what? Liberia? What?"

"No, no, the cafeteria. Where we eat. You can get ice cream there, and fried chicken, and they even have a salad bar."

"A bar? You goin' to the bar already, Marcel? You supposed to be in school!"

"No, no, Maman! I just meant—they have different kinds of lettuce, and—well, you give my love to everybody, okay, Maman? Tell everyone I called from America!"

And he hung up the phone. Tell everyone I miss them, and I miss you, and I don't know how I'll ever dance without Grandma's singing and Sebastian on his drums, and I wish they had papayas here. And please tell Dad these shoes hurt like holy hell.

***

Back in his dorm room, Marcel flopped down on his bed, his hands behind his head. He was exhausted, but too wound up to sleep. At last, at last, he's here and his parents are not. Oh, my God.

***

Chapter 1 Study Questions
THE SOCIOLOGICAL PERSPECTIVE

1. What is Samantha's major, what is her professional goal, and how will sociology help her to achieve this goal? What is **sociology**?

2. Criticize the statement, "Individuals create their own destiny." How do the social contexts in which one lives influence whether one goes to school, is occupationally successful, or lives a long life? Define sociological imagination.

3. What are three major sociological perspectives? Define each.

4. Psychology focuses on the individual. What does sociology focus on?

5. What philosophy did Mrs. Cahill display by insisting on smoking with the windows rolled up?

6. Define group. How was this a source of Mrs. Cahill's view that college was for a woman to find a husband?

7. Specify the basis for Mrs. Cahill's stereotyping comments.

8. Define achieved status and ascribed status. Which applies to Mr. and Mrs. Cahill, respectively? Explain.

9. Define primary group and secondary group. What is an example of Samantha's primary and secondary groups?

10. Give an example of how one's social context affects one's personality.

11. Define self-concept and specify its source. Samantha is beginning to feel uncomfortable with what aspect of her personality?

12. Define role, role strain, and role conflict. Give examples using Samantha and her mother/father.

13. Define manifest function and latent function and offer examples in reference to education.

14. Where is Marcel from, and how many live in his house? Compare the folk society where he grew up with American society.

15. What are norms? Give an example of a norm regarding bathroom use.

16. What is the term that describes unclear norms? How did this apply to Marcel and bathroom use in the dorm?

17. What is the name of Marcel's roommate? How did he treat Marcel the first time they met?

18. Give instances of Marcel being homesick.

CHAPTER 2

Weirdness in the World
Culture

"COME ON, SAMANTHA," said Dash Goldman, "Get your nose out of the books and get your ass out here. We're gonna meet the geeks and goddesses of Emerson Hall."

Even though classes had not yet begun, Samantha was already reading the first chapters in her textbooks. If she was going to be a lawyer, she had to begin to act the part by immersing herself in her work responsibilities. This was how she involved herself in **anticipatory socialization** (the process by which people prepare for future roles before they actually enter those roles); reading, studying, and acting, as she had seen her father and his associates do.

Samantha turned around in her chair and saw her roommate standing in the open doorway to their room. Dash leaned insolently against the doorframe, one hand on her hip, the other playing with her spiky blond hair. Low-slung jeans and a short tank top exposed her midriff, which sported a ring with a tiny dangling skull in her navel. She was wearing thick black mascara, in such stark contrast to her white-blond hair and pale pink lipstick that it appeared as if her eyes were just visiting from someone else's face. She loved dressing this way and upsetting her parents' values of being clean-cut and proper. **Values** are ideas about what is considered good versus bad; right versus wrong; desirable versus undesirable. Dash's value for self-expression is reflected in her unconventional appearance.

"Come, come," said Dash, entering the room and crossing to Samantha's desk, where she closed the textbook lying among the notebooks and pens. "You said you wanted to meet people in the dorm, and nobody starts reading their textbooks before classes even begin. You think you're going to become a lawyer tomorrow?

"People are gonna start thinking you're a geek instead of a goddess and *we don't want that.*" She pulled Samantha up by the elbow out of her chair and snatched the pen out of her hand. This language reminded Samantha of the Sapir-Whorf hypothesis. **Language** is a shared system of words that have agreed-upon meanings and enable people to express and communicate ideas and feelings. Although "geek" is a slang term that originally referred to a carnival performer whose act involved biting the head off a live chicken or snake, Samantha knows that the word geek today means someone who is not popular, fun, or cool. The **Sapir-Whorf hypothesis** is the idea that language shapes our perception of reality. For example, the words geek and nerd in US culture leads to the perception that some students are geeks and nerds.

"Con—" Dash flicked the pen into the trash where it pinged against the metal rim "—fiscated!"

Laughing, Samantha allowed herself to be dragged out of their room and into the corridor of Emerson Hall's third floor. She wanted to belong, to be a member of a primary group.

"Hey, Dash," said a guy in a towel and T-shirt emerging from the south end bathroom. "Hey, Brett," Dash answered. "Brett, Samantha; Samantha, Brett." Dash waved her hand back and forth between them as if herding names through the air.

"Hi, Brett," Samantha smiled at him.

"Hey, Samantha, you must be the bookworm roommate," he answered. Samantha blushed and glanced at Dash. What had she been telling everyone? Dash was unrepentant and only shrugged.

"What's the number for?" Samantha pointed at a round blue sticker stuck to Brett's forearm with the number 4 on it. "Oh, that's from Daly's ... thing, whatever you call it. I got a four for singing "Jingle Bells" in Japanese and having a pet tarantula."

"*Here?*" demanded Dash. "You have a tarantula here?" Brett laughed. "No, I didn't bring it. My little brother has it back home, don't worry!"

"Well, thank God for that!" said Dash. "Sasha's snake is cool. Tarantulas are *not* cool. I'm checking into a motel if you ever bring that thing in here! There oughtta be some law against tarantulas." She called after him as he headed into his room.

Brett laughed and waved her away. **Laws** are social norms that are instituted by political action and enforced by political authority, such as police or other agents of the state.

"Someone has a snake here?" asked Samantha, trying to keep up with her roommate, who was on a mission, dragging her down the hall. "Shhh! Nobody's supposed to know!" hissed Dash. "The RAs, I mean. It's really cool, though; I'll show you later. She feeds it rats. Right now we're going to see Daly Brown to get you a number, but I don't think it will be very high." Dash rolled her black-rimmed eyes at Samantha, who had no clue what she was talking about.

***

It seemed to Marcel that he would never get to dance. He had been to endless meetings, orientations, and his other classes in the five days since arriving at school. Everyone he met seemed to have some very specific task to accomplish with him, and then he was hustled to the next person and the next office, where they completed one small task and sent him elsewhere to get a signature or complete another form. There was a glitch with one of the scholarship forms he had turned into one office, so he was sent somewhere else where they dealt with that particular form. It was in a different building, and by the time he'd gotten back to the first office, they had closed for lunch. The organic solidarity of US society was certainly much different from the mechanical solidarity of Martinique.

The term **solidarity** refers to a sense of social unity, cohesion, and sense of belonging among members of a society. Sociologist Emile Durkheim (1858–1917) noted that solidarity in traditional agricultural societies differs from solidarity in modern, industrialized societies. In traditional societies, most people live in small villages where everyone depends on farming for a livelihood. All adult members of the society perform similar work roles based on traditional routines and procedures that have been handed down from previous generations. According to Durkheim, in traditional societies such as Marcel's home country of Martinique, social unity, or solidarity, is based on similarities among people in their activities and values. Durkheim called this type of solidarity **mechanical solidarity.**

In contrast, modern, industrialized societies such as the United States are characterized by what Durkheim called **organic solidarity**, social unity based on mutual dependency and the need to cooperate in order to survive. Modern societies are characterized by a high division of labor and specialization of work roles; rather than adults working in similar livelihoods, there is a wide range of occupations in modern societies. Although workers in modern societies are specialized in their occupations, they are not self-sufficient—they depend on others to produce and distribute food, clothing, housing, water, heat, and other goods and services. This mutual dependency provides the basis for social solidarity in modern societies.

Now Marcel was sitting in the office of the school guidance counselor, the one who had helped arrange his scholarship and transportation. Marjorie Trask was about 45, with permed auburn hair and a bright smile.

"Please, call me Marjorie, Marcel. All of our international students do. Have you met Ben Williamson?"

"No, ma'am."

"Marjorie, please! Ben's wonderful, you'll like him. He's one of the other Black students here on campus. We do have 11 Black students. Or do you prefer 'African American?'"

"Black is fine, ma'am."

This wouldn't be the last time Marcel would encounter confusion between his race and his ethnicity. **Race** is a socially defined category of people who are believed to share distinct physical characteristics that are deemed socially significant. Because of Marcel's dark skin and hair texture, he is categorized as "Black." Racial categories are often imprecise and misleading. For example, some of Marcel's classmates may categorize Marcel as "African American." However, Marcel's ancestors are not from Africa; they are from Martinique, so Marcel is not African American.

Ethnicity is a shared cultural heritage or nationality. Ethnic groups may be distinguished on the basis of shared language, religious beliefs and practices, dietary customs, forms of family structure and roles, music and dance, and national origin. Marcel's race is Black, and his ethnicity is West Indian as he was born on Martinique in the West Indies and shares the cultural heritage (language, dietary customs, etc.) of other West Indians.

"Well, 11 Black students, of course, plus 10 Asians and one Israeli. And we want everyone to feel as though you're part of a family while you're here at school. An international family. You know, you're the first student we've had from the West Indies." This had been a feather in her cap, and she beamed at him. "I know adjusting to a new place and a new culture can be difficult, Marcel." Marjorie Trask's eyes were full of compassion. "Do you have any issues you wish to share?"

Culture is the ideas, material objects, and ways of life that characterize a society. Culture includes knowledge and beliefs, values, technology, symbols (including language), and norms. Marjorie knows that Marcel comes from a culture whose beliefs and norms are different from those found in the United States. For example, traditional Martinique culture includes the belief in and practice of voodoo. Most Americans believe that voodoo is a silly and superstitious practice found in primitive cultures.

"No, ma'am."

"Oh. ... Well, here's my card, Marcel. You can call me anytime, if you have any questions, or if you just need to talk."

"Thank you, ma'am."

She sighed. "*Marjorie*, please, Marcel. I want you to feel you can come to me anytime. Okay?" She smiled broadly, her eyes searching his face and a friendly hand on his shoulder.

"Yes, Marjorie, ma'am. Good-bye, ma'am," he said to Ms. Trask as he left the office and headed over to the music school.

***

The instructor for Jazz Dance was Esther Cady. She was a very small woman of about 50, with close-cropped gray hair, large tortoiseshell glasses, and a throaty, booming voice, molded by three decades of dance studio acoustics. In fact, her size was the only thing small about her; the way she seemed to fill up a room and draw everyone's attention reminded Marcel of his mother, who could have picked up Esther Cady under one arm. But he wouldn't advise trying it.

He'd been on pins and needles at the guidance counselor's office, dying to finish up and get to the music school. Now he was finally here, in the Jazz Dance studio with Esther Cady and 18 other students. Modern Dance would begin tomorrow, and Marcel felt the stirrings of trepidation tug at his stomach.

"I expect everyone to be warmed up by the time class begins," announced Esther Cady. "You don't need any hand-holding through stretches and warmups, and if your schedule has other classes back to back with dance, change it. You'll need at least half an hour beforehand to get properly prepared. Remember, your body is a precision instrument, deserving of respect. Itzhak Perlman wouldn't perform a concert without carefully tuning his violin first, and you should all see your bodies the same way. Even if you think you're just practicing, every time you step onto the dance floor, you need to prepare your mind and body as if you're doing a sell-out engagement at Carnegie Hall." Professor Cady stood perfectly straight in the center of the dance floor, all 5 feet 1 inch of her; chin up, looking each student in the eye as she spoke. Or rather, made her announcements; each statement was definitive and vitally important socialization, the words carefully chosen and fired off like artillery. **Socialization** is the process by which individuals learn and generally accept the culture and expectations of a particular society or social group. Professor Cady is socializing her dance students according to her expectations about student performance in her classes.

Marcel, suddenly an uncharacteristic bundle of nerves, wondered if she was like this at home—*I am now going to cook breakfast, dear, and it will be the best breakfast it can possibly be. It may look like toast and oatmeal, but if centered and prepared properly, it will become champagne and caviar.*

Professor Cady began walking slowly up and down the line of hopeful young dancers as she spoke. Her trim body, clad in a black leotard and bright red sweat pants, seemed to glide over the floor. "If you're looking for two hours of goofing off every Wednesday and Friday, you're in the wrong place. If you feel like skipping dance class because you were out partying the night before, you won't find any sympathy here. Either this is your reference group or you need to do something else in life. If you want a lot of hand-holding, if you're content with mediocrity, you might as well leave now." A **reference group** serves as a model for our values, beliefs, and behaviors. A reference group may be a group to which we belong, such as Professor Cady's dance class. A reference group may also be a group that we identify strongly with even though we are not a member of it.

The silence in the studio was palpable as all 19 students watched the fiery professor. Marcel was aware of dryness in his throat and the pulsing of blood at his temples. This was the kind of authority he remembered from his grade school days in Martinique—he and Professor Cady should get along very well.

"But you aren't here for any of that!" thundered Esther Cady. "You're here because you're driven, you're powered by the dance, you have the seeds of excellence in you, and you cannot rest until you've coaxed them into bloom! Your role will be to work hard, harder than you've ever worked. Your body will fight you, your balance will elude you, your spirit will flag, but if you have the drive and the attitude, my role is to help you every step of the way."

Marcel found himself looking into Professor Cady's electric blue eyes as she came to a full stop directly in front of him. Taking him by both hands, she pulled him out of the lineup into the center of the dance floor, never breaking eye contact. A flush of perspiration prickled at the back of his neck.

Dropping his hands, Esther Cady stood back and smiled. "All right, let's see your moves, Jamaica." She turned and motioned to a guy in a black T-shirt sitting in the sound booth.

Music began to play, keyboards and percussion; Marcel didn't recognize it. He closed his eyes. This was it; this was what he'd been working toward for the last 10 years of his life. He'd been counting the days until he could leave Martinique, the island of his birth, the island of his imprisonment. It had seemed so small and confining, especially for the last year, definitely after he'd gotten word that he'd received a full scholarship to come here. He was finally on his way to becoming a member of a dance group, to becoming a great dancer, and someday he would be on Broadway.

Eyes still closed, Marcel drew in a smooth, warm breath full of light. A pulse beginning in his feet moved up his legs and spine and unfolded his arms like the release of a bowstring, and he began to dance.

***

Daly Brown's room was at the north end of the third floor hall. He shared it with Kevin Bittner, a biology major from Pennsylvania. The door was ajar as Dash and Samantha approached.

"Daly!" said Dash, as she barged into the room, pushing the door all the way open. "We got a virgin here."

"What? Dash!" Samantha tried to get her friend's attention, but Dash ignored her and made brief introductions. Samantha was shocked. There seemed to be nothing Dash wouldn't talk about, to anyone! Samantha was not at all comfortable talking about virginity and other sexual topics so openly. Growing up in her parents' home, the discussion of sexuality was considered a **taboo**. This is a norm that prohibits certain behaviors. Samantha's parents taught her that open discussion of sexuality is forbidden; thus, talking about sexuality or using sexual terminology was a taboo in Samantha's family. She did not realize that Dash was just joking and used "virgin" because Samantha had not been tested by Daly's Bizarrotron.

"Samantha, Daly Brown. That's Kevin." She motioned to a reclining figure on one of the beds, who hid behind a magazine. Daly was sitting in a chair, wearing what looked like a pair of orange silk harem pants. He had scraggly reddish hair down to his shoulders and a goatee. Samantha couldn't help staring at his chest, which was completely covered with tattoos: flaming skulls, barbed wire, a swastika, a nun with a spear through her head (which raised questions about his beliefs), all splashed across his skinny chest like a billboard for a horror movie marathon. **Beliefs** are ideas about what is true and not true. Beliefs are a component of culture; they are learned through socialization, guide our behavior, and change over time. A spiral snail shell dangled from one ear, and a purple rabbit's foot hung on a chain around his neck. Flames from the skull tattoo looked as if they might ignite the rabbit's foot at any second. Looking at Daly's appearance, Samantha wonders what Daly's beliefs are concerning religion, humanity, and conformity.

Samantha had never met anyone like Daly Brown. She'd seen people like him in New York City, Mohawk-wearing pierced and tattooed members of a subculture or maybe a counterculture of self-expression, but she'd never seen such body art close up. A **subculture** is a group within a dominant culture that differs from the larger culture in one or more important ways. Daly may be part of a youth subculture that embraces appearance norms that differ from those of the mainstream culture. **Counterculture** is a subculture with values or beliefs that oppose those of the mainstream culture. A subculture is different from the mainstream culture, but a counterculture actively opposes the mainstream culture, often through organized rebellion or political action. Samantha doesn't know Daly well enough to say whether he is a member of a subculture or a counterculture.

Daly said nothing but analyzed Samantha with his light blue eyes. He observed her gestures, her language, and the way she carried herself. *Classic WASP material. Very cute, button-down shirt, jeans, natural long hair, probably shows jumping horses or something. I'm guessing a three.*

Samantha grinned nervously and said, "Hi, Daly. How's it going?" The other guy—was his name Kevin?—remained buried in his magazine, so she didn't say anything to him.

"Samantha's gonna be a lawyer like her dad," offered Dash, seating herself on the edge of the empty bed.

"Mmm-hmm," said Daly, as he picked up what looked like a ray gun or an elaborate squirt gun from his desk. It was bright green plastic with *things* on it, and he fiddled intently with the little knobs and … things, as if making careful calculations.

Apparently satisfied, he turned his attention to Samantha again and pointed the contraption at her chest.

"Well, we'll just see what the *Bizarrotron* has to say, shall we?" he said. His face was dead serious.

"The—what? What is that thing?" Samantha asked.

"Excuse me, *I'll* be asking the questions here," said Daly, and made another small adjustment. "Hmm. She doesn't look very weird, does she?" This was apparently directed at Dash, who shrugged, and grinned at her roommate. "So," back to Samantha, "got any disgusting habits? Can you floss your nasal sinuses with a spaghetti noodle? Belch the national anthem?"

Giggling, Samantha shook her head. "Nope. Sorry." She tried not to violate **folkways**. These are norms that reflect the customs and etiquette of a society. Belching in the presence of others, such as Daly is suggesting, is a violation of a folkway.

Daly sighed, a pained expression on his face. "Okay, we'll start slow here. Do you eat your own boogers? How about other people's boogers?" Giggling, Samantha kept shaking her head no.

Leaning forward, his light blue eyes intent, Daly continued. "Ever been abducted by aliens? Been struck by lightning and come back to life with psychic powers? Had baby spiders hatch out of any orifices? Killed anyone with a toilet plunger?" No, no, no, and no. She certainly did not violate **mores**. Pronounced morays, these are norms that reflect a society's morals and are considered very important for the well-being of society. For example, murder, stealing, and child abuse are violations of mores; these are unacceptable behaviors that are considered immoral and harmful to society. Violations of mores can also be violations of the law, as is the case with the examples of murder, stealing, and child abuse. But not all mores are laws, and not all laws are mores. For example, many college students engage in underage drinking (a violation of law), but they do not consider their behavior as immoral (a violation of mores). And obtaining a legal abortion is not a law violation, but some consider abortion to be immoral and thus a violation of mores.

Daly leaned back, looking faintly disgusted. "Okay, we got a real lightweight here. Have you ever done anything even *slightly* weird? Please don't say 'no' or we'll have to kill you."

Samantha looked at Dash and they both burst out laughing. Then Samantha got serious, and thought hard. "Well, I can balance a stack of twenty-five quarters on one elbow. ... And I once gargled with baby oil."

Daly raised one reddish eyebrow at her. "I thought it was Listerine."

He sighed heavily and shook his head. Fiddling with the *Bizarrotron* again, he coaxed a little blue sticker out of it, and stuck it on Samantha's shoulder.

"A two!" exclaimed Samantha. "Dash, I only got a two!"

Dash covered her face, laughing. "It's your own fault, Samantha! You've gotta get out more. And how do you think I feel, having a two for a roommate? I could die of boredom, you know! Or embarrassment."

"Well, what did *you* get?" demanded Samantha.

"A seven for my pierced nipples. Five for the pierced nipples, plus two for showing him," said Dash proudly. Samantha grinned; she knew Dash was planning on having her tongue pierced next, and two of her friends at home had joined the body-piercing **fad** (a pattern of behavior that, while short-lived, spreads quickly and is strongly embraced). Samantha didn't think she'd like the tongue piercing, but a navel ring might be kind of cool.

"This could be bumped up to eight if you'll do it again," offered Daly Brown.

"No way!" said Dash. "You'll have to get in line like everyone else."

"*Damn* it," muttered Daly. Turning to Samantha, he told her, "I don't usually do this, but I'm willing to work with you here. Three more points if you show me your nipples, with or without hardware."

Samantha grinned, and Dash grabbed her arm, whispering hoarsely at her ear. "*Not without dinner and a movie first!*"

"Not without dinner and a movie first," said Samantha.

"Hmmph!" replied Daly. "All right, here's your assignment for this week: go out and bite a perfect stranger on the ear. Extra points if you draw blood."

Samantha considered this; until now she'd never heard of socialization that would suggest biting people as an appropriate form of behavior.

"Come on, Samantha, let's go, we've got places to go and people to meet." Dash pulled Samantha along and out the door. "Thanks for the two, Daly," called Samantha. "Bye, Kevin, nice meeting you!"

A pair of brown eyes peered furtively from behind the magazine on the other bed.

***

Marcel was at the cafeteria, having dinner with two of the students from Jazz Dance. Outwardly he looked calm and collected, but inside he was back to the low-level anxiety which had hardly left him since his arrival. For a moment while he'd been dancing, he'd felt something else, a sense of balance and excitement, the freedom of his body clearing his head. But what of the professor and the other students? They had applauded after he'd finished dancing, and some had smiled at him. But many wouldn't look him in the eye, and he felt their coldness. A few more students had been asked to "show their moves," and then the whole class had done an hour of basics. Afterward Marcel had been surprised when a couple of the other students had invited him to come along to the cafeteria.

"Hey, Marcel," said Drew Hastings. "When did you get here from Jamaica?"

"I'm not really from Jamaica," he answered. "I'm from Martinique."

"Martinique? Where the heck is that?" Drew demanded. He had been the first to speak to Marcel in class after he had danced: "Some moves, man! I think Cady likes you." Drew was of medium height and had blond tips on his dark brown hair. He had an intense, wired quality to his body and expression and said whatever was on his mind.

"It's down in the south of the Caribbean. Closer to South America," explained Marcel, toying with his beef stroganoff. One thing he'd noticed about American food was that the meat was all very soft and mushy, hardly different from the limp noodles on his plate. The meat back home was nice and tough, something you could sink your teeth into.

"Oh. Well, you talk Jamaican. Hey, mon! Hey, mon!" Drew said, grinning.

"My parents went to Antigua once," offered Connor McIlwaine, Drew's friend, a dark-haired guy with a pierced ear and a mesh tank top. Marcel nodded briefly and turned back to his stroganoff. He didn't know what to say.

"What did you think of our dance class? Cady's quite the drill sergeant, isn't she?" asked Drew. "She reminds me of my teachers back home," said Marcel. "But I think she is too small to beat us." The other two burst out laughing. "Beat us?" exclaimed Drew. "Well, she won't have to, she scares the devil out of me already!"

"I like her," said Marcel with an uncertain smile; he wasn't sure what the others found so funny. "But I don't think the other students like her much. Or me either."

"Don't worry, Marcel," said Connor. "They're just jealous. You blew everybody away. How did you learn to dance like that?"

Marcel didn't answer, embarrassed. The other students were cold to him because they thought he was good? This made no sense!

"Ah, they're a bunch of nellie crybabies," said Drew. "You probably won't have to put up with them anyway, once you're in Intermediate." Marcel knew there would be auditions next week; Professors Cady and Howe would be dividing the classes up into beginning and intermediate based on their performance. There was also an advanced level for both Jazz and Modern, but freshmen students were never placed there. Drew seemed to think Marcel would make Intermediate, and he hoped Drew would be there too if it turned out that way. Marcel could only do his best and hope he made it; in fact, he'd signed up for practice time in the studio that night after dinner.

"You're in Harrison Hall, right?" asked Drew. "I'm on the first floor. Have you seen Mark Manning's new wheels? Brand-new red RX-7."

"*Hot*, that boy is *hot*," said Connor.

Marcel had no idea what either one of them was talking about, but their easy camaraderie made him nostalgic for the friendly Gemeinschaft relations of his home. This is the German sociologist Ferdinand Tönnies's (1855–1936) term that refers to societies characterized by close personal relationships. **Gemeinschaft** relationships (similar to primary group relationships) are typical in traditional societies, rural villages, or small towns. Marcel misses the close personal interaction, or Gemeinschaft, that characterizes Martinique.

Until now, most of Marcel's interactions with Americans—bus drivers, dorm supervisors, and the cashier at the cafeteria—have reflected the Gesellschaft of US society. Gesellschaft is Tönnies's term that refers to societies that are characterized by impersonal formal relationships where the purpose of interaction is to achieve some particular, often economic, goal. **Gesellschaft** relationships (similar to secondary group relationships) are more characteristic of modern societies, such as the United States. Marcel is unaccustomed to such impersonal relationships, and this contributes to a sense of isolation in his new environment. Americans, Marcel has observed, seem impersonal and focused on doing their job. But now it was nice to just hang out with friendly people, even if he was clueless about the things they talked about.

Drew went on. "He got it for his 18th birthday. I think he threw away the convertible he got when he was 16."

Oh, cars. They were talking about cars. "It must have cost a lot of money. How can he afford such a car?" Marcel asked.

"No problem, he's a member of the Lucky Sperm Club," said Connor.

"The Lucky what?"

"You know, the symbol, born into megabucks. *Lucky sperm*. He is a Manning of *the* Mannings of Martha's Vineyard." A **symbol** is anything that denotes a particular meaning recognized by people within a culture. Symbols include language, gestures, and objects whose meanings are commonly understood by the members of a society. Marcel is finding out quickly that he doesn't understand many of the symbols his new American friends are using in this new context.

Marcel laughed and shook his head. Americans! Lucky Sperm Club; the material culture and non-material culture were so foreign to him. **Material culture** refers to all the tangible things that people in a society make or use, from simple things used in everyday life (such as clothing, food items, chairs, soap) to more sophisticated technological innovations (like airplanes, computers, and cell phones). Marcel is unfamiliar with some aspects of material culture in the United States. In Martinique, Marcel never encountered a drink called latte or recycling containers.

Non-material culture includes the nontangible aspects of culture, such as the beliefs, values, symbolic meanings, and norms. Marcel is unfamiliar with much of the non-material aspects of culture in the United States. For example, earlier in the story, Marcel was not familiar with the norms concerning what to wear when walking from the shower to his dorm room. He is also unfamiliar with many of the symbolic meanings and language used in the United States (for instance, the use of the word "issues" to refer to problems and the meaning of the Lucky Sperm Club).

They put too much milk in their coffee and called it *latte*; they had special trashcans for special kinds of trash; they had issues instead of problems; and now they even had lucky sperm. He found himself wishing for the sensible world of Martinique, where trash was trash and sperm was, well, just what it was. Why did Americans have to complicate things so much? No wonder they had so many issues. At that moment he didn't realize how ethnocentric he was being. This is the practice of viewing one's own culture as "normal" and superior and viewing other cultures as "weird" and inferior. Marcel thinks the norms and behaviors in Martinique make more sense than those he finds in America, and are therefore better. He is being ethnocentric.

Here he never knew what would come up next, and in fact, the **culture shock** was starting to make his head hurt. This is the social psychological stress caused by being in a totally unfamiliar cultural context. In coming to America, Marcel is thrust into an unfamiliar culture, creating stress and confusion.

"Marcel, do you know Ben Williamson?" asked Connor.

"No, should I?"

"Oh, you should meet him, you'd like him."

"I would? Why is that?"

"Well, he's ... you know ... Black."

***

Samantha and Dash burst into their dorm room, still giggling after making the rounds of Emerson Hall. Samantha had met Annie Hawkes and her twin brother Amory from a potato farm in Idaho. They had big plans to go to business school and then open a Far East import-export company.

"Dash," cried Samantha as she flopped onto her bed. "Nobody else has a two! I'm the only one with a two. Even the potato twins had a three and a four!"

"So, Samantha, we just have some work to do. But don't worry, I want you to know I'm here for you."

There was a knock at the door. Samantha opened it to find a brown-haired guy in a Grateful Dead T-shirt and corduroys standing there, staring at her. He looked vaguely familiar.

"Oh, hi, Kevin," called Dash from her bed.

This was Kevin, from Daly Brown's room, the guy with the magazine. Samantha had barely noticed him, caught up as she'd been with the Daly Brown experience. And of course she was still trying to come to terms with the humiliation of being a two, so she was distracted.

"Are you, um, going to the Crow's Nest tonight?" Kevin asked. "There's a bunch of people going to the Crow's Nest tonight. It's in the Student Union, at the top. I mean the top floor of the Student Union. That's why they, um, call it the Crow's Nest."

"We know where it is," said Dash, sitting cross-legged on her bed.

"It opens at six o'clock. Will you be there at six o'clock? Or later? I could be there later, if you can't make it at six." He shoved his hand into a baggy pants pocket and then handed Samantha a wadded-up piece of paper. "I wrote down my cell phone number, you can call me in case you can't make it at six." He held up his cell phone for her to see, his favorite possession, in case she doubted he really had one.

He continued, in a hurry to get everything said. "Or if, you know, you, um, end up coming later. You can call me. Sometimes the phone is out of range; there seems to be, um, pockets of reception on the campus. But if it doesn't go through, you can just try again in a few minutes. I move around a lot. Well, okay, um, bye."

And Kevin Bittner scurried down the hall to his room, hands in his pockets. Samantha hadn't said a single word. She closed the door and turned to Dash, catching her eye and holding out the wad of paper.

"I think this is for you."

They both erupted into gales of laughter.

"Oh, no, girlfriend, I'm sure that's for you," said Dash.

"No, really, I think he wants to see your nipples!"

"I think he wants to see your pocket of reception!" Dash screamed back at her, and they fought over the note, Samantha trying to force it on her and Dash laughing as she pushed it away. Dash rolled over on the bed and ended up facing out the window.

"Hey, look, there's that Black guy. Marcel something-or-other. Sounds French."

Samantha looked over Dash's shoulder and saw three students walking up the steps to Harrison Hall. One was the guy with dreadlocks, the one she and her mother had seen on the day she'd arrived. The one her mother had thought was so fortunate to be coming here, since he *obviously* couldn't afford it. Her mother saw dreadlocks as a symbol of a counterculture rejecting the proper dress and hairstyles of America.

"He's gorgeous," said Dash. "He's from somewhere in the West Indies, some place I've never heard of. Not Jamaica, though, he gets pissed off when people call him Jamaican."

"Great dreadlocks," commented Samantha. "My mother would hate him. She needs to develop some **cultural relativism**. In other words, get a clue." This is the understanding of a culture (or a member of a particular culture) according to the beliefs, values, and norms of that culture. Samantha wishes that her mother would view Marcel according to the beliefs, values, and norms in Martinique rather than from the vantage point of her own culture.

"Lisa Schift is in his dance class. She says all the girls and most of the guys think he's way hot." Dash glanced up at Samantha's face. "But don't get your hopes up, honey, he's probably gay."

"Why do you say that?"

"He's a dance major, isn't he? And look who he's with."

Samantha watched Marcel enter Harrison Hall with Drew Hastings and Connor McIlwaine. They were lovers and openly gay.

"Oh," said Samantha, and turned away from the window. "Well, I'm gonna make a phone call," Samantha told her. "I'm going to call Kevin and tell him you'll meet him at the Crow's Nest and you want to have his baby."

"In your dreams, girlfriend!" Dash called after Samantha as she left the room.

***

There were phone booths near the stairwells on each floor, and Samantha sat down in one, pulling her calling card out of her wallet. Most of her friends had cell phones, but Samantha refused to have one; they seemed so intrusive. She'd be talking face-to-face with a friend and they'd put her, a live human being, on hold while they answered their cell phone. So she used the more cumbersome pay phones at the end of the hall, believing them superior to an annoying device that could interrupt your life 24 hours a day.

Samantha's face was flushed and bright. She was bursting and couldn't wait to call her parents. Her professor was engaging, she had a great idea for her term project, and her dorm-mates were fruitcakes. Samantha wanted to pierce her navel. Her mother would just die.

The phone rang and rang. Maybe they weren't home, but the answering machine should pick up. Finally, Samantha heard her mother's voice.

"Hi, Mom, it's Samantha!"

"Oh, Sammy ... honey. I was just—where are you calling from?"

"I'm at my dorm. You won't believe what Sasha Lowe has in her room. And I got rated a two, and—Mom, is Dad there?"

There was a pause. "No, he's not here, Sammy. He won't be, either."

"He won't be? Is he on a business trip or something?"

Samantha's mother laughed, a hollow, mirthless sound. Her voice sounded strange. "No, I mean he won't be coming back here. Your father's moved out, Samantha."

An odd sensation of numbness spread through Samantha's chest. "He's moved out? What do you mean, Mom? Why?"

"We're getting a divorce, Sammy. We were waiting for both you girls to get off to college. We were going to tell you sooner, but we didn't want to spoil your first day at school."

***

Chapter 2 Study Questions
CULTURE

1. Is Marcel's family a reference group as well as a **membership group** for him? How about Samantha's family? Why or why not?

2. Does Samantha apply **cultural relativism** to her assessment of Daly Brown? Why or why not?

3. Give two other examples of **material culture** in this chapter (besides Kevin Bittner's cell phone).

4. How would Marcel violate a **folkway** in Professor Cady's dance class, within the context she describes? A **more**? A **taboo**?

5. Give two examples of the use of **language** in the chapter, one where the meaning is understood by both parties and one in which it is not, and explain why.

Through the Window

Socialization

T HEY CAN'T DO *this, they can't do this to me,* Samantha thought as she stalked across the lawn in front of Emerson Hall. She had no particular destination in mind, she just had to get out and walk. She shoved her hands into the pockets of her denim jacket, her fists balled up, keeping her head down as she walked, not wanting to talk to anyone.

Her parents were *married*. Among their friends and neighbors, she and her sister were some of the very few whose parents were still together. They had never had to go through the agonies of stepparents, stepsiblings, weekend visits and jockeying for position between domestic enemy lines. Samantha realized she had always derived a sense of satisfaction from being in a family whose parents were still together; it somehow made her look more mature, more successful, more ... like a real person. Now who would she be, as the daughter of divorced parents? This was really the **looking-glass self**. This is Cooley's term for the social self—that is, for the self-concept people develop on the basis of how they perceive other people view them. Samantha is confused about her self-concept, which she feels will be negatively affected by the divorce. Samantha understood that her self-concept is affected by how she thinks she appears to her friends. She now felt worse as she imagined that others would disapprove. She felt ashamed.

Her parents were *married*. Wasn't that the function of marriage, for parents to stay together? To provide a sense of emotional stability?

She and Audrey had cousins, Jeremy and Jen, their uncle Doug's kids. Both Ed Cahill and his brother Doug had married girls from wealthy socialite families from Cape Cod, but Doug and Patricia Cahill had separated when Jeremy was ten and Jen was eight, and their father had moved to Texas. The two kids had gone to Texas for every holiday and school break and most of the summers, and she and Audrey hardly ever saw them anymore, but when they did, they'd seemed to be doing well enough. When they were 14 and 12, their father had remarried, and his new wife didn't want the kids hanging around. She wanted to start her own family. So the Texas visits had fizzled out, and what had been a relationship with their dad had gradually become replaced by excuses and gifts sent at Christmas and birthdays. By the time Jeremy and Jen were 18 and 16, birthdays were forgotten and Christmas gifts had turned into cards with a check. They had two new half brothers they'd never seen.

Jen spent a month in a private psychiatric hospital when she was 15 after a suicide attempt, and Jeremy had been arrested three times by the age of 18. Then he joined the army and hadn't been heard from since. The family dysfunction had certainly left its mark.

Samantha had always felt lucky to have escaped a similar fate; sure, her family had their problems, but it had never come to this. Her family had provided the function of sustaining each other's well-being. Or did they? At least they spoke to each other, they spent holidays together, like families were supposed to. True, her mother was a bitch and her father was an alcoholic, and maybe real happiness was too much to ask.

But hadn't they at least had a semblance of it? Ever?

Samantha tried to think of times when her family had been happy, and her paced slowed as she realized with horror that she could hardly think of any. A parade when she was 11; she and her mom and dad watching Audrey twirl her baton. A trip to Cancun when she was seven and Audrey nine, but she couldn't remember much of that, mostly playing on the beach and a beautiful red parrot in the hotel lobby; they'd had their pictures taken with it. A birthday party at home when she'd turned 10; they'd gotten a karaoke machine and had giggled and sung songs for hours.

Was that it? Memories that could be counted on one hand of a happy family? Were most families like this? Was happiness a chance occurrence, coming up once in a blue moon to mark off long stretches of just surviving? How had she managed to find a halfway decent self-concept behind enemy lines? **Self-concept** refers to the ideas and images individuals have of themselves. Samantha has cultivated an idea of herself as a relatively happy and stable person and wonders how this could come out of a family of unhappiness and emotional instability. This could be because of the choices she's made as she's grown into an independent entity, maximizing the positive and minimizing the negative influences of her family. She may also have had other positive role models who helped strengthen her self-concept.

Her dad had gotten drunk at the birthday party with the karaoke machine. He'd gotten louder and louder and then dropped the microphone into the punch bowl, and her mother had screamed at him. Her friends had all left early. Audrey had locked herself in her room. Samantha's heart grew heavier as she realized that these kinds of interactions were the norm for her family. **Interaction** is the reaction of people to others on the basis of their interpretation and definition of the symbolic meaning of the actions of others. Samantha's mother screams at her drunk husband out of frustration and embarrassment; the friends go home early due to discomfort with the drunkenness and screaming; Audrey isolates herself out of anger and a sense of helplessness that there is nothing she can do to alter an uncomfortable situation. Each of the actors reacts to the situation based on their interpretation of the actions of others.

But they'd had fun for a few hours, hadn't they? Did it usually last longer, with other families? Did other people have parents who talked to each other, who sat together after dinner watching television and baking cookies, who enjoyed each other's company? She thought of her friends and their families, looking for signs of real life, but could only come up with disjointed fragments: tennis lessons, appointments with therapists, trips to Europe, and smoking pot while the various parents and step-units were out of the house.

Samantha stopped walking for a moment. We never had any "in" jokes. Not even me and Audrey. We never had any private family jokes we could titter about, smug with the knowledge that we shared a camaraderie that others weren't part of. Tears flowed as she realized that each member of her family was a completely separate entity, taking great care to keep his or her own territory sharply defined. There was hardly any crossover, no time she could think of when the boundaries softened and they created a space where they could all be together and enjoy each other's company. They had spent so many years on their own border patrols that they had no energy for worrying about someone else, whether her dad or Audrey might need some support or a sympathetic ear.

***

The push-buttons of the pay phone blurred through a tear-filled gaze as Samantha jabbed at them with a forefinger. The phone rang several times, and Samantha took deep breaths, willing herself to stay calm.

"Hello." Leslie Burns Cahill's voice sounded a little sleepy, without its usual edge. She usually sounded curt, as if whomever was calling had better get right to the point.

"Mom, were you ever happy?"

There was a pause. "Who's this? Sammy? Samantha, 'sat you?"

"It's me, Mom. Were you?"

"Where are you calling from? Are you at school?"

"Yes, I'm at school, Mom. I just want to know: were you ever happy?"

Another pause. "What do you mean?"

"*Happy*, Mom. I want to know if you were ever *happy*."

"Well, I don't know how I'm supposed to answer that. How can I? How can I? Did your father ever ask me that? I guess he didn't! He never asked me because he—he didn't, your father never cared!"

Her mother sounded weird. She sounded like she'd had too much to drink. Or forgotten to take her medication. Or both. For heaven's sake, thought *Samantha, it's only been a couple of hours since I last spoke to her, and she's already drunk?*

"But Mom, I'm not asking about Dad. I want to know ..."

"He never once! Did he? Why should he care about his wife? When he had— plenty, plenty of other—he had his girlfriends, didn't he? Well, he's happy now, isn't he! Who cares if I'm—"

"*What*?" Samantha couldn't believe her ears. "Mom, what are you talking about?"

"That bastard! Never loved me! I wanted to, I wanted to be ... He wouldn't listen. He never did. He just went out, all the time, told me he was going to meetings, you know, but he was meeting her. I told him for years that I didn't trust him, that I knew he was out seeing other women, that he would leave me."

"Who, Mom? *Who was he meeting?*"

"Lindsay!" Her mother was screaming into the phone by now. "It was Lindsay! He lied about it, but I know! Why don't you call and ask her if she's happy! Men are pigs, it's no use trying to be nice to them, they just go find themselves a girlfriend anyway." Samantha considered the possible **self-fulfilling prophecy** her mother's emotions suggested. This is when a false definition of a situation produces behavior that, in turn, makes the originally falsely defined situation come true. It is possible that Mr. Cahill was not unfaithful, but that Mrs. Cahill falsely accused him of infidelity. This false definition could have led Mrs. Cahill to express distrust and resentment, which, in turn, could have led Mr. Cahill to seek intimacy outside the marriage.

"Mom! Mom? How do you—Mom!" Samantha called into the phone but there was no reply. Her mother had put the phone down and was walking around the room, Samantha could hear noises but couldn't understand what she was saying. "Mom, pick up the phone!" Samantha cried in exasperation, but finally replaced the receiver on its hook.

Lindsay Geffler? One of her dad's secretaries? She couldn't believe it. She'd seen Lindsay several times at her dad's firm, with her coiffed hair and long pink fingernails. Come to think of it, the last time she'd seen her, Samantha had admired a diamond brooch on Lindsay's blazer. Lindsay had smiled and told her it was a gift from her father. *What kind of employer gives his secretary an expensive piece of jewelry?* Was this symbolic of something more than friendship? Samantha knew that certain messages and expectations are entwined with the giving of jewelry; diamonds given to women are usually seen as a romantic gift, and the more expensive the more serious the message. Diamond rings are an ultimate symbol of commitment and are part of material culture in American society.

The conversation, if it could be called that, left behind a sour taste and a vague feeling of dread. *But now I know more than before I called her*, Samantha thought grimly. She felt her mother's unhappiness keenly, clear as day even without answering the question, and she wondered if her mother knew how much she pushed her father away by her behavior, all the while blaming it on him. But what could she say?

***

Samantha made another phone call. Her sister Audrey picked up on the second ring; she was at school in Amherst and had her own apartment.

"Hello?"

"Did you know about this?"

A pause. "Hi, Samantha."

"Did you?"

"Did I what?"

"Oh, come on! Dad's moved out! They're getting a divorce! For God's sake!"

"Yes, *for God's sake*, Samantha! Of course they're getting a divorce! I can't believe he stayed with her as long as he did."

"And you didn't tell me?" Samantha was practically screaming into the phone. "I can't believe you didn't tell me!"

"Tell you what!" Audrey yelled back. "Tell you what anyone with half an eye could see? They were miserable. They made us miserable. What more do you want?"

"What more do I—Audrey, did you know Dad had a girlfriend?"

"That woman from work? Lindsay? That's old news, Samantha. She isn't the only one."

"*Audrey*! I can't believe this! How can you condone him? He's cheating on her!"

"Oh, for God's sake, Samantha. Do you remember when you were in third grade and I was in fifth and Mom refused to leave the house for five months?"

Samantha paused. "It wasn't five months. She wasn't feeling well."

"It was FIVE MONTHS, little sister. She barely said two words to him and spent all day reading paperbacks. Every day. She never cooked, she never cleaned. He should have left her back then."

"She didn't have to cook and clean! She was having trouble with her medication, remember?"

"I do remember. I remember that she didn't have to cook or clean because I did most of it for five months. You played with your Barbie dolls."

"I ... what?" What was she talking about? It hadn't been that bad, had it? Had Samantha been remembering things through rose-colored glasses?

"Audrey, do you have Dad's number? I want to talk to him."

"Get it from Mom. I don't have it." And the line went dead.

Hanging up the phone, Samantha leaned back against the phone booth, her arms folded inward on herself, as if she would disintegrate if she relaxed. The truth settled in on her with sickening finality, as if she'd been the last to finally realize what the whole world already knew: No, there never had been any real happiness. They'd all just been going through the motions. She and the **significant others** in her life, although she loved them, all held each other at arm's length. These are important people in an individual's environment who serve as models for social learning or socialization, and who help shape the individual's self-concept. Samantha's parents and sister are significant others to her and she to them; they influence each other and act as social models, for better or worse. Even though she concludes that happiness in her family was illusory, there are doubtless other benefits she's reaped from her relationship with her significant others.

She decided to call herself Sam. She'd always been Samantha, or the less desirable Sammy, and had always thought of herself as Samantha. But Samantha was a little girl whose heart was breaking; Sam was someone different, someone older, more sophisticated, someone who wouldn't go overboard about a divorce that should have happened years ago. Samantha had believed that an occasional peck on the cheek between her parents was real affection; Sam knew better and understood that she was now on her own. Whatever happiness and affection really looked like, she would have to find out for herself. Samantha would have thought this a hopeless task, but Sam thought she could hold up and at least find comfort in the looking.

***

"Hey, Kyle," Marcel said to his roommate, "I got to go downtown to Webber's. I'm supposed to get dance shoes for my classes, we all got to wear a special kind."

Kyle remained bent over his desk, his nose nearly touching the paper he was writing on.

"Because of the floors. The dance floors in the studios, they tell us we got to wear special shoes. ... I just wondered if you want to come downtown."

Kyle shook his head without looking up, and Marcel sighed, picking up his jacket where he'd left it on his bed. His roommate appeared to be engrossed in his books and taking notes, a dedicated student. You had to read a lot of books to study political science. But Marcel had accidentally seen Kyle's notebook yesterday, and the pages were completely covered with doodles and drawings. It was a strange way to study. In his school on Martinique he would have had his backside tanned for wasting so much paper.

It was his second time on the bus. As with the first time, coming from the airport, he marveled at how clean the bus was and how quiet. Thinking of riding buses on Martinique made him smile, and he wondered what the passengers on this bus would think if they were to suddenly be transported to an island bus.

The last time he'd ridden a bus on Martinique he'd been going from Macouba, where his family lived on the north of the island, to the capital town of Fort-de-France. They didn't actually live in Macouba; the Devereaux family resided in the little village of Toussaint about 10 miles away. It was too small to have a post office, so all of its residents had to use Macouba addresses. Marcel and his brother Sebastian would be stopping to pick up the mail at the Macouba post office on their way back home after spending the day traveling to Fort-de-France and back. They had left their house at dawn for the 10-mile walk to the bus station, carrying bags of clothing made by their sisters to deliver to an aunt's boutique in the big town. Nobody ever called it Fort-de-France, just "Big Town."

"You gone to Big Town today, boys? You tell you Aunt Cécile to come an' see me sometime. I *know* she's a lonely woman and I got what she needs!" This from their neighbor, Alphonse Thibodeaux, who'd had a thing for their widowed aunt forever.

Marcel and his brother had laughed and waved him off. "Why don't you come wit' us, Alphonse? You can tell her your own self!" Marcel had called to him, but of course Alphonse had never moved from his chair on the front porch.

"Like Aunt Cécile would even want him, so he could sit on her porch drinking the whole livelong day," Sebastian had chuckled. The Thibodeauxs' unmarried uncle was an institution for the kids in the village; he always had a smile and a joke but never did a lick of work in his life.

There were a dozen other tasks to be taken care of during their trip. They would go to the town of Ajoupa-Bouillon to deliver a basket of vanilla beans to a merchant there, which would be added to his international shipments; they would be able to redeem their voucher once the buyer in Big Town sold the shipment. There was eye medicine to buy for Daria's little son, letters to drop off, relatives to visit. They'd be drinking cups and cups of tea wherever they went—it would be unheard of to just drop in and out without sitting for a spell and sharing tea and johnnycakes. Ignoring the value of hospitality would be like a slap in the face to the members of their community, to those particular people, and to the unnamed **generalized others**. This refers not to any specific individual but to other people in general, who represent the general norms and values of the culture. The process of socialization involves individuals becoming aware of the expectations of others in general and acting according to those expectations. Although Marcel and his brother might not have an intimate relationship with everyone they met during their trips, they behave in a way that shows respect to people in general in their society.

The Devereaux women rarely went on these excursions to Big Town. They were busy sewing clothes and working in their gardens; Mariette had a special vanilla patch and grew other spices, but Daria and Maman Devereaux stuck with hardier crops like pumpkins and papayas.

"Mariette, my girl, I don't know how you coax dem fancy vanilla beans to grow. They got more temperament than a red-headed ballerina wit' tight shoes," Maman would say to her. "You give me a nice patch of pumpkins, they'll just grow right up big as you please and thank you for pickin' 'em."

Marcel wondered what jobs his mother and sisters might have done if they had lived in America, where there is a high **division of labor** compared to that of Martinique. This refers to the number of occupations and roles and degree of occupational specialization in a society. Societies with relatively few occupational roles and little occupational specialization have a low division of labor. Societies with many occupational roles and a high degree of specialization have a high division of labor.

Sebastian and Marcel couldn't carry the pumpkins to Macouba, so their father would borrow one of the village's two cars for their transport. As it happened, Marcel and his family had crammed into this same car for the trip to the airport, and he'd still had some squashed pumpkin on the bottom of his new shoes when he'd boarded the plane.

In Macouba the two brothers had joined the throng of people at the bus station, tromping through the sun-heated garbage and elbowing their way in to the crowd, shouldering their bags and baskets. In America Marcel had been amazed at how quietly and patiently people had waited in line to board the bus; in fact, he quickly discovered that not waiting one's turn generated glares and grumbles. They were all getting on the same bus, but it seemed very important that it be done in an orderly fashion, one at a time, and don't get out of place. He'd love to see the Americans on this clean and quiet bus cope with the Macouba bus station, where they'd be left standing in the fly-covered trash puddles as everyone else barged onto the buses.

And the noise, he missed that too. Every rickety bus on the island was driven by committee; the driver himself plus three or four of his friends or relatives ("touts"). These were an endless supply of cocky young men who helped load and unload goods and luggage, collected the bus fares, and who kept cranking up their own stereo or boom box louder than the next bus. On the one Marcel and his brother had ridden, they'd spent the 3-hour ride listening to a scratchy Whitney Houston tape over and over until someone had finally donated another tape. It turned out to be bagpipe music, so Whitney Houston was quickly resurrected.

The touts hung off the steps of their vehicles and shouted at the crowd, advertising the merits of their own rattletrap bus over the others at the station, trying to cram as many passengers as possible inside. Once on the road, if the aisle of the bus was filled with standing passengers, the touts would motion for them to all duck down as they passed police stations so they wouldn't get arrested for overcrowding. Well, they wouldn't really get arrested since the officers would most likely be relatives, but they'd certainly have to pay a "fine" if caught. The fine would go into the pockets of the officers.

Marcel shook himself out of his island reverie as the city bus arrived downtown. He disembarked at his stop and turned to watch the bus drive away. Its roof was bare, no bags of palm leaves or dried fish or rice tied willy-nilly all over it, no loads of bananas, secured in baskets made of their own leaves, no banged-up cages of live chickens. The bus itself was a uniform gray color with one purple stripe and a tasteful Transit Authority logo—no hand-painted murals of palm trees and people dancing or slogans with lots of exclamation points: "When your there, your there!!!" "Trust in Jesus Express Bus!!!!" "Macouba-Big Town Space Shuttle!!!" Here in America, you waited in line and you didn't paint your buses.

At Webber's, where he'd been told he could buy the required dance shoes, he was appalled that they cost $56. He didn't even want to wear shoes when he was dancing, and he was sure his bare feet wouldn't hurt the special finish on the studio floors. But they all had to get them. He'd been a little chagrined on the first day of dance class when the other students had shown up with all kinds of special clothing and outfits: leotards, sweatbands, tights, leg-warmers, bandanas tied on heads, and cut-off shirts carefully draped off one shoulder. Marcel had simply worn loose black cotton pants and a sleeveless shirt, made lovingly by his sister out of alternating strips of different-colored cloth. Some of the other students had stretched and practiced while wearing headphones so it hadn't been very easy to talk to anyone, but a couple of them had been friendly and asked where he was from.

At Webber's Marcel idly wandered through the racks of dance clothes, but decided he'd have to manage with what he had as he looked at the prices. How did they do it? He wondered incredulously. Remembering some of the other students in his Modern Dance class, they must have been wearing over a hundred dollars' worth of clothes at once. He couldn't justify spending this kind of money on clothes for only himself, remembering how his mother had scraped and saved for new shoes for him and his father. Each pair had cost about $15. As much as he wanted to fit in to his new **peer group**, he couldn't wear the same clothes as them. This is a group made up of individuals who are very similar in interest or age. Marcel knew that clothing and appearance make an impression on members of his dance class, who are about his age and share an interest in dance. But he didn't have money for expensive clothes, and he wondered how his peer group would react to his dress and appearance.

Standing in the clothing store, surrounded by all-white faces and expensive merchandise he couldn't buy, Marcel was acutely aware of his class and his minority status in a way he'd never felt in Martinique. **Class** is a ranking in a stratification system based on socioeconomic and economic factors of educational attainment, occupation, and wealth (money and material possessions). Marcel's lack of wealth placed him in a lower class than his peers. A **minority group** is a group that has less access to wealth, power, and prestige compared to the dominant group within a society and that experiences prejudice and discrimination. Minority group status is often based on race and ethnicity but may also be based on sexual orientation, age, and disability. Marcel was a member of the Black majority in Martinique; he was now very aware of being a member of a minority group, through no choice or fault of his own.

His passion for dance would have to make up the difference; it always had been and would be his sense of power and identity. He left the store and kept walking.

He did buy a pair of sunglasses for $5 at a convenience store next to Webber's and a bag of marshmallows and then walked around downtown for a little while. There were pigeons and squirrels everywhere, like on campus, only he didn't see anyone throwing rocks at them. In fact, he was surprised to see a few people sitting on benches feeding the birds from paper bags. Feeding birds! No wonder they looked fat and lazy.

He loved the vinyl record shop and spent a long time listening to all the different kinds of music—R & B, soul, pop, rap, reggae, Latin, hip-hop, country, folk, jazz, and classical—discovering a love of Mendelssohn. He didn't have the money to buy anything, but the selection was incredible, and he wished his brothers could see this. There was a shop that sold nothing but different kinds of candles, and a pet shop with puppies and fish and iguanas. The fat, furry puppies in the store window looked clean and well fed, not like any dogs he'd ever seen back home. He had to admit they were cute, but couldn't imagine spending $400 for one of them. He smiled to himself, imagining his family's reaction if he were to call them up and tell them he'd just spent half of his semester's stipend on a … what was it? A golden retriever puppy. They'd think he had lost his mind.

On the bus coming back to campus, the seats were all full, so Marcel stood but didn't hold on to any of the bars. He liked working his legs and feet on keeping balanced and as an added challenge put his hands into his jacket pockets, so his back and legs would have to work harder to remain balanced as the bus moved and lurched.

Something was in his right jacket pocket, and he withdrew a crumpled piece of paper. It had been torn off a bottom corner of a sheet of notebook paper much like his roommate's. Opening it up, he read the following words printed in block letters: "PLEASE KEEP YOUR JACKET AND OTHER CLOTHING HUNG UP IN YOUR CLOSET."

***

It began to rain, but Samantha didn't want to go back to her room yet. She found herself outside the music school, and the light and music emanating from the grand old building only seemed to heighten her loneliness. She could go inside, but the building seemed full of life and people and she just wanted to be alone. So she climbed down into a window well and sat down in the leaves at the bottom, kept dry by an overhang. In fact, the 3-foot-deep well made a nice little cave, sheltering her from the storms outside trying to find her, and her heart calmed as she leaned against the sturdy brick wall, her arms wrapped around her bent knees. Her hair was a mess, her eyes puffy and raw, and she wiped her nose on the back of her hand.

God, families! Who needs this?! She wondered how the social organization of her family had ever come to this. **Social organization** is the order of a social group as evidenced by the positions, roles, norms, and other constraints that control behavior and ensure predictability. The members of Samantha's family all have well-defined positions and roles, and she wished she knew how these all developed into a system that did not function well.

She closed her eyes and rested her cheek on her knees, listening to the music and feeling the warmth of the room on the other side of the window wash over her. Someone was playing "Ivy" by Frank Ocean, one of her all-time favorites, and the knot of hurt and anger in her breast began to slowly unclench.

The music was turned up loud, the way she liked it, and the windowpanes resonated in rhythm. Opening her eyes and looking in through the window, an amazing sight gripped her.

A tall Black man was dancing by himself. He wore black cotton drawstring pants and nothing else, and his bare feet hardly seemed to touch the smooth wooden dance floor. He had a lean, whipcord-slender body, and Samantha could see his muscles flex as he whirled and arced. His face was impossible to read as he moved, sometimes hidden by his hair, and for a moment lifted to the light, eyes closed. The wild mane of dreadlocks seemed to be performing its own parallel dance as he spun and turned. His arms traced an arc through the air as they began behind his hips and then swept up in front, crossing in front of his face, while his upper body rotated, perfectly balanced. It was incredible to Samantha that he could move so many ways at once with so little effort and yet create the effect of a completely unified whole, blending completely with the light and music.

His dancing was the second most beautiful thing Samantha had ever seen, second only because he had come along after the first thing.

This had been a young chestnut mare on the farm where Samantha had kept her horse two years earlier. It was late May in northern New Hampshire, an exquisite time of year, fresh and fertile and green, and the sun-drenched air seeped into everything, imbuing the horse and the watcher, Samantha, with the magic and glow that had been missing all winter. The heavy gray lethargy of winter had left traces of its somnolence around her heart, but this day was one of the first she'd felt truly awake and aware. It was one of those days where she just wanted to rest her cheek against everything the sun touched—the weathered gray side of the barn, the silky flank of a grazing horse, the wide green leaves of the lilies by the pond. On that day Samantha had been in no hurry and had leaned against the fence, watching the mare in a grassy meadow.

She was a young mare, just approaching her prime, her glossy copper-chestnut hide reflecting like bronze in the sunlight. She was full of the promise and delight of spring, Samantha could see it in the toss of her head and the bounce of her step. Apparently some midsummer gremlin was whispering nonsense in the mare's ear, because she suddenly picked up a long branch and carried it around, a very un-horse-like thing to do. She waved the supple, leafy branch in the air, looking quite pleased with herself, a gleam in her eye as she gripped the branch in her strong teeth. Then a breeze sprang up and ruffled the dangling ends of the branch, like the sudden wave of a big green hand near her neck, where she couldn't see it well.

The mare exploded into action, galloping and snorting across the meadow, her eyes wide and nostrils flared, golden-auburn tail flying. Her whole body took flight and heaved and flowed under the late spring sun, powerful muscles under a shimmering skin alive with split-second reflexes and a deep grace that spoke of primal freedom. She ran with no hesitation, no care for anything else in the world at that moment. Finally, the horse slowed down and stopped, looking surprised, only to go charging off when the mysterious green wind-hand swatted at her again. She went on like this for a long time, cockily waving her branch and then panicking when she scared herself with it, and Samantha laughed until her face ran with tears and she had to hold herself up against the fence. The life and beauty of that day had filled her spirit, and the memory of it always lifted her.

But it wasn't as if she could return to that same pasture again. It had been the whole setting and her receptiveness to it; the alchemy of the sun and green grass and a waving branch; her awareness of the moment had transformed the whole experience as it wouldn't have on a different day, watching a different horse.

She felt like that now, as if the rawness of her heart and the ache of the day's events had left her too drained to do more than live from moment to moment, and this moment had found her down in a window well watching a dancer. His freedom of movement reminded her of that other day, of that dancing mare in the meadow; as if the music and emotion inside him expressed itself directly as it came, without censure or translation. It was a freedom and grace of being that Samantha didn't have, having been coached for years into second-guessing, subterfuge, and stealth by her family. The knowledge that she would probably never experience this state of weightlessness suddenly seemed unbearably sad, and tears threatened again.

The music stopped. Samantha closed her stinging eyes, resting her head on her knees.

A soft scraping sound brought her head back up, her hazel eyes open wide. He was there, standing right in front of her. He had opened the window and was regarding her with a slightly bemused expression on his narrow face, one hand on a slender hip. A sheen of perspiration made his upper lip glisten and dampened his chest. Up close like this she could see that his skin was an unblemished warm brown, and his dark eyes were slightly almond shaped.

"You have the best seat in the house. Most people pay a lotta money (mon-ney) for seats like this (seats like dis)." The dancer's voice was velvety, the Caribbean lilt rolling off his tongue like a stream over polished stones.

"You're not from Jamaica," she answered. He shook his head, the dreadlocks rustling back and forth, caressing his shoulders. They were narrow locks, about the size of her little finger, not big matted ones. They sprouted from his head in a dense cascade, as if a fountain of black ribbons had been stopped in midair. She wanted to touch them.

"You're not from Jamaica (*Ja-MEE-ka*) either," he said.

Nope. I'm from New Hampshire. The thought formed but wasn't spoken; Samantha used to be from New Hampshire. She used to have a family. Instead, she asked him, "Are you from Montserrat?" Marcel's eyes opened slightly wider, the only sign of surprise. He slowly shook his head.

"Nevis?" He shook his head again, the dreadlocks dancing. She wondered what they'd feel like in her hand, against her face.

"Dominica?" No again. The hint of a smile played at the corners of his mouth.

"Antigua?" Samantha sighed, shrugging her shoulders in mock exaggeration. "I give up! Where *are* you from?"

"But you were doing very well (*var-ry well*)," Marcel said quietly, his eyes twinkling. Inside him a knot he'd had with him since his arrival started to unwind. Like a tiny sigh of relief, an ember glowing among heavy logs of tension.

In spite of herself, Samantha smiled. Here she was, committed to a really foul mood, and this guy, this non-Jamaican, was spoiling it by making her smile.

"How do you know so much about Caribbean islands? Have you been there?" he asked her. It sounded like a phrase from a song.

Samantha glanced away briefly. She felt ridiculous for having Googled them yesterday, but wild horses couldn't drag this from her. "I've never been to the

Caribbean. I've heard the islands are beautiful, though." She leaned forward, her hazel eyes lit up by the lights from the studio. "But you haven't answered my question. Where are you from?"

The smile still playing at his lips, Marcel shook his head again. "Come, one more try. You were var-ry close."

Samantha laughed, a nervous eruption. She buried her face in her hands, pretending to think hard, and realized her heart was pounding. Then she looked back up at him, suddenly thinking she must look like a complete freak with her swollen eyes, tear-streaked face, and crazed hair. She spoke: "Martinique."

The word hung in the air between them, halfway between the rain of the September night and the warm glow of the light from the dance studio. The smile playing at Marcel's lips broke through and spread, and his face was transformed.

"I am Marcel," he said.

"I know. I'm Sam."

***

Chapter 3 Study Questions
SOCIALIZATION

1. Discuss how the **looking-glass self** relates to Samantha and her parents' impending divorce. Also explain how the concept relates to Marcel and his peer group of the dance class.
2. Identify five **agents of socialization** that taught Samantha that marriage means "till death do us part."
3. Give two examples of behavior described in this chapter that are shaped by expectations of the **generalized other**.
4. In comparing Marcel and Samantha's socioeconomic status, which of them belongs to an upper **class** and which to a lower class, and why?
5. What is the difference between a **generalized other** and a **significant other**? Give an example of each from the chapter.
6. Who are Samantha's **significant others**?

The Raindrop

Sex and Gender

T HE CROW'S NEST was on the fifth floor of the Student Union, a convoluted attic space with odd little nooks and corners. There were pillows and over-stuffed chairs under dormer windows, a small bar at one end, and a pool table right in the middle. Marcel and Samantha were soaked by the time they got there, the intermittent rain having finally made up its mind and come down with a purpose as they had walked over from the music school.

"Come on over here, we can stand by the stove," Samantha told him and led him through the crowd to a wood-burning stove on the back wall, its cast-iron doors open to reveal a crackling fire inside. Her honey-brown hair hung in limp strings around her shoulders, and Marcel could see remnants of raindrops on her eyelashes. She had large, innocent-looking eyes of an unusual hazel color and just the faint-est splash of freckles across the bridge of her nose. He wondered if she knew how beautiful she was.

"I love fireplaces," Samantha said, as they crowded together in front of the stove. There were a lot of people in the Crow's Nest, making it a little difficult to hear each other. Marcel leaned forward to tell her, "We don't have them in Martinique" and caught a fragrance from her wet hair—jasmine? Fresh-cut grass? The aroma of moist papayas just after they've been cut open? A powerful image from his home suddenly filled his head: sitting cross-legged on the ground with a spoon and a papaya in his lap, carefully scooping out the fat black pips nestled inside like a nest of shiny tadpoles.

"Have you ever eaten a papaya?" he asked her. The glow from the cast-iron stove warmed him; the downpour had turned chilly and he wasn't used to it.

"No, I haven't. They grow on trees, don't they?"

Samantha wished she could touch the locks of hair hanging over his forehead. Tiny orbs of rainwater perched on the dreadlocks like glass beads; a crazy thought occurred to her as she imagined him shaking his head and sending the little glass beads flying in all directions. They would make a miniature symphony as they scattered, a crystal shower only she'd be able to hear.

Marcel nodded in answer to her question, and several beads of rainwater coalesced to form a large drop hanging from the end of one lock. "We have papaya trees outside my house." He suddenly felt silly; why would she be interested in that? She seemed to be staring at his forehead; did he have something on it? Should he excuse himself to go find a toilet? Wait—didn't they call them bathrooms here? But it was so pleasant standing by the fire with her that he didn't want to leave. But he'd kick himself later if he really *did* have something nasty on his face like a leaf or a spider. Or a big blob of mucus. Marcel started to reach up to his face to brush at it, and found that Samantha's hand was already on its way to his forehead. *Oh my God, there IS something there! What is it? Is it something nasty?*

"Sorry!" said Samantha, touching the end of the dreadlock. "You have a ... a raindrop! It's hanging over your eye, I thought ... I thought it would fall in your eye. ..." Well, that was sure lame. He probably thought I was going to poke his eye out. For God's sake, Samantha.

She held up a forefinger, glistening with a drop of pure rainwater. Marcel felt his breath tighten as she put her finger in her mouth and licked it clean, daintily, like a cat. They both laughed, a nervous release.

Thank God it was only a raindrop!

Marcel was smiling at her, a quizzical look on his face. He nodded his head and glanced to her left, and she realized he was indicating something behind her. Turning around, Samantha gasped as a face loomed in her own, about 2 inches from her nose. Kevin Bittner, Daly's roommate from Emerson Hall, was standing right behind her.

"Oh! Hello, Kevin, I, uh, didn't see you standing there." Samantha smiled nervously and edged away, trying to reclaim her personal space.

Kevin was not a happy man. "It's 9:35."

"Oh. Is it?"

"I was here at six o'clock."

"You were?"

Oh, brother. Who IS this guy?

"I had my cell phone with me the whole time." He held up the device so she could see it clearly, 2 inches from her face. *Exhibit A. Cell phone. Right here.*

Samantha looked at Marcel and then back to Kevin. *Kevin, I think it's time for you to crawl back under your rock.*

"Didn't you have my number?" he persisted. "I gave it to you!"

"Oh, was that for me? I thought you wanted to meet Dash here. So I gave *her* your number." *Nice recovery!*

Kevin continued to loom in her face. "Who's he? Are you together?" He indicated Marcel without actually looking at him. Samantha glanced at Marcel.

Marcel leaned forward. "I am Marcel Devereaux. Yes, she is with me. It has been a pleasure meeting you." He linked his arm through Samantha's and pulled her away. "Let's go sit down." His **gender identity** led him to take the initiative, assuming that he should make decisions and be assertive, especially in the presence of another male. This is the psychological state of viewing oneself in a particular way as either masculine or feminine. Marcel sees himself as a man, with certain expectations of behavior that other men and women would have of him.

Laughing, Samantha sat down cross-legged on a large pink pillow under a dormer window. It reminded her of the window well at the music school, and the memory of his dancing was still with her, fresh and fine and unblemished, even by the little encounter with Kevin. She was glad that Marcel had smoothly gotten her out of an uncomfortable situation, although she knew that some might see this behavior as verging on sexism, assuming that she couldn't make decisions on her own, and understood that there are differences in gender roles in different societies. **Sexism** is an attitude, action, or institutional structure that subordinates or discriminates against an individual or group because of their biological sex. Samantha knows that she could have gotten herself out of this uncomfortable social situation without Marcel's help and that some would have interpreted his taking action without consulting her as expressing an attitude that women need men to make decisions for them.

"Is he a friend of yours?" Marcel asked with a smile, settling himself on another pillow. "Hardly!" Samantha laughed. "He lives on my floor. His roommate is this really weird guy, he has this ... this thing, I think he calls it a Bizarrotron. You get a number from it, I only got a two, but my roommate Dash got a seven ..." Samantha realized she was babbling as she recounted her experience with Daly Brown, but Marcel didn't seem to mind. All she could think about was the way he listened with his head slightly cocked to one side, the drying dreadlocks hanging over one eye.

She asked him about Martinique, and he told her about growing up on his island home. About how strange it was coming here, how different and how exciting, and how he'd been dreaming of coming to America ever since he was knee-high to a grasshopper.

She loved listening to him talk. The rolling cadence of the islands held her captive under some kind of spell. It *must* have been a spell because a few minutes after they'd sat down, she looked up and saw with a shock that it was after midnight.

***

It was one o'clock when Marcel made it back to his dorm. Kyle, his roommate, was an unmoving lump under the covers, and Marcel tried to be quiet and not turn on the light. Something crinkled when he sat on his bed. *This better not be another stupid note.* But it was. He unfolded it and held it up to the pale light coming in from the window. It was in all capital letters again, as if he were shouting.

"I DON'T APPRECIATE YOU COMING AND GOING AT ALL HOURS OF THE NIGHT. PLEASE LEAVE ME A NOTE IF YOU ARE GOING TO BE COMING IN AFTER 11:00 P.M."

Marcel sighed, crumpled up the note, and tossed it on the floor. What difference did it make when he came in? He tried to be quiet. He tried to be considerate. It occurred to him that he and Kyle had not actually spoken to each other in days, and he started feeling irritated. Then he pushed this away—nothing could spoil this evening, nothing could dampen the memory of Samantha's smoky hazel eyes or the way she brushed her hair back over one shoulder. Not even Kyle.

"Kyle," whispered Marcel. "Where I come from we just say something if we want to say it. If you have any—issues—you can just tell me, okay? You don't have to write me notes."

There was no answer, although he was sure Kyle wasn't asleep. Marcel undressed and slid under the covers of his bed, forgetting his roommate and thinking only of Samantha, who had captured him with her intelligent eyes and her sweet, sweet smile. He would have to ask her when he saw her again about her intended major, sociology: what the heck was it? But his thoughts, as he drifted off to sleep, were not exactly academic.

***

Professor Guy Rourke was 53 and mostly bald. But what little hair he had left he wore with pride; several strands were carefully combed from one side over the top to the other side. Samantha had always found this very cute on balding men. It was the second week of classes, and sociology, her intended major, was the best class so far.

Professor Rourke leaned back on the edge of his desk at the front of the classroom, looking deceptively casual, with his hands folded across his chest. Samantha knew this was just a cover, in a few minutes he'd be unable to stop pacing back and forth, waving his arms in the air, seized by the passion of his words. She watched and waited.

He looked out across the room, and then looked down at the floor intently, as if there were some universal truth carved into the scuffed gray tiles. Or an obscenity, perhaps. Suddenly he raised his head up, inhaled sharply, and demanded,

"Who in this room considers themselves an individual?"

There was silence for a moment, and then several hands went up. More followed, until everyone had raised their hand, including Samantha.

"So," declared the professor, who stood up and uncrossed his arms. "We have here a room full of individuals, yet you've all just exhibited a group behavior, each person doing what everyone else is doing."

There were a few titters as the hands all sagged and then wilted back down.

"If each of you is truly an individual, wouldn't it have made more sense to do something nobody else is doing? I didn't ask anyone to raise their hand, I just wanted to know who considers themselves an individual! Now, let's try it again: *who in this room considers themselves an individual?*"

Amid giggles and snickering, several students stood up. A few sat on the floor, one girl opened a book and placed it upside-down on her head, and Samantha sat on her desk, her back to the front of the classroom. One guy stood and said "Yo!" And another belched "Yes, sir," and another guy took his shirt off.

"All right," the professor grinned. "I get the point. You can sit down now. And put your shirt back on." He started his pacing, his hands behind his back.

"We live in an individualistic society! We believe individualism is important, yet we're all conditioned to do certain things, to react in certain ways, because of our socialization. Because of this we've all come to learn that certain things are acceptable and certain things are not. Because we were born into American culture, we share certain beliefs and norms, which most of us have internalized as the truth. If we were born into another culture, we would have internalized other beliefs as the truth, and we wouldn't question it. In fact, if we were from another culture, we would look at American culture and think the differences we see are *wrong*."

Now he was really getting going. The hands had become unclasped from behind the back, the face was getting a little red, one arm was showing signs of waving.

"When children are born, they are dependent upon their parents to survive. They have no knowledge. They will soon learn the language, values, beliefs, and norms of their culture. As you will learn in this course, the society and culture in which you live affects your behavior, your choices, your beliefs, values, and attitudes, and even your self-concept—how you view yourself.

"For example, how many men in here view themselves as emotional and nurturing?"

No hands went up.

"Interesting," continued Professor Rourke. "How many women view themselves as emotional and nurturing?"

About half of the hands in the class raised their hands.

"Uh-huh! Why is it that many of the women in this class but no men view themselves as emotional and nurturing?"

One guy slouching in the back replied, "'Cause we're guys."

"Okay," said the professor. "But the male **sex** is a biological term which means that you have XY chromosomes instead of XX, and you have different physical characteristics and reproductive organs. But what does your biological makeup have to do with your psychological and social traits or characteristics, such as being emotional versus rational, or nurturing versus independent? Being male is not the same as being masculine, and being female is not the same as being feminine. Sex is not the same thing as **gender**." These are the social and psychological characteristics associated with being male or female. In American culture, characteristics associated with being female include being nurturing, emotional, and cooperative. Gender characteristics associated with being male include being independent, unemotional, and aggressive. Male gender characteristics are collectively known as masculinity, female gender characteristics are known as femininity.

"Now, how many students in here are majoring in early childhood or primary grade education or nursing?" Of the dozen or so hands that went up, only one was a man's.

"Why is it that most education and nursing majors are women? Has society taught you that these roles are 'women's roles?' Yes, indeed, in every society, members are taught what behaviors and roles are expected of females and males. These are what we call **gender roles**." These are behaviors and roles assigned to men and women in a society. There is debate as to whether the biological differences between men and women are largely the cause of gender roles. Since women are healthier, live longer, and biologically bear children, this explains to sociologists why they eventually develop in the division of labor roles of child rearing, cooking, and weaving. Men, being more muscular and aggressive, tend toward hunting, building, and dominant positions. However, sociologists generally argue that any differences are learned. The context has prepared roles for men and women, and our biological differences are not sufficient to explain gender roles in general or power differences in particular. Men dominate in all areas of the social structure.

"Different societies have different gender roles. In American society young women are expected to pursue an education and a job or career. In some societies, however, women are either not allowed to attend universities or are discouraged from doing so. Societies also have their own beliefs, values, and norms that they accept as reality and socialize their children to accept. How many people in this room have ever eaten a dog?"

A few people snickered and made faces, but no one raised a hand. "I'd be surprised if anyone had because eating dogs is not part of our culture. In other cultures it's perfectly acceptable and even desirable, and they don't have a problem with it.

In fact, they wonder why we think it's disgusting. Now, we know there are all kinds of cultural differences between societies, but how about similarities? Is there one cultural norm that is found in every society known on Earth?"

One student volunteered. "Shaking hands?"

Professor Rourke shook his head. "Nope. If you put your hand out to an Inuit Indian, he will just look at it, and wonder why you're not rubbing noses with him. No, I am thinking of a taboo that is found in some form in every known culture. Anybody know?"

Samantha raised her hand. "**Incest**?" The term refers to sexual relations between certain categories of kin, generally those of close blood relationship. Some form of incest taboo is found in all known societies, although the relationships that the taboo covers vary.

"Yes! The **incest taboo**. It takes different forms with different societies, but it's there, a strong social force that prohibits us from having sexual relations with our own relatives."

One woman in the front row had a question. "Professor, isn't that something genetic? If it's found in all societies, avoiding incest is probably some kind of natural instinct, isn't it?"

"Is it?" The professor resumed his pacing. "How about animals? Do animals naturally avoid incest?"

No one seemed to know.

Professor Rourke answered himself. "No, they don't! Animals have no problem with sons and mothers mating, fathers and daughters, grandparents and grand-children, you name it. The incest taboo for human beings is a social phenomenon, most likely arising out of a need to avoid complicating familial relationships. Certain types of incest, such as cousins marrying, have been allowed or even desired in some societies, especially with royalty and the upper classes in Europe, but again it was for social reasons—consolidating property, making political alliances, et cetera. We do what we do because of our socialization. Because of those forces outside ourselves which shape our experience and our beliefs from the day we're born."

He faced the classroom. "We are born into a society. When we get up in the morning, we do not begin the day as individuals, and as individuals carve out how we're going to live our day. We may be under the illusion that we're individuals about to begin a day of making our own choices as independent entities, but what we're really doing is waking up and taking part in pattern-recurring social relationships. Much of the decisions we think we're making on our own are already programmed into us by social forces we unconsciously take to be true. Our realities are already shaped by the society into which we're born.

"Does this mean we're a society of brainless automatons, unable to even think for ourselves? No, it doesn't. People have different motivations, different IQs, different perceptions. These are internal forces that guide our behavior, and if we were studying these we'd be psychologists.

"But we're sociologists, so we're interested in the external forces that shape our behavior: status, role, and power. We're interested in the **institutions** (an established order comprising rule-bound and standardized behavior patterns for smooth societal functioning) of our society. These are the kinds of concepts we'll be exploring in this sociology class, and it won't be just me telling you about them in the classroom. We are all social actors; we are all members of a society; and in order for you to really learn sociology, what makes us tick as social creatures, you will have to get out there and delve into pattern-recurring social relationships."

A hand went up. "Professor Rourke, since I'm a social actor, I'd like to study myself at home watching TV, and not come to class."

The rest of the students laughed, and the professor rolled his eyes. "Oh, yeah, you're the one who took his shirt off. You get an F. But you can redeem yourself by handing these out." He gave a stack of papers to the TV-watching student, who arose from his slouch and began distributing them around the room.

"For your first assignment, I want you each to choose a topic from the list and write up a proposal for a term paper based on your research. The key point here is that your paper will be based on field research, not just library and textbooks. You will have to go out in the real world and make observations. Follow the example provided for the first draft proposal. My office hours are posted if you need help.

"You could choose to focus on how males and females interact differently, for instance, how greetings are conducted in different social settings depending on gender. Or you could compare males' and females' different ideas about what constitutes sexual double standards by conducting interviews and then comparing responses according to sex. There are endless possibilities, but our point for today is to start learning how to focus on a topic and organize it into a coherent study."

Sexual double standards are the different standards applied to the sexual behavior and expression of men versus women. For example, it is more socially acceptable for men to have casual sexual relations with a variety of partners than it is for women.

"We're going to take the last half hour of class time today to break into small groups, say about six people each. You're going to discuss the topics on the list that most interest you and come up with a hypothesis for the basis of a proposal. Each person in the group should come up with one. You can look over the examples on page two, and I'll be circulating among the groups."

Samantha's head was spinning as she looked over the list. She'd been thinking about her sociology project since the first day of classes and knew her volunteer work in a soup kitchen back home would be a good foundation. She read through the list: crisis hotline, court-ordered teen substance abusers, home for pregnant teenagers, juvenile detention centers, AIDS education, teen crisis center, halfway house for adult alcohol abusers, working with court-ordered children and teens who have suffered abuse, a battered women's shelter, police-community relations, working in a homeless shelter.

That was it. The plight of homeless people had always weighed heavily on her; she always wanted to do something when she saw some forlorn-looking derelict huddled on a sidewalk or a park bench. But what? How much would a dollar or 5 dollars or even 50 help the guy on the street who has no job, no income, no place to live, and no future? Working at a homeless shelter would be a good way to figure out the social conditions that got them there. Then she might have a chance of making a difference, especially when she got her law degree.

For the next half hour Samantha and her partners hashed out hypotheses for their topics; some half-baked and some halfway decent. Samantha came up with a null hypothesis, "Incidence of drug abuse is no higher in homeless populations than in the population at large."

A student sitting next to Samantha turned to her as they were finishing up. "You know, there's a homeless shelter downtown on Miller Street. I'm going there tomorrow to talk to the supervisor about getting permission to conduct a survey. I talked to Professor Rourke about it last week. You can come with me if you want."

Samantha regarded her. She was older than many of the other students, probably in her late thirties or early forties, a slender woman with curly dark brown hair. She'd had a lot of good suggestions during their group discussion of their topics and hypotheses and was also going to study homeless people.

Samantha smiled. "Thanks, that's a great idea. I'm Sam, by the way."

"I'm Jill Hathaway."

***

Dash was in their room when Samantha finished her classes. She dropped her backpack on the floor and sat down on her bed. Dash looked up from her book.

"What are *you* so happy about? A person with a rating of 'two' doesn't deserve to look so smug."

Samantha grinned. "Oh, nothing."

Dash slammed her book and sat up. "What, 'Oh nothing?' I don't think so! Come on!"

"Hey, I saw your boyfriend last night! At the Crow's Nest! He was so mad that you didn't call him."

Dash looked at her blankly. "Oh, for crying out loud. *Kevin*? No, no, he's *your* boyfriend, my dear. Don't tell me you didn't show up at the Crow's Nest at six o'clock? How rude of you! And you didn't call him? You are a gravy-sucking swine of a bitch!" She threw a pillow at Samantha, who laughed.

"I was busy. I couldn't call him."

"Busy doing what? Not studying, I hope. Do not tell me you were studying, or I will have to kill you."

Samantha smiled a Cheshire-cat smile. "He's not gay."

"Who, Kevin? Are you kidding? That doesn't apply in his case; I don't think he's gotten beyond farm animals yet."

Samantha just kept smiling.

"All right, *who* then? Who's not—oh, my God, you don't mean who I think you mean. The dancer? The gorgeous Caribbean guy? You're kidding!"

"I kid you not. And I'm telling you, he's not gay."

Dash sprang up from her bed and flounced onto the foot of Samantha's bed.

"So, out with it. Do you have *first-hand knowledge* of this? Where did you do it? Does he have a private room?"

"No, we didn't do it! We didn't do anything. We just talked, at the Crow's Nest. I met him at the music school. And oh, my GOD, Dash, you should see this guy *dance*. He's unbelievable."

"You saw him dance? How? Did you go to his class? What's his name again, Marcel? Come on, girl, out with it!"

"Marcel Devereaux. He's from Martinique."

"And you haven't done it yet."

Samantha laughed and covered her face with her hands. "Dash, for God's sake! I've known the guy for like 20 hours or something."

"Well, you don't want to sit around too long discussing the weather, now do you? Do you have any idea how many other babes and butches are out there waiting to get into his pants? Hey, maybe he's bi."

"Well, I'll be sure and ask him next time I see him!" declared Samantha. "I hope it's pretty soon. I gave him my phone number."

"Well, he probably won't call today, that's too soon. He won't want to look desperate. But maybe that's how they do it in Martinique. Where is Martinique, anyway?"

"It's in the Lesser Antilles, an island chain in the Caribbean. Martinique is near Barbados."

"Well! Aren't you suddenly the geography whiz! You must really like this guy. He'd better call you soon, maybe tomorrow. Oh, that reminds me, you have a message. Your father called, there's his number." Dash pointed with her chin to Samantha's desk, where a scrap of paper had been left.

Her father had called. Samantha picked up the scrap of paper and didn't recognize the number on it; this must be wherever it was that he was living now. She suddenly wondered if he was staying with her, with Lindsay. Images of her father and his secretary flooded her mind, and she even imagined him chasing her around his desk with the office doors closed. Could her father even be guilty of *sexual harassment*? This constitutes sexual comments, gestures, or physical contacts that are deliberate, repeated, and unwelcome. If Mr. Cahill had made sexual relations a condition for Lindsay keeping her job, he would have been guilty of sexual harassment with his secretary. Samantha remembered the symbol of the diamond pin her father gave Lindsay and from this concluded that her father's attentions were not unwanted.

"Samantha, you okay?" asked Dash.

"What? Oh, yeah, sure." She stared at the phone number, her buoyant mood dissolving in seconds. She hadn't spoken to her father since finding out about the divorce last week. She looked at the foreign numbers written on the paper until they started to blend into a haze. Then she stuffed the note into her desk drawer.

***

Marcel stood at the phone booth at the end of the second floor hallway of Harrison Hall. In his hand he held a crumpled piece of paper with a phone number written on it. His other hand rested on the receiver, still in its cradle, waiting.

Should he do it? He'd only met her last night. What if she had a boyfriend? Of course she didn't have a boyfriend, or she wouldn't have given him her number. She wouldn't have given him her number if she didn't want him to call her. Sure, she wanted him to call her, she wasn't just being polite. He could tell.

But how did they do it here? What if he turned her off by calling too soon? Was he expected to call her today? Or in a few days? He really wanted to see her today, he wanted to keep talking to her, he wanted her to look at him again with those lovely eyes, the way she'd looked at him last night. She'd kept saying she must look awful, but she hadn't. At all.

Damn it! Thank God we didn't have to go through this on Martinique! Hardly anyone had phones anyway where he lived, and if you were brave enough (or dumb enough) to try calling a girl, you'd have the whole family and three neighbors listening in. No, there were plenty of other ways of approaching girls there. And he hadn't had too much trouble. So what was his problem now?

Picking the receiver up, he took a deep breath and dialed the number. One ring, two rings, three rings. A connection was made, a little fuzzy.

"Hello?" a male voice answered. *Hmm, hadn't expected this.*

"Hello, I'd like to speak with Samantha Cahill, please."

There was a silence. "Who is this? Is this a joke?"

Didn't this guy's voice sound familiar? Oh, God, it was him—the guy last night at the Crow's Nest, the guy who was there at six o'clock! Marcel quickly hung up the phone and looked at the piece of paper again.

Samantha had given him Kevin Bittner's cell phone number.

Chapter 4 Study Questions
SEX AND GENDER

1. How might Samantha's and Marcel's **socialization** have been different to result in different ideas about gender roles?
2. How are one's **gender identity** and **gender role** different?
3. What **taboo** is found in some form in every known culture?
4. Explain the difference between **sex and gender**.

Seventeen after Two

Research Methods

J ILL HATHAWAY AND Samantha sat on rickety folding chairs in the office of the
Miller Street Shelter. The shelter's director, Mr. Stroud, looked over their paperwork, a copy of the assignments from their sociology class, and a short bio and study
plan they'd each written up. He laid the papers down on his cluttered desk and
looked at them over his bifocals. Mr. Stroud had a sad, hound-dog face, with tired
eyes and a kindly expression. His voice never wavered above a solemn monotone.

"So tell me, Ms. ..."—he glanced down at one sheet—"Hathaway. Why do
you want to do **field research** on homeless people?" This is a method of research
in which researchers study social activities or groups in their natural setting (as
opposed to a research lab or other artificial environment).

Jill met his gaze candidly. "Children, Mr. Stroud. I have two of my own and I'm
doing my best to make sure they get the love and care they need to become whoever
they want to be. I worry about the children in trouble, children in places like this
who are disadvantaged before they even have a chance. I want to help them get a
chance. But I'm not sure if what I want to do is macro or micro sociology." **Macro
sociology** is concerned with the big picture: large social structures such as social
institutions (family, education, religion, economics). **Micro sociology** has a more
narrow focus and is concerned with behavior, interactions, and experiences of individuals and small groups in specific situations.

Samantha glanced at her lap. Jill sounded so together, so focused. She hoped
he wouldn't ask her the same question, but he did. "I used to volunteer at a soup
kitchen," Samantha told him. "I always wondered who the homeless people were,
what their names were, and where they came from. I want to understand the social
issues that led to their becoming homeless, so I can find a way to help. Even if it's
only in a small way."

Mr. Stroud leaned forward, tenting his fingers together and pursing his lips.

"We do have students coming here from time to time. But you have to understand, the people who live here, temporarily or long term, get tired of being studied. They don't always appreciate being asked a lot of questions by people they'll never see again." This was a long speech for the taciturn Mr. Stroud, and he paused.

Samantha tried to read his face. What was he thinking? Would he let them come? Had they already had too many students? The silence stretched out. Thoughts of Marcel superimposed themselves on her mind, as they did often, and she hoped there would be a message from him when she got back to the dorm. She could see him in her mind's eye, bare-chested and whirling to the music. ... Mr. Stroud finally spoke again, bringing her attention back.

"You can come and do your research as long as you obtain informed consent from all residents of the shelter that you include in your study. **Informed consent** means that the residents agree to voluntarily participate in research after being informed of the nature of the research. Research must also be objective. **Objectivity** is the scientific principle that research should not be influenced by one's own personal beliefs, values, and biases.

"Thank you, Mr. Stroud," said Samantha. "The first part of our assignment is observation only. Can we maybe just observe for the first week or so?" Samantha was asking Mr. Stroud if she could do **non-participant observation**: the researcher observes a group or activity he or she is studying without participating in the group or activity.

"You could, but what works better is to start doing some kind of work and let people get used to having you around. Of course, that makes it **participant observation** instead. What students usually do is a case study (a method used to do a detailed and thorough study of an individual, group, or event) here at the shelter, using participant observation and surveys." A **survey** is a scientific research method using interviews and questionnaires to obtain answers to questions. **Interviews** are a direct research method in which a researcher questions a respondent directly. Interviews may be conducted face-to-face or over the telephone.

He smiled for the first time, seeing their surprise. "I guess I can find my way around a sociology assignment. I have a master's in social work, and I did a lot of undergraduate work in sociology and psychology. Trust me, the people here will open up to you much better if you don't stand on ceremony. Once they know you well, you'll get more valid responses from them."

"Mr. Stroud. I ... am ... here. Mr. Stroud." A raspy voice at the open doorway caused the two women to turn around in their seats, to see a small, thin man with oversized work pants and several dirty sweaters on. He was oddly bent, as if he'd gotten out of bed the wrong way a few years ago and had never straightened up. His eyes were red rimmed and teary, and he glanced furtively at Samantha and Jill, repeatedly dropping his gaze to the floor.

"Hello, Winston," said Mr. Stroud. "Is it 2:17 already?"

"Yes! Mr. Stroud, yes! ... 2:17, right here." Winston pointed to a cracked wrist-watch fastened to his skinny wrist.

"Well, that's fine, Winston, just fine. I wish everyone around here would be so punctual." He pushed himself back from the desk.

"Punctual, yes! I'm punctual, Mr. Stroud. I'm the mostest ... punctualest ... person here. ... Ah!" He stared at his watch, astonished. "Two-eighteen! It's 2:18, Mr. Stroud!"

"So it is. Time to show our new students around the shelter. Can you do that for me, Sir Winston? Ms. Hathaway, Ms. Cahill, meet Winston Churchill."

***

"Marcel, how nice to see you again." Marjorie Trask, the guidance counselor, stretched out her hand and Marcel shook it. He wondered what this meeting was about; she'd just called and asked him to make an appointment at his earliest convenience. Was there some problem with his scholarship? Some technical detail he wasn't aware of? He'd already filled out stacks of forms and paperwork. Maybe he'd missed something.

"So, how did your first week of school go, Marcel?"

Was this going to be a weekly thing? Was he supposed to share his issues? "Fine, ma'am. It went fine."

"Oh, come now, Marcel, I'm sure you know my name by now! Please call me Marjorie."

"Yes, ma'am, Marjorie."

"Now. I just want to remind you that we're here for you in case you need anything, any counseling or assistance. We are able to refer out to psychologists who specialize in gender issues, if that's necessary."

Didn't we have this conversation last week?

"Thank you, ma'am. Marjorie."

Marcel simply couldn't get around the fact that the guidance counselor—synonymous with teacher—was being friendly and wanted to help. Most of the experiences he'd ever had with teachers had been on the receiving end of their authority. Without thinking, he slid his left hand over his right; he'd learned to protect his writing hand from the sharp rap of the ruler. Mr. Marchand especially had been faster than a striking snake with it, and it was hard to do his homework if the knuckles on his right hand were bruised. *Rap!* For looking out the window. *Rap!* For poking his friend Anton between the shoulder blades with his pencil. *Rap!* For laughing at the girls. And forget telling your parents about it when you got home: two more raps *for giving your teacher a hard time, wasting all the good money we spend on books and school fees, bless the poor man for having to pound the education into that thick skull of yours ...*

"Marcel? Are there any issues which you feel we haven't addressed? Anything you'd like to share? Special needs, **sexual orientation**?" This is the classification of individuals as heterosexual, bisexual, or homosexual based on their emotional and sexual attractions, relationships, sexual behavior, and self-identity.

What?

"Um ... no, ma'am." *What kinds of things did students TALK about here? Sexual WHAT?*

"Oh. I see." Ms. Trask looked somehow disappointed, as if she'd expected more.

Perhaps Marcel just wasn't giving her a chance to do her job. Maybe there was something he could tell her, some issue he could share.

"Ma'am?"

"Yes, Marcel?"

"Well, there is my roommate. ... His name is Kyle Parker? He, uh, he doesn't talk much. In fact, he really doesn't seem to like me."

"Oh, well, I'm sorry to hear that. I'm sure if you just give him a little time, once he gets to know you, he'll open up." She flipped through her notes on Harrison Hall residents. *Kyle Parker... bipolar disorder... on medication.* "Maybe I can have a little chat with Kyle and see if he's having any problems."

"Thank you, ma'am."

She picked up a colorful leaflet and gave it to Marcel. "Maybe you'd like to take this, it really is an excellent organization. They meet every first and third Tuesday of the month in the Student Union. There's a café on the fifth floor, the Crow's Nest?"

"Yes, ma'am, I know it."

"Well, thanks for dropping by, Marcel. You just call me if you need anything."

"Thank you, ma'am."

Outside the office, Marcel stuffed the flyer into his shoulder bag and headed down the steps. He knew very well where the Crow's Nest was, and the thought of it sent his mind reeling. Samantha had seemed so ... friendly, so interested. He'd really thought there was something there, and yet she'd given him a bogus phone number. Maybe since Samantha was the first person who'd really listened to him since he'd gotten here he was reading too much into it. He tried to shrug it off as he made his way over to the cafeteria, but the feeling of disquiet would not leave, making him moody and sullen as he remembered her damp hair, the crackling fire ... and a single raindrop.

***

Jill Hathaway dropped Samantha off at Emerson Hall and went to pick up her children from day care. As she climbed the stairs to the third floor, Samantha found a little knot of tension fluttering in her stomach, growing with each step closer to her room. What if he'd called and left a message? What if he had called but had decided not to leave a message? What if he'd called and left a message, but she didn't get it? He'd be expecting her to call back, but she wouldn't have his number. *Damn it, I should have gotten his number, too, when I gave him mine. What if he hasn't called at all?*

"Dash, what's up?" Samantha practically swung the door off its hinges as she entered their room.

"Not much. S'up witchoo?"

"I just got back from the Miller Street Shelter. I went with Jill Hathaway, she's in my sociology class. We're going to do a case study there for our term papers. You should see this guy who showed us around. He's a scrawny little guy who calls himself Winston Churchill and thinks he can make things invisible, and—Dash, I don't have any phone messages, do I?"

Dash regarded her friend with velvety purple-shaded eyes. This suited her better than the black mascara. She had tied a long pink silk scarf around her neck and was playing with the ends of it. "He hasn't called. Don't get your knickers in a twist. But there's another message from your dad." She pointed to a note on Samantha's desk. Dash grinned. "And may I just say that I am, of course, delighted to be your personal secretary."

Samantha sat down heavily on her bed and stared at the note. Marcel still hadn't called. And her dad had left three messages now. One of these days she was going to have to talk to him; she couldn't put it off forever. Damn it, she'd been in a pretty good mood when she'd come in the door; *it's amazing how much power a little piece of paper can have. Wouldn't I feel a thousand percent better if that note was from Marcel?*

"Sam?" said Dash. "Did I say something wrong? I was just kidding."

"What? Oh, no, don't worry. I was just ... thinking. Hey, you want to go get some dinner?"

"Okay. You're not gonna call your dad first? He seemed kind of anxious."

Samantha picked up the note with his phone number and looked at it. The unfamiliar number seemed to taunt her, and she stuck it into her jeans pocket.

"I'll call him later. Let's go."

***

"Mind if I sit down?"

Marcel looked up from his cafeteria dinner to see a large Black man standing at the table, carrying a heavily loaded tray. He was a little taller than Marcel, about 6 ft, and about 50 lbs heavier, with rounded shoulders and a spare tire. He had an open, easygoing expression and an engaging smile. Marcel gestured to the empty chair across from him.

"Please." He'd been picking at his food, in a funk, not looking forward to finishing up his—what was this stuff called? Lasagna?—and returning to his room with Kyle the Hermit still not speaking to him. Well, he'd only be there long enough to shower and change before going to the music school for dance practice anyway. His mood started to lift as the man set his tray down and took a seat. There was something very friendly and comfortable about him.

The man extended a hand and said, "Ben Williamson. Nice to meet you."

"Marcel Devereaux."

Ben looked around the cafeteria and then grinned at Marcel. "This must be the Black folks' section, huh?"

Marcel smiled and kept picking at his lasagna. "Mon, I tell you, never have I seen so many white faces. On my island, there is black from coast to coast."

"That sounds just *fine*. You're from Martinique, right? But everybody thinks you're Jamaican?"

"Yes, how did you know?"

Ben chuckled as he dove into his chili and cornbread. Marcel was amazed at the amount of food that could be crammed onto one tray: baked beans, broccoli, three different kinds of bread, chili, mashed potatoes, corn on the cob, two chicken legs, peas and carrots, and fruit cocktail. Ben looked like he planned to eat every last bit of it.

"Oh, I've been hearing about you ever since I got here from Atlanta. That's in Georgia, down south—peach trees and pecans and all that. 'You gotta meet the Jamaican guy, you gotta meet the guy with the dreadlocks, man.'"

"How did you know I'm from Martinique?"

"The guidance counselor told me." Ben laughed as he saw the recognition and a slightly pained expression on Marcel's face. "Oh, yeah, you know her! I know you do!"

Marcel smiled. "I'm supposed to call her 'Marjorie.'"

"Just like all the other minority students, right?"

"She wants me to share my issues with her." Marcel pulled the flyer Ms. Trask had given him out of his backpack. He hadn't really looked at it yet, and he saw that it had the words "Free to Be" emblazoned across a rainbow background. "Did she give you one of these?"

Ben took the flyer from him and looked it over, shaking his head.

"Aw, man, she just thinks you're gay. This is a support group."

"She what?" Said Marcel, surprised.

"You're a dance major, fer cryin' out loud. Plus, you got on them tight-ass black jeans. The whole administration has their panties in a wad about discrimination: they get one whiff of racism or discrimination against gays and it's front-page news. They avoid that like the plague. They don't keep their gays and Blacks happy, they're in deep dog-doo." **Discrimination** is the unfavorable treatment of individuals because of their membership in a group. Many forms of discrimination are illegal in the United States. In colleges and universities, discrimination based on race, national origin, religion, gender, age, and disability is against the law. Some, but not all, colleges and universities have policies prohibiting discrimination based on sexual orientation.

"What!" exclaimed Marcel. "She thinks I'm gay? Ah, mon, she asked me about my 'sexual orientation.' I thought she meant was I right-handed or something!"

Ben threw his head back and laughed, a rich, deep guffaw. He had a big man's laugh; it was full and loud and took no prisoners. He suddenly put on a very solemn face. "'Yes, Ms. Marjorie, my sexual orientation sure is right-handed, Ms. Marjorie, but only in the shower and never on Sundays.'" Ben's brown eyes twinkled.

Marcel couldn't help himself. The thought of saying something like that to the guidance counselor, or—God forbid—his teachers back home was simply beyond comprehension. He shook his head in disbelief.

A terrible thought suddenly struck him.

"Oh, no!"

"What?" asked Ben, a chicken leg halfway to his mouth.

"This girl, I met this girl the other night. She was all right, let me tell you. We hung out at the Crow's Nest, and I thought, you know ..."

Ben laughed. "Oh, yeah, I know! I got to beat the women off with a stick, too. So what's the problem?"

"Well, she gave me her phone number, only when I tried calling it ..."

Ben put his chicken leg down. "Don't tell me, it was some horse hockey number. Man, that's *harsh*. Cute chick?"

"Oh, yeah. But now I'm thinking maybe she thought I was gay! Does everyone here think you're gay if you're a dancer?"

Ben shrugged his shoulders. "Well, I don't know, man. Tell you what, though, you come shoot a few hoops with me—you got basketball on Martinique? You use coconuts or something?—I'll teach you how to use a basketball, man, then we'll go have a few beers. And put on some baggy pants, for Pete's sake! You just stick with me, you'll be all right. Have some chicken." Ben handed him the remaining leg from his own plate. "You're way too skinny."

Marcel laughed and took the chicken leg. It was impossible to stay depressed around this guy.

Ben went on. "I'm telling you, man, that chick will be way sorry she gave you the wrong number!"

***

Samantha and Dash set their trays down on a table near the front door of the cafeteria.

"Not very hungry, I see," commented Dash as she surveyed Samantha's tray. It contained a carton of milk, a bowl of fruit cocktail, and a muffin.

"I guess not," replied Samantha, and she stared off into space as she fiddled with the milk carton. Milk began to dribble out and onto the table as she pulled at the opening.

Rolling her eyes, Dash took the carton from her. "Give me that. You're gonna spill it all over yourself." She got the carton open and gave it back to Samantha. Then she looked her in the eye. "So. Are you going to tell me what's up, or do I have to lock you in a closet and beat you with a rubber hose?"

Samantha smiled ruefully. "Oh, Dash, I guess I'm turning into a basket case these days. My dad keeps calling and I just … My parents are getting a divorce and I just can't deal with it."

"Sam, I'm sorry." Dash put her fork down and touched Samantha's hand.

Samantha shrugged and looked away, blinking to keep back the tears. "They were waiting for both my sister and me to go off to college before they did it. I don't know how long they've been planning this. A long time, I guess. I feel like a jerk because I didn't know. My sister is a jerk because she knew and she didn't tell me." She bit her lower lip, struggling to keep her composure. Her gaze traveled around the cafeteria.

"Oh, my God," said Samantha, as she recognized Marcel, sitting on the far side of the room with another Black man.

"What?" Dash shifted in her seat and followed Samantha's gaze. "Oh. The man himself. The guy who hasn't called you."

"I hope he doesn't see me," Samantha said as she hung her head down over her tray.

"Why not?" asked Dash. "Why don't you go talk to him? Just be friendly."

"I just can't. Not right now. What if I go talk to him and he's all cool and distant? I'd probably burst into tears. I'm such a mess."

"Hey, you want me to go ask the dancer man how come he hasn't called you in three days?"

"Dash! No!"

"Just kidding, girlfriend. Relax. Maybe he lost your number or something."

"Yeah, maybe. You know, Dash, I'm really not very hungry. I think I'll go to the library for a while, I have to do some research for this sociology project. I don't know the difference between quantitative and qualitative sociology. I'll see you later, okay?" **Quantitative sociology** emphasizes studies that apply mathematical and statistical techniques to empirical observations of society. A quantitative study on homelessness would focus on the number of homeless people, their sex, income levels, and jobs. **Qualitative sociology** (Verstehen method) is a way of gaining insight into human action by understanding the sociocultural setting in which it occurs. The researcher is concerned with how the social setting is understood or interpreted by the actors. A qualitative study on homelessness would capture how it feels to be a homeless person.

"Okay, I'll create a diversion while you make your getaway. I could stage an act of spontaneous human combustion."

"Very funny. I'll see you back at Emerson." Samantha stood and picked up her backpack, glad they'd happened to sit so close to the exit. Marcel was on the far side of the room and probably wouldn't see her.

"I wouldn't do it for just anyone, you know!" Dash told her as she left. Samantha waved to her and slipped out the door.

***

Sitting at a table strewn with open textbooks and scribbled notes, Samantha leaned back and stretched. She had tried to come up with one hypothesis to test to explain homelessness, but could not find an **independent variable** (a variable that influences the dependent variable). A **hypothesis** is a scientific prediction about the relationship between two variables that can be tested through empirical research.

She would have to find a **variable** (a characteristic or property that varies or is subject to change) to explain it, something that might cause her dependent variable, homelessness, to occur. **Cause** is the scientific view that two variables are related and that one produces the occurrence of the other in a predictable manner. The **dependent variable** is presumed to be the outcome or consequence of some cause (independent variable: Samantha knew homelessness might be correlated with medical problems, poverty, worker layoffs, general hard times, or even having too many children, but which variable should she concentrate on?) **Correlation** is a statistical measure in which change in one variable is associated with change in another.

Samantha needed a theory of homelessness, something that would help provide an explanation or understanding that might guide her research. **Theory**, in sociology, is a set of ideas or concepts that are useful in understanding and explaining a broad range of social phenomena.

Immersing herself in books for an hour had helped to clear her mind, but Samantha knew she couldn't put off calling her father any longer. She wouldn't freak out about it, she'd just have a nice short conversation with him and get it over with. There was a pay phone in the lobby of the library, and she walked down the stairs with her calling card in her hand. A lump began to form in her throat. *I will be calm about this, I will be calm. People get divorced all the time. I will stay calm.*

While the phone rang, Samantha hoped desperately that there would be no strange female voice picking up. That would just be too weird. *Hi, I'm Samantha Cahill. Are you my dad's girlfriend?* To stop fidgeting, she stuck her right hand in her jeans pocket.

But there was no one home. Voice mail picked up and a polite recorded message instructed her to leave a message after the tone. The beep came and went but Samantha didn't notice, her attention was riveted to a scrap of paper she had just discovered in her pocket. Finally, she hung up the phone without leaving any message.

What on Earth? What is this doing here? She was staring at her own name and phone number. She had written this for Marcel when they were at the Crow's Nest, and she had given it to him, *she remembered giving it to him!* Wait, she had pulled a piece of paper out of her pocket; it was the one with Kevin Bittner's number on it (like she would ever want to call it) and she had torn off the bottom half of the paper, which was blank. She'd used it to write her name and number, and she'd handed it to Marcel!

Now she remembered that she'd been looking at his face when she'd given it to him, and had stuffed the remaining scrap of paper back into her jeans pocket. Now she had this in her hand, and it was her own number, the one she should have given to Marcel.

And she'd been too cow-eyed at the time to see that she'd given him the wrong piece of paper.

***

Esther Cady stopped by the dance studio as she sometimes did in the evenings to see how the new students were shaping up, not so much to see what they were doing, but who was there. She tried to apply scientific reasoning often in her assessment of students. They all told her they came often, but she questioned the validity of their comments. By dropping in frequently, she could get a more reliable feeling. **Validity**, in research, is a measure of truth. It is difficult or nearly impossible to investigate drug use and know the answer we obtain is true or valid. Very often, we are forced to obtain a measure of reliability rather than validity. It is **reliable** (not necessarily valid) if the same answer is given several times. Reliability is an attempt to ascertain how truthful (valid) an answer may be by obtaining the same answer or measure at two or more times. If the same question elicits the same answer two or more times, it is said to be reliable. If it is reliable, it may be valid. If it is unreliable, it is not valid.

The lightweights would only be showing up for the Wednesday and Friday afternoon classes, the middleweights would sign up for an occasional evening practice session, and once in a while a really serious dancer would be there night after night. If these students had some real talent as well as discipline, *well, then*.

A tiny smile played at her lips as she recognized the West Indian student, Marcel Devereaux, practicing his heart out for the fourth night this week. It was too soon to tell—experience had taught her not to get her hopes up too quickly—even a promising student could burn out, drop out, decide to go to business school instead. But this one, this Black student, he sure had some moves, and it was clear that dance was in his heart and soul. She'd known students who wanted more than anything to be great dancers, who practiced all the time and had plenty of determination. But if they didn't have an innate and elusive quality, a certain X factor that the natural dancer had and the hopeful could only try to copy, they would never be great dancers. It was something you were born with or you weren't, some kind of direct communication between the spirit and the physical body, something that took place on some mysterious dimension when the music began. It was an eternal joke on Esther Cady that she did not herself have it, although she could fool the untrained observer. But she knew what it looked like, and this young man from the Caribbean was the closest she'd seen in a long time.

Marcel danced as if he were the only one awake in the world or as if he had stepped into a dream and everyone else only thought they were awake. As Professor Cady watched him, he caught her eye and stopped. He walked to his phone on the floor and turned off the music. Wiping himself with a towel, he approached Esther and offered his hand.

"Professor Cady, good evening. Nice of you to come."

He was always so polite! "How are you, Jamaica?" She knew where he was from but liked the sound of Jamaica.

Marcel grinned. She was the only one allowed to call him that. "Just fine, ma'am, and you?"

"Fine, fine, Marcel. Just leave the music off for a minute and repeat your last sequence for me."

Connor and Drew, the two other students practicing in the studio, stopped to watch. After Marcel had whirled through a minute-long sequence, one they had learned in class, the professor called them over.

"All of you, positions, and on my count, do it three times in a row."

As she watched the three students, it was clear who had the natural ability and who didn't. But they were all learning, and she was a teacher. She addressed the three young men who waited expectantly after finishing their routine.

"The purpose of practicing is to get your moves down, to train your body, and learn to respond to the music as if it were second nature. But there is another element, another level of the dance, indeed of any task that you set your heart and mind to and aspire to excellence." The diminutive professor slowly walked and turned as she spoke, her hands clasped behind her back.

"In the art of Zen archery, the most important thing one has to learn is to stand with the bow fully drawn and release the arrow spontaneously at the point of maximum tension, without any deliberate effort." She stopped and looked at them. "Sounds easy. It isn't. It took me more than four years to learn. My teacher, a Tibetan monk, likened this process to snow falling off a bamboo leaf. The leaf bends lower and lower under the weight of the snow until the snow suddenly slips to the ground by itself, without the leaf having exerted any pressure.

"When you dance, you do have to train your muscles, fine-tune your balance, study the routines. But you must keep training your mind, you must keep going to the point where we don't see you dance anymore. The deliberate effort involved is transcended, you get beyond the routine, and you are truly dancing. This is what you keep in your mind and heart as you practice. Good night, gentlemen."

Marcel watched thoughtfully as the professor left the studio. *Snow.* He'd never seen it. It now had a magical quality, elusive and shrouded in fantasy. *I want to see snow.*

Drew and Connor picked up their jackets and bags.

"On that note!" said Connor, slinging his backpack over one shoulder. "Marcel, you coming?"

"Oh. Yeah, I'm coming." Marcel picked up his pack and started toward the door.

He happened to glance over at the window as he often did while he practiced, and stopped in his tracks when he saw a figure crouching in the window well. *Samantha*? She had her hand up against the window, holding something small and white.

"Um, you guys go ahead. I'll catch up later," he said to Drew and Connor, who shrugged and left the studio.

Marcel approached the window and looked at her. She was just as he remembered, but her hair was dry this time and fell over her shoulders in a casual silky tumble. Standing in front of the window, he saw that she held up a small piece of paper.

"This is for you. I gave you the wrong number by mistake." Marcel studied the scrap of paper silently. There was a phone number written underneath *Samantha Cahill* and under that was a hastily drawn little heart.

His eyes met hers. Samantha realized that her heart was pounding, and she couldn't read his face. Maybe this had been a mistake; she shouldn't have come. She should just make an excuse and leave.

"Wait right there," said Marcel, and he disappeared.

Samantha was left sitting in the window well, the phone number still in her hand. Where was he going? The lights in the studio went off, and she could hear the echo of the heavy wooden door closing. Now what? Was he coming? Should she just keep waiting? If anyone had come along and asked her what she was doing huddling in a window well outside the music school with her phone number in hand, she wouldn't have been able to say. *I'm not exactly sure what I'm doing here ...*

Soft footfalls approached. A figure appeared at the edge of the window well, and she could see the unmistakable outline of dreadlocks silhouetted against the night sky. Marcel dropped his backpack into the window well and climbed down inside, kneeling in the leaves next to her.

"Marcel, I'm ..." She didn't get any farther with her apology, unable to speak with Marcel's soft lips covering her own. The aroma of his skin was intoxicating; two hours of dancing had given him a moist, salty fragrance, and she could taste him as she returned his kiss. Leaves crackled as he shifted to enfold her in an embrace and she sank her hands into his thick black mane.

Apparently her apology had been accepted.

***

Chapter 5 Study Questions
RESEARCH METHODS

1. What is the difference between **macro** and **micro** sociology?

2. Why is **objectivity** important in research? Do you think it is possible for a researcher to be totally objective? Why or why not?

3. Why does Mr. Stroud recommend that Samantha and Jill do **participant observation** research rather than **non-participant** observation research at the homeless center?

4. Describe three different types of **survey research**. Which type of survey research is best suited for studying residents at a homeless shelter? Explain your answer.

5. Suppose Samantha wanted to find out what percentage of homeless shelter residents currently use illegal drugs. Which type of research discussed in this chapter would probably provide the most **valid** data? Why?

Yes, We Have No Papayas

Organizations

T HE DOOR TO Samantha's room creaked open and she peered inside. It was dark.

"Dash," she whispered. "Are you in here?"

Pushing the door all the way open, she led Marcel inside by the hand. She left the lights off. "My roommate's out," she whispered, and he closed the door. Standing close and taking her face gently in both hands, he kissed her lightly and then pulled back to look at the way the glow from the window made her eyes shine. The warm tropical rain was soaking into his spirit, a welcome relief after a long drought.

Holding his gaze with her eyes, Samantha turned slightly and bit the fingers cupping her face, and he gasped slightly. Pulling her close, Marcel wrapped himself around her, and the tropical rain stirring in them both rose to tempest force.

***

The light clicked on, making them both squint and snatch at the blankets.

"Hey, girlfriend—whoa, whoa, whoa." Dash was back, larger than life in lime-green stretch pants, a black-and-white sweater, and a beret. She stood with her hands on her hips in front of the two of them, taking in the overcrowded bed, the tangled sheets, and the clothes flung everywhere.

"Hi, Dash." Samantha smiled weakly and waved her fingers. Marcel was frozen in surprise, his arms wrapped around Samantha and her head on his chest.

"Oh, no, don't get up! And don't mind little old me, I'd never think of intruding on such an intimate moment." Dash picked up a lacy bra and held it up. "Nice!"

Marcel pulled the blanket up higher but one long leg was still sticking out. "Um, Dash ..." began Samantha.

"Far be it from me to barge in, you know, on a private happening," Dash went on, but she grinned irreverently and made no move to leave them alone. "I'd never want to bust up some heavy breathing." She picked up a pair of lacy panties. "Very nice!"

Samantha could feel Marcel's chest twitch as he started to laugh.

"Dash, do you mind ... she tried again. She snatched at the panties, but Dash held them out of her reach. "Looks like you're out of uniform, my dear!" She giggled and tossed them out into the hallway.

"Dash, you complete witch, get outta here!" Samantha, laughing, threw a pillow at her as she finally headed for the door.

"You know, if you leave these out in the hall like this, people are gonna think you've been playing hide the sausage," Dash called over her shoulder on her way out of the room.

"Dash!" Samantha leaped out of bed and flung herself at the closing door.

"Riding the baloney pony," Dash giggled and zipped out the door as Samantha slammed it. She turned around and leaned against it, and looked at Marcel. They both burst out laughing.

"That was my roommate."

***

"Hold his feet up, like this." Jill Hathaway was showing Samantha how to change a diaper. They'd been volunteering at the Miller Street Shelter for a couple of weeks, and Samantha had been dreading this particular chore, but she wanted to show that she could pitch in and do everything. She gingerly took the baby's feet from Jill and started cleaning him up. *This isn't exactly what I had in mind when I set out to save the world, she thought ruefully, but I guess this is where it all starts!*

The child's mother, Letitia, was 19 years old and had a toddler as well as this baby boy. She was a recovering crack addict, and her children had already been taken away from her once. Letitia sat by a window, a dispirited look on her face as she gazed through the glass at nothing while the students cared for her baby.

The baby was strangely pliable as she changed him, soft and boneless, like a rubber toy. His brown eyes were dull and glassy, and he rarely cried. His mother had been drinking and doing crack cocaine while she was pregnant with him, and he had spent the first two months of his life in intensive care. Now he was 11 months old but looked much younger, about six or seven months. His two-year-old sister played quietly on the floor near her mother, and she screamed and cried whenever Letitia was out of sight. Samantha wondered what kind of lives these two children would have, given the probable retardation of the little boy and the emotional and economic circumstances of their mother.

Samantha sat on the floor and cradled the baby in her lap, looking around the shelter. There were a lot of older people, lost and forgotten by their families, people with no money and no one to look after them. Some were middle-aged, like Barry, who had lost his hand in a motorcycle accident, and Stephen, an alcoholic. Letitia was one of four mothers currently at the shelter, and her two babies were the youngest children. She was apparently in a state of alienation and didn't talk much to anyone, not even to her own children. **Alienation** is a sense of powerlessness and meaninglessness. To Karl Marx, alienation characterized the condition of the workers in a capitalist society whose work failed to provide a meaningful expression of self or of one's relationship to fellow humans and nature. Letitia is alienated from society by her homelessness, drug problems, and her difficulty in caring for her two young children. There are undoubtedly many social factors contributing to her state of alienation: coming from a poor socioeconomic status, inadequate education, and a possible history of abuse and neglect.

Jill had gone to sit at a table with an elderly man and had gotten out her notebook. Today they were interviewing residents, using questions they'd worked out the night before at the library.

"Hey, little man," Samantha said softly to the baby in her lap. "Shall we go interview your mama?" The child regarded her with his inscrutable brown eyes.

Samantha carried him over to the rocking chair by the window and gave him back to Letitia, who said nothing. "He's a good baby, isn't he?" said Samantha. "He didn't fuss at all." Letitia idly rocked the chair with one foot and didn't answer. She was of medium height, with creamy light-brown skin and close-cropped black hair.

Perhaps she was biracial? Samantha wasn't sure. She had a somewhat chunky build and a scar on her forehead near one eye. Samantha wondered if she'd been beaten.

"Hey, Letitia, you know I'm a student from the university, right?"

The young woman shrugged. She kept rocking the baby in her lap.

"Well, I was wondering if you could help me with one of my assignments. It's a project? For my sociology class?" Samantha knew this was a big stretch, having observed Letitia's antisocial demeanor, but maybe it would be good for them both if she talked a little.

Letitia shrugged again.

Is this a yes? I feel like I'm intruding. Samantha glanced over at Jill, who seemed to be deep in conversation with her subject, an older man with frizzy reddish-gray hair. She was taking copious notes, and Samantha wondered how she always seemed to get things together so quickly.

Taking a deep breath, Samantha pulled a notebook out of her backpack. "I really appreciate it, Letitia. This is an important project; it's 30% of our grade. Can I ask you some questions?"

Finally, Letitia nodded.

Last week Samantha and Jill had done an observational drawing, making a diagram of the setting and describing what was happening. Then they'd done the participant observation; Samantha had helped Winston Churchill sweep and mop the floors and had helped make lunch (pea soup, bread, and Jell-O). She and Jill Hathaway had spent hours in the library reading up on research methods so they would have a good plan for their studies.

Now it was time to move on to the interview, and Samantha found herself a little nervous. "Letitia, can you describe to me what you do during one whole day here, from when you wake up to when you go to sleep?" Samantha sat poised with her pen and her notebook, shifting uncomfortably as the young woman regarded her with expressionless eyes. After this, she would ask her for five things she liked best about the shelter and five things she didn't like. Then she would follow up with the five things she liked best and didn't like about living on the streets rather than the shelter, so she'd be able to compare homelessness on the street with homelessness within a **formal organization**. This is a social structure deliberately created to achieve one or more goals. The Miller Street Shelter was created to provide homeless people and their families with food, shelter, basic medical care, clothing, group support, and referrals to other social services, such as job training and substance abuse counseling.

Letitia looked down at her son, now dozing in her lap. Her eyes never leaving the baby's little round head, covered with tiny brown curls, she began to speak. "I had my first baby when I was 17. That's my baby girl, Shanya Lynn. I smoked some reefer when I was pregnant with her, but nothin' much. I didn't do no crack or nothin', not then. Her daddy was working down to the lumberyard, and he said he was gonna marry me when I got pregnant with Shanya."

Samantha wondered if she hadn't understood her request; she was supposed to get a description of a day in the life of a resident. But she didn't want to interrupt, so she kept taking notes as the young mother continued.

"He always did drink a lot, and a coupla times he beat me up. He didn't know what he was doin'. Then he got hisself thrown in jail, and I never did see him after that. I moved in with my sister and had Shanya, and then we got evicted. I didn't have no money, so I started turning tricks. We was all staying with my sister's friend; she had a house trailer, and her boyfriend starts bringing this crack home and doin' it in the trailer. I was pretty drunk most of the time, and once I got started on that stuff, well, it just kept coming, as long as I did a trick or two with him, and I just kept flyin'. I didn't even know I was pregnant again until I was five months gone. My sister's friend threw us all out, including the boyfriend, when she found out he was sleeping with me. I tried to get off the crack, but that's a powerful wind that blows right through a body, it ain't so easy. When Lucius was born they had to keep him in 'tensive care for two months on account of the crack. They said he might be brain-damaged."

Letitia paused and sighed, as if exhausted. She rested a hand on the sleeping baby's little curly head. "They got to do some more tests on him when he's older. If he's hurt bad, it's his own mama what did it to him. For the rest of his life, ain't nothin' can change that, his own mama hurt him. That thought never leaves my mind, from the time I wake up to the time I go to sleep again. It's all I can think about."

Letitia sighed again, her eyes dull and vacant. "So that's what I do, from sunup to sundown."

Samantha put her pen down. She didn't know what to say. She couldn't imagine living with this knowledge, every minute of every day, as Letitia did. Suddenly she felt intrusive, out of place. How had she ever thought this would be easy? She would return another day for the interview. She put the notebook away.

"Letitia, I'm sorry," Samantha told her. "I hope Lucius will be okay."

The young mother nodded, and looked her in the eye. "Now can I ask you some questions? I ain't gonna grade you or nothin'."

"Sure."

"Have you ever been raped?" Samantha shook her head *no.* "Have you ever watched your mama get her head split open by her boyfriend? Have you ever had to make porridge out of crackers and hot water for your babies, 'cause there wasn't no more food?" *No* and *no.*

Letitia nodded again, her face still expressionless. "I didn't think so."

***

"I had lasagna last week at the cafeteria," Marcel was saying as he and Samantha looked over the menu at an Italian restaurant.

"I guess that makes you an expert on Italian food!" said Samantha with a grin. "No lasagna on Martinique? Not even pizza?"

"We have pizza, but not like here. And I couldn't believe it—the other night, a guy in my dorm had a pizza delivered right to his door!" Samantha laughed. "You can get just about anything delivered to your door: pizza, Chinese, Vietnamese, Thai, even Burger King."

Marcel, smiling, shook his head and looked through the menu. "Doesn't look like they have a salad bar. I don't know what to order. What's lin-geen?"

"Lin-gwee-nie," Samantha giggled. "Long, flat noodles. You can get it with marinara sauce, clam sauce, or mushroom sauce. They're all yummy."

Marcel leaned forward and smiled at Samantha. His white teeth were dazzling, and Samantha's breath caught in her throat. *I can't believe I'm sitting across from this gorgeous guy. And he's even more gorgeous without his clothes on.*

"You pick something," he told her, with a twinkle in his eye. "But it better be good, or else!"

"Oh, I'm scared!" replied Samantha, and studied the menu very seriously. "Hey, look, Marcel, how about linguine with papayas? Spaghetti with coconut sauce? Pizza with coconuts and papayas?"

"You wench!" said Marcel, tossing a napkin at her. "You can't even get good papayas here."

"How come? We get all kinds of other good things—mangos, bananas, pineapples. Why can't good papayas be shipped here like everything else?"

Marcel thought for a moment. "They are too soft. Even before they ripen they start getting mushy; they are a mess to transport. Even on Martinique they're usually just sold at local markets because it's too much trouble to transport them very far. But there are papaya trees everywhere; most people just walk out their back door and pick one."

Samantha leaned forward with her chin on her hands, her face radiant. "It sounds wonderful. I would love to pick a papaya." Marcel imagined spoon-feeding her the succulent, sweet fruit and watching the juice run down her chin. *I can't believe it! I'm sitting right here with this beautiful girl.* The thought of her in a bikini on a beach on Martinique, with him kissing the papaya juice from her lips, was taking his breath away.

The waiter came. Samantha ordered some strange-sounding dishes, which she insisted he would love. Marcel worried about the cost, everything seemed so expensive, but Samantha said she'd just use her plastic.

"But you still have to pay later, don't you?" he asked.

"Not me. My dad pays it. The bills go right to his address anyway. Except I don't exactly know where that is right now. He doesn't live at home anymore."

"Yes, you told me. I am sorry about that. How are your parents doing?"

"Oh, I don't know," Samantha sighed. The whole situation made her head ache. "The last time I talked to my mom, she was making all kinds of accusations, and whenever I try to talk to my dad, he's drunk."

"What about your sister? Can you talk to her about it?"

"Yeah, one of these days. She seems to be mad at all of us right now, so I'm letting her cool off for a while. We're not exactly a happy family. How about you? Are your parents divorced?"

"No, I think they'll be married forever. They're pretty content."

"How about your brothers and sisters? Are any of them married?"

"My oldest sister Daria is married; she has a little son and another on the way. My sister Mariette has a baby daughter, but she's not married. The rest of us are too young to get married."

"The rest of us ... How many siblings do you have?"

"Six inside, two outside."

"What? Outside what?"

"Outside the marriage. My mother and father have seven children (inside), and my father has two others, with two other women (outside)."

Samantha stared at him. "You mean, like before he married your mother?"

Marcel shook his head. "No, my half brother is 15 and my half sister is 10."

"And your mother? Does she know about these children?"

"Sure she does. Everyone knows. We don't talk about it much."

"But what does your mother think? Doesn't it upset her, your father having children with other women?"

"Well, it's hard to explain. I don't think she likes it, but there's not much she can do about it. I don't think my father is still seeing those two women. I've never talked to them about it."

Their dinners were served. Steam rose from the fettuccine Alfredo and linguine with marinara sauce, and the aroma was heavenly.

"Well, that's just so … bizarre!" said Samantha. "My mother found out my dad's having an affair with a woman at his office and she's divorcing him and causing a lot of commotion. I'd say she's very upset about it. Here, do you want to try the fettuccine?"

They were quiet for a few minutes as they dug into their pasta. Marcel was surprised to find it delicious, especially the creamy Alfredo sauce.

Samantha remarked, "You know, I was interviewing a woman today at the homeless shelter who had to feed her children crackers and water because she didn't have any food. It makes me feel guilty, eating all this good food now."

"Why were you interviewing her?"

"It's part of my term project for sociology. We were doing qualitative unstructured interviews, but mine sort of got off track. I was supposed to ask her about five things she likes best and five things she doesn't like about living at the shelter, but I just didn't have the heart after she told me about her life and her babies. One of them might be brain damaged."

"What do you do with this? The five questions and the interview?"

Samantha put her fork down. "Well, we're doing a case study at this shelter. We have to design and carry out a research project in five stages. First, state the problem. Mine is that drug use in homeless shelter populations is no greater than in the population at large. Then design the research; this will be interviews in the shelter and surveys outside the shelter. Then we collect the data; that's what I'm doing now. Finally, analyze the data and come to conclusions. That will be the hardest part. It's not so tough asking people questions, but then I have to come up with something intelligent to say about it all."

She picked up her fork and dug into her pasta again. She glanced up at Marcel, to find him watching her with a funny little smirk on his face.

"What?" she demanded.

Marcel smiled at her. "How did you get to be so smart?"

"How did I—oh, for heaven's sake! You should have seen me with the unstructured interview today! It was so unstructured I couldn't get anywhere." She paused. "Well, that's not really true. This woman, Letitia, did tell me what I needed to know."

"Are you going back there tomorrow?" asked Marcel.

"No, tomorrow I'm going to the county courthouse. I have to do some non-participant observation exercises so I'm going to sit in on a trial. It's a child molestation case."

"Child molestation! Samantha, you have a stronger stomach than I."

Samantha looked at his empty plate and grinned. "Looks to me like your stomach is doing just fine."

***

It was dark when they drove back to campus in Samantha's car. Marcel had loved the long days here when he first arrived; on Martinique, darkness came at seven o'clock year round, so he'd been amazed to find the sun still up at 9:00 p.m. in early September. But now, in late October, the days were shorter and the air crisp and cold, especially at night.

They sat in darkness in the parking lot for a little while, across from the residence halls. With the engine running, the heater on (Marcel thought he would die if the temperature got below 75) and Frank Ocean playing, they were snug inside their own little nest. Marcel stroked Samantha's silky, honey-colored hair. He had never seen anything so beautiful and loved touching it.

"Marcel," Samantha whispered. "I wish I had a family like yours."

He laughed. "What, and never get to use the bathroom? Brothers stealing your underwear? Maman making you get up at 5:30 in the morning and wear tight shoes?"

"They sound like great people. Fun people. I'm just dreading going home for Christmas. My mother keeps asking me about it, but I don't want to go. It won't be the same without my dad around, and the thought of two weeks cooped up in the house with her ... I just can't bear it."

"Won't your mother be lonely if you're not there?"

"She'll have my sister. I can't deal with them right now. Did I tell you my mother wants me to testify against my dad in court? To say that he was abusive and an alcoholic?"

"No, you didn't tell me." Marcel frowned and pulled her closer, rubbing her shoulder. "Are you going to?"

"No! He was never abusive! It's just my mother's ... well, she twists things around. She has to have things her way, and now she's mad at me because I don't want to go to court."

Samantha sat up straight and looked at Marcel. "You don't have anywhere to go over the Christmas holidays, do you?"

Marcel smiled. "Martinique is too far away; my stipend won't cover the airfare. I was going to ask Ben if I could stay with his family in Georgia. We have to get out of the dorms for those two weeks."

"Marcel, why don't we go somewhere? We could drive to New York City. I have friends there; in fact, I think my friend Shelby will be spending the holidays with her folks in Ithaca, so she'd probably let us use her apartment. It's in Queens. You've never been to New York, have you?"

Marcel smiled. Her enthusiasm was infectious. New York City! Of course he hadn't been there, but he'd been dreaming of it for years. That's where he was going to end up, living in Manhattan, dancing on Broadway. New York City for him was people and lights and the roaring applause of the crowds. Just the thought of it made his heart beat faster.

But it would be expensive. Gas for the car, eating in restaurants. He didn't have a lot of money to spare. Samantha knew this and was generous with her dad's credit card. She insisted that it wasn't a problem. He had to admit that it made him a little uncomfortable, the kind of money she spent and her penchant for doing expensive things. Marcel had never had money to speak of, and his idea of relaxing was to be outside, hanging out with his friends, dancing, playing sports, or just walking on the beach. She didn't seem as interested in these kinds of things—she was in the habit of spending money. She loved eating in nice restaurants and going to concerts and movies, and she bought new hoes and clothes regularly.

But New York City! How could he pass up a chance like this? It would be incredible.

"Well, what do you think?" asked Samantha, her eyes bright.

"Will there be snow?"

"For you, Marcel, there will be snow at Christmas in New York." And she kissed him long and deep.

***

There was a knock on Marcel's door. He rolled over and looked at the clock; it was only 6:30 in the morning.

"Marcel Devereaux, phone call," came a voice from the other side of the door as the footfalls receded down the hallway. Marcel put on his robe and went out to the phone at the end of the corridor.

"Hello?"

"Marcel, it's Ben. How ya doing? Hey, sorry to call so early, but have you looked out your window yet?"

"What? I, um, no, I haven't. What's outside my window?"

"Dude, just look. And meet me at the cafeteria at noon today." The line went dead.

Bewildered, Marcel replaced the receiver and returned to his room. The door creaked and groaned as he closed it, but these days he wasn't too worried about disturbing Kyle. His roommate slept a lot, and he always made sure to slam the door whenever he came and went, regardless of whether Marcel was asleep. He had said maybe 10 words to Marcel in the weeks they'd been roommates.

Marcel pulled up the window shade and looked outside. At first he didn't see much, just the street below, the manicured lawns and sidewalks, and a few early morning joggers.

Then he saw it, in green spray paint, scrawled across the brick wall outside the parking lot across the street: "NIGGERS—EAT SHIT! NIGGERS—GO BACK TO AFRICA!"

Marcel stared in disbelief. He didn't know what to think. He'd never seen such a thing on Martinique and hadn't expected it here. He sat down on his bed, a pulse pounding in his temples and a warm, uncomfortable flush creeping up his neck. *Why?* What had he ever done? He was starting to really like it here, and now he was angry that some idiot was trying to ruin it.

That's all it is. Just some loser, someone without a life, someone screaming for attention. Whoever had done the spray-painting was just some loser who didn't speak for everyone, and if Marcel allowed him to get under his skin that was just what the jerk wanted. He forced himself to calm down, to breathe deeply, centering himself as he did before beginning to dance. *Just some nobody,* he thought. *You can't touch me.*

***

"Yo, Marcel!" called Ben. "Island boy!" Marcel saw his friend waving at him from a table in the corner of the cafeteria. He was sitting with three other students, all Black. It was a few minutes after noon.

"Marcel, meet the founding members of "Double Black": Raymond Pierce, Michelle Jackson, and Radcliff Sutton." Marcel greeted the three other students and sat down. They didn't seem to share Ben's affable nature; in fact, they seemed tense and preoccupied.

"What's 'Double Black?'" Marcel asked.

"The newest racism awareness group on campus," answered Cliff Sutton. He was slight and thin, with a flattop haircut and the sides of his head shaved. He was naturally tense, one of those people with energy to burn. Although they were the same color, Cliff and Ben were as different as night and day.

Ben looked at his watch. "Now five hours old."

Cliff continued. "W. E. B. Du Bois described the identity of being Black and an American as a double consciousness. We are not free to just be who we are, we are always living a parallel existence as Black and American—we are first and foremost Black, and second, African Americans. Double Black."

"Who's W. E. B. Du Bois?" asked Marcel. Even Ben's eyes widened a little at this. He placed a large hand on Marcel's shoulder and gave him a friendly squeeze. "Marcel, my man, I can see we got a lot of work to do here!"

Michelle spoke up. She was a pretty, dark-skinned woman, with long straightened hair pulled back from a pleasantly round face. "W. E. B. Du Bois was a Black sociologist. He was one of the founding members of the NAACP." She watched Marcel's face for recognition (*don't tell me he's never heard of the NAACP!*). But Marcel nodded; he knew it.

"He was a poet and a philosopher," continued Raymond. "He did all kinds of research on Black society in America; he thought social science could provide answers to racial problems." Raymond Pierce was as tall as the affable Ben but didn't seem to share his appetite for food. He was slender but well built and wore round, silver-rimmed glasses.

Cliff leaned forward, his face close to Marcel's. "But it didn't, did it? Even Du Bois himself concluded that in the hostile climate of America, the only way to bring about social change was through agitation and protest. He finally got so disgusted that he moved to Ghana, renounced his American citizenship, and joined the Communist Party."

"Drake goes on vacations in Ghana," said Ben. Cliff smiled. "He's the *man*, and I'm gonna hang *out* with his ass when I move to Ghana!" The others laughed.

"You do know who Drake is, don't you?" Ben asked Marcel with a grin. "I know, I know!" Marcel replied.

"We're forming Double Black to demand that the university sit up and take notice. Racism should not be tolerated in the educational institution. University officials have the power and authority to do something about it," said Michelle. An **institution** is an established and enduring pattern of statuses, roles, and social relationships designed to meet basic human and social needs. Five main institutions in society are family, religion, politics, economics, and education. **Power** is the ability to impose one's will upon others, even if they resist. Power resides in social statuses, such as mother, professor, employer, or physician. The president at Marcel's university has power to order an official investigation of racism on campus and to institute policies that prohibit and punish racist acts. **Authority** is power that is considered legitimate. The members of Double Black believe in the authority of university officials; that is, they view the power of university officials as legitimate.

"If they don't get so bogged down in red tape that they can't move on it," added Cliff. "That's why we'll be doing a little publicity of our own to keep the school motivated." **Red tape** refers to official procedures that can become so time-consuming that they interfere with the efficient functioning of a formal organization.

Cliff fears that the university administration may refer the racist issue to so many committees and require so many signatures that nothing will actually be done to the perpetrators.

"Michelle's already been down there documenting the vandalism. She took pictures, and we're going to three local news services," said Raymond. "If the bureaucracy of the university fails to do its job, we'll do it for them." **Bureaucracy** is a large organization that is designed to perform tasks efficiently and that is characterized by a hierarchy of authority and explicit rules and regulations.

"We're not letting anyone off the hook on this," said Ben. "Until we get the power elite to sit up and take notice, racism will just continue to be swept under the rug, like it always has been." The **power elite** is a small, powerful group of people exercising influence on the affairs of a society or community. Sociologist C. Wright Mills suggests that the power elite who control US society consists of those in positions of economic, political, and military power. In our novel, Ben uses the term power elite to refer to the people in the upper levels of administration of the university.

Marcel looked around the table at their faces. They were angry, as if they had personally been insulted. In his mind, the vandal was some pathetic social reject who shouldn't be getting the time of day from them, someone who probably belonged in a **total institution**. This is an organization in which people are isolated from the rest of society and are under the control of the organization's staff and administrative officials. Examples of total institutions include prisons and mental hospitals.

"I don't think we should take it personally. It's just some jerk trying to get attention," he said. Cliff Sutton's eyes flew open wide and his nostrils flared. "We *should* be taking it personally! Every insult, every slight, every racist statement ought to be fanning the flame of everyone's consciousness—some brainless bigot uses a brick wall to express racial hatred, and we use the media to retaliate."

"But that's what he's after, and if we make a big deal of it, then we just give him what he wants," Marcel responded.

"Then we just pretend it doesn't exist? We pretend that racism isn't still alive and well in America, like a dirty cancer no one wants to talk about?" asked Michelle.

"I'm just saying I don't think whoever did it speaks for everyone. If we respond in a big way, then won't it look like we're taking him seriously? Like he's a spokesman for all Americans?"

Cliff Sutton leaned forward, his face close to Marcel's. "Why do you love White people so much, anyway?" Marcel thought of all the White people he'd ever known, which weren't many. He couldn't think of a really bad experience with any Whites on Martinique; there had been tourists, a writer, a few hotel owners, and a couple of fairly harmless missionaries. There had been one Australian who claimed to be looking for bat caves in order to start a company exporting guano, but his research seemed pretty much confined to bars and night spots. He'd been fun, a real character. And now he'd met a lot of White people at school: Professor Cady, Marjorie Trask, who had helped get his scholarship and travel money, and Samantha. ... Finally, he answered Cliff's question.

"They are genuine. They already have everything, so they have nothing to prove." Cliff leaned back, regarding Marcel with surprise. "I guess you haven't been around America for the last hundred years."

"Didn't they have slavery in Martinique? Don't they have sugar plantations there?" asked Raymond. Marcel nodded slowly. "There's a fort in Big Town. That was supposed to be where the slaves were bought and sold when they came in on the ships."

Ben spoke up. "The Middle Passage, Marcel. Those were the survivors of the Middle Passage, arriving on your own island."

Marcel looked at him. The Middle Passage? Yes, it was true, there had been slavery on Martinique, generations ago. It was a terrible blight on the history of human beings, and it occurred to him that he really didn't know that much about it. At home and in school, they'd never talked about it much; it was in the past, and they were all moving on with their lives. This whole discussion of putting pressure on the university and using the media had caught him a little by surprise; on Martinique, **traditional authority** usually dealt with problems. This is power that is legitimized through respect for cultural traditions. Marcel thinks that on Martinique, the perpetrator would likely be rooted out through the island grapevine and dealt with informally rather than resorting to official means.

He had a lot to learn about America, especially the **Iron Law of Oligarchy**, the tendency for power within organizations to be concentrated in the hands of a few. The other members of Double Black understand that few people in the university administration have the power to develop policies concerning racism on campus.

Marcel suddenly felt uncomfortable and glanced at his watch. "I got a meeting with my dance professor." He stood up. "When you have another meeting, I'd like to come."

***

Marcel found the door to Professor Cady's office open. "Professor? You wanted to see me, ma'am?"

"Good afternoon, Jamaica. Please sit down."

It felt different to be sitting across a desk from Professor Cady. Marcel was usually towering over her in the dance studio, sweating and working as hard as he could, while she marched smartly around and called out commands: "Get that leg up! Not so fast, draw it out, smoothly, smoothly ... wait to look up, now the arms. Oh, for Pete's sake, Jack, start the music over! Everyone! Pay attention, on my count!"

From any other person, this behavior would have been abrasive and seen as coercion, but Esther Cady's charisma superseded everything. **Coercion** is the use of power to force an individual or group to behave as another individual or group desires. Professor Cady really isn't forcing anyone to do anything, so she is not engaged in coercion. She has already made it clear that if the students plan to just slouch through her classes, they should just drop the class. **Charisma** is an extraordinary and appealing personal quality. Individuals who have charismatic authority use their extraordinary qualities to exert power over their followers. Professor Cady uses her charismatic authority to motivate students to work hard in her class. In contrast to Barack Obama, Donald Trump is not thought of as having charisma.

Now Marcel was in her office, and the office reflected her. Neat, precise, not given to unnecessary frills. Framed pictures of Esther Cady as a young dancer adorned the walls, along with an autographed photo of Alvin Ailey.

"Marcel, I wanted to talk to you about your dancing."

"Is something the matter, Professor?"

Esther Cady laughed. "On the contrary, Marcel. I want to know what your plans are. What do you intend to do with your dance career?" Without hesitation, Marcel answered, "I'm going to dance on Broadway, ma'am."

The professor burst out laughing. "That's what I like to hear!" She leaned forward, more serious. "And I'm going to come and see you on Broadway. But there are a few details to think of before you get there."

She leaned back. "Every spring we perform a dance showcase here at the music school. This is what we'll start working for in earnest after the Christmas break. Most of the numbers will be group dances, but I want you to do a solo piece. I'll help you with it, but I want it to be your own choreography."

Marcel's jaw dropped open. "Me, Professor? A freshman student?" Freshmen never did solos at these dance concerts. "Yes, Marcel. As much as I enjoy teaching you here, I am not sure this is the best place for developing your talent. There's another reason why I'm asking you to do this. I'm inviting an instructor from Juilliard to come to the spring showcase. You have heard of the Juilliard School, haven't you?"

Marcel's mouth went dry; all he could do was nod.

"Good," said the professor. "She's an old friend of mine, and I've told her about you. If she likes what she sees, she'll recommend you for an audition at Juilliard. I'll talk to Marjorie Trask about the possibility of transferring your scholarship if you're successful. Since it comes through the National Endowment for the Arts, we might be able to get it reassigned to Juilliard with some phone calls and paperwork. Would that be acceptable to you, Marcel?"

Marcel looked at her, his eyes aglow and his heart about to burst. He would have to start rehearsing right away—he was already thinking about the choreography and the music; he'd have to sign up for more studio time; there was all day Sundays, and how long until the spring showcase? Six months? Would that be enough time? Should he concentrate on familiar and well-polished moves or work on new ones ...

"Yes, ma'am, that would be acceptable."

***

Samantha got up from her dorm room desk and stretched. She'd been writing up her notes from the Miller Street Shelter with a growing sense of dissatisfaction. Her original premise seemed so dry, so pedantic. There was so much more going on, so much more she could get into, that her hypothesis didn't cover. She would have to go see Professor Rourke about revising her project.

There was a knock on the door. "I'll get it," said Dash. Today she'd frosted her spiky blond hair with a spritz of magenta color and around her neck was a studded leather dog collar with a tag: "Bosco, please call 777-2434."

"Hey, Daly," said Dash as she opened the door wide. Samantha came to the door to find Daly Brown and Kevin Bittner in some kind of toga get-up. It looked like they had taken white bed sheets and were going for a Lawrence of Arabia look, or perhaps tried to get out of bed without actually getting out of bed.

"Is this your Halloween costume? Don't tell me, you're the Ku Klux Klan," said Dash. "I hate to tell you, but that's been done. I might point out that it's more than a bit tacky, too."

"*Hardly*," declared Daly Brown, offended. "The KKK is a bunch of misguided bigots who thrive on hate. My name is Brother Destiny, and these are not Halloween costumes. We are Warriors with the Truth of Love, and we're spreading love to our fellow human beings. Raj Ramahatrian, the Truth of Love Warrior King, says that the world is a mess because we're too passive about love, so evil takes over. We have to be proactive and make an effort to spread love; we have to make it our priority. Just as the warriors of primitive times were vital for protecting their societies, today we Warriors of Love are the only hope for modern society. Brother Tree?" He nodded to his roommate, Kevin, who was hovering in the corridor, clutching a wad of large dried leaves. After several attempts, he lit the leaves with a cigarette lighter, and they started smoldering.

"Brother Tree, the blessing, please," said Daly. Kevin stepped forward, tripping on his bed sheet, and waved the smoking bundle in the girls' faces. They coughed; the smoke was thick and oily.

Kevin cleared his throat. He waved the leaves back and forth with each declaration:

"Truth! Love! Peace! Um ..."

"Serenity," prompted Daly.

"Serenity! Um ..." he glanced at Samantha and blushed. "Love!"

And the fire alarm went off, a deafening Klaxon bringing everyone out of his or her dorm rooms, cursing and grumbling.

Chapter 6 Study Questions

ORGANIZATIONS

1. What is **alienation**? Which character in this chapter is described as being alienated?
2. What are the goals of the Miller Street Shelter?
3. What are the five main **social institutions**?
4. Is the Miller Street Shelter a **total institution**? Why or why not?
5. What is the meaning and origin of the term Double Black? Are the members of Double Black planning on using **coercion** to achieve their aims? Explain your answer.

CHAPTER 7

Snowflakes

Population and Social Change

ELLO?"

"Hi, Mom, it's Sam."

"Sammy. I was expecting you to call three days ago. Didn't you get my messages?"

Samantha frowned, rubbing her temple. "Yes, I got your messages. I've been busy." *Please, can't we just get on with this? Do we have to have a play-by-play of how everyone lets you down?*

"You've been busy. I've been busy. Everyone's busy. Michael Feinstein tells me you never return his calls, either."

"Mom, don't start on that again. I've already told you I'm not testifying, so there's no point in me talking to your attorney!"

"But you don't seem to have a problem talking to your father's attorney." Samantha could hear the acid in her mother's voice.

"It was just a few questions, and anyway, that's my business!" Samantha could hear her own voice start to rise, the defensiveness surging—a push-button reflex.

"It just seems a little unfair, don't you think, that you're willing to talk to your father's attorney and not mine?"

"Mom, never mind about the attorneys. Okay? Can't we just have a simple conversation? I'm calling about Christmas."

"Christmas. I see. Well, when are you coming home?"

Samantha took a deep breath. "I'm not. Coming home, I mean. I have other plans for the Christmas break."

A very chilly silence followed. Finally, her mother spoke.

"I see. You're not coming home for Christmas. Audrey's coming, but you have other plans. Do these other plans which don't include your mother involve going to see your father?"

"I'm going to New York. I don't know if I'm going to see Dad or not. Anyway, if I see him or not, isn't that my business?"

"I guess there's not much these days that's worth sharing with your mother. Everything is none of my business, isn't it."

Well, not exactly. There IS something I can tell you!

"Don't you want to know what I'm doing for Christmas? I'm going to New York City with my boyfriend. Remember the Black guy with the dreadlocks? The one you thought was so fortunate to be coming to school here? That's him, and we're staying in Shelby's apartment in Queens."

"Mom? ... Mom? Are you there?"

The line had gone dead.

***

Back in her room, Samantha smiled to see Marcel sitting on the floor surrounded by wrapping paper and boxes. He looked up as she entered. "Did you talk to your mother?"

"Mmm-hmm." Samantha cleared a space on her bed and sat down. Dash was out with friends until late. She had winked outrageously at the two of them when she'd left, reassuring them that she definitely wouldn't be back until late. Really late. Really, really late.

"Well, what did she say?"

"She said …" Samantha looked at his sweet face, full of concern, "She said, Merry Christmas and she hopes we have a good time."

Marcel rose up on his knees in front of her and slid his arms around her waist. "Really?" he asked. Samantha nodded, her head dropping low. Marcel gently lifted her chin with one hand and touched the corner of her eye with a forefinger. Delicately, as one would pick up a newborn mouse. "Then what is this?" he whispered. "A drop of rain?"

Samantha looked into his face, her eyes full of hurt. He seemed to be able to soak it up, to take in her pain and still radiate warmth, when she felt only cold inside. "Must be," she whispered.

"Shall I take it from you?" he asked, his voice like velvet against the rough serrations of her soul. She nodded slowly, and without taking his eyes from hers he placed his finger to his lips and sucked the teardrop from it. Samantha leaned forward and rested her head against his shoulder, soaking him up, surrounding herself with him.

"Sam," he whispered, "I am having a terrible trouble only you can help me with." She leaned back and searched his face questioningly. He picked up a Christmas present and showed it to her. It was a mess; it looked like a three-year-old had tried to wrap it and then sat on it.

Samantha burst into laughter. "Marcel! What happened! Did a horde of Vikings attack you while you were wrapping this?" She took the package from him, examining the rumpled corners, the wads of sticky tape sprouting from its surfaces like fungal growths, and the white scars where he'd tried to rip the tape off.

"The tape is very sticky," he said sadly. "Never in my life have I done the wrapping; my sisters always did it." He looked so helpless that Samantha put her arms around his neck and kissed his cheek.

"I will wrap this for you," she smiled into his ear. "Will you? I was hoping you would, said Marcel. "I would like this to be a nice surprise for my family." He gestured to the chaos on the floor, and Samantha had to laugh.

They had spent the afternoon Christmas shopping and were now getting packages ready to send off to their respective families. It had only taken a few minutes for Samantha to gift-wrap her three packages and tape them up into little boxes for mailing. Three small gifts, going to three different places. Then she'd gone down the hall to call her mother.

Marcel, on the other hand, had surrounded himself with great swaths of wrapping paper, tape, boxes, and bags. It was the first time he'd really been able to buy anything nice for his family, and he glowed with pleasure thinking of how pleased they would be when they received this big box. His brothers would have to go to Macouba to pick it up, and he was including a pack of cigarettes for the inspections officer so he wouldn't be inclined to take anything else. But there were bags of candy, marshmallows, and Oreo cookies as well; they could give the officer a bag to take home to his kids. It would probably take his brothers Sebastian and Loïc most of the day to pick up the package and take it home.

"They're going to love these," Samantha said, climbing down onto the floor with him, picking up a pair of baggy 501 jeans. "Who are these for?"

"My brother, Sebastian," answered Marcel. "Loïc is getting some, too. And these are for Mariette and Daria," he said, showing her the earrings, and the faux pearls for his mother, and a tweed cap for his father. Toys for a nephew and a niece, a Pez dispenser for a little brother, and a paint-by-number set for a little sister. Samantha watched his face as he handled each item lovingly, as if wishing he could give each one to its intended owner himself. It occurred to her that Marcel's whole box of gifts had cost less than the necklace she'd bought for her mother.

Laughing, she held up a half-empty bag of marshmallows. "What happened here? I thought you were sending these to Martinique!"

Someone knocked at the door. A mild wave of irritation erupted in Samantha. She was enjoying this time with Marcel, and no one else was part of it. *Whoever you are*, she thought, *I'm busy*!

Kevin Bittner stood in the hallway, his hands behind his back. "Um, hi, Samantha." Lank brown hair fell over his eyes. He flicked his head frequently to shift it, but it always fell right back to the same spot. He wasn't wearing his Love Warrior bed sheet today.

"Hi, Kevin."

"Um, how're you doing?"

"I'm fine."

"Oh. That's great. That's really great, you're fine. Well, I'm doing okay myself."

Samantha glanced back at Marcel in his nest of Christmas cheer on the floor. He was unwrapping the gifts he'd already done so she could redo them. She turned back to Kevin, closing the door a little more.

"Did you want something, Kevin?" *I hate to be rude, but is there a point to this?*

"Oh, uh," Kevin smiled nervously, "it's Brother, Brother Tree …" He produced a little paper flower from behind his back and held it out to her.

"I was, um, wondering if you would, you know, like to come with me. Raj Rama-hatrian is giving a talk on campus, it's Thursday night, he's going to talk about the commercialism of the Christmas season, and you know, how we should be just loving each other and not bothering with, you know, material things, how, um, buying gifts, um, trivializes the grand design of, um, love …" He trailed off, standing there in the vast sea of the hall corridor, looking at Samantha as if she were a life raft and he about to drown.

Samantha took the flower from him. She couldn't let it just hang there in a vacuum. "Well, I'm pretty busy, Kevin, I don't think so. But thanks for asking. Bye, now," and she closed the door gently.

"One of your many admirers?" asked Marcel wryly, looking at the little paper flower. "Oh," laughed Samantha, "He's just a guy who lives down the hall. There's some talk on Thursday by this kook," and she handed him the flower. There was embossing on each of the four paper petals.

"'Raj Ramahatrian,'" read Marcel off the petals. "'December 11, Love is Every-thing, Truth of Love Warriors.'"

"It's this group or religious sect or something," said Samantha. "Kevin showed up with Daly Brown the other day, and they were both wrapped in sheets and preaching love and peace and everything. They called themselves Brother Tree and Brother Destiny," she giggled, taking the flower from him and tossing it in the wastebasket.

"I guess you're not a religious person," commented Marcel. "Nope. I haven't gone to church in a decade. My mom used to try to get us to go to church when my sister and I were younger, but I just didn't see the relevance. It just didn't seem to provide anything I needed. I think religion is more for older people who have less complicated lives."

"Is this the Daly Brown with the *Bizarrotron*?" asked Marcel, and she nodded. "When do I get to see this thing? When do I get a number?"

"One of these days, don't worry!" said Samantha. "Now, let's see what can be done here." She surveyed the clutter of gifts, paper, ribbons, and tape. "This is a tough job, but I think I got here in time."

***

Two weeks later, with packages sent off, papers turned in, and exams taken, Marcel and Samantha set off for New York in her car. Marcel tuned in an oldies station on the radio, where "Say You, Say Me" by Lionel Ritchie was playing.

Samantha smiled. "You like that '80s music, don't you?"

"Mmm-hmmm."

"Don't you listen to Beyoncé, or Japanese Breakfast or anything?"

"I eat breakfast. I listen to Lionel Ritchie. I dance to everything."

"What are you going to use for your solo piece in the dance showcase? Don't you think Juilliard will be more impressed if you're versatile, if you use newer music instead of just '80s stuff?"

Marcel had already been thinking of this. "Yes, I think so. I want to use a combination of different pieces, but they have to flow together. It's not easy picking the right ones. Maybe you can help me with current music."

"Sure! I can make you a playlist with a bunch of good new music."

"That sounds *fine*. Hey, where are we going?"

"I want to get the car washed." Samantha pulled into a drive-through car wash.

"What? Do we have time? I thought you wanted to get to the city before dark."

"Oh, we will, this will only take a few minutes."

They entered the car wash and Marcel stared around him in disbelief. They were inside a giant machine! Like a washing machine, for cars. "You Americans have a machine for everything!"

Samantha laughed at the look on his face. "Well, how do you wash cars on Martinique?"

"You have to drive your car down to a river, and you can wash it yourself or pay the guys there to do it. It takes about an hour."

"You drive it into a river?"

"Yes."

"Don't the cars get swept away?"

Marcel burst out laughing. "They're shallow rivers. You just drive into the edges where it's about a foot deep. Then you go to the market or something while the guys wash it."

"In the river. You leave your car in the river, and some random guys wash it. And you go to the market and eat papayas!"

"Yes, papayas! And breadfruit! And sour sops!"

"What the heck is a sour sop?!" laughed Samantha.

"Oh, they're so good. They grow on trees, and when they're ripe they turn black and mushy. They look like rotten potatoes."

"Sounds, uh … wonderful. Well, in New York we'll have to go to a sushi bar, and there's this place in Queens that has the best pizza, and we definitely have to get lox and bagels at a deli."

"Ben told me I have to eat New York cheesecake, and he's a man who loves his food."

"Of course, cheesecake!"

"And Broadway. I have to see it, even if only to walk on the sidewalks." The shows would be too expensive, but just to be there, just to see the lights and the people. ... Marcel could hardly imagine it.

"Oh, we'll do Broadway. And Central Park, and the museums. I just wish we had more than two weeks!"

***

"We're eating with sticks?" asked Marcel. "Even the soup?" They were at a little Chinese restaurant near Shelby's apartment in Queens. They had arrived after dark, and it had taken half an hour to find a parking space on the street, four blocks from the building. Marcel was amazed by all the people and the traffic; he'd never been to a **megalopolis** before. This is a continuous metropolitan region, in which the outer rings of the adjacent urban areas merge. New York City is a good example of a megalopolis.

They'd gotten the apartment keys from a neighbor and walked to the restaurant, not wanting to give up the precious parking space.

"The soup you can eat with a spoon," said Samantha with a smile. "Here, hold the chopsticks like this."

Marcel tried eating his Mongolian beef and fried rice with chopsticks, but gave up after a few minutes.

"I will be here all night if I am eating this one rice grain at a time," he said ruefully to Samantha, and he asked the waiter for a fork. "If I were back home, I'd just eat it with my hands," he told Samantha. "But it's delicious!"

She grinned. "Aren't you glad you came here to New York with me instead of going to Atlanta with Ben?" He smiled back at her. "Yes, Sam, I am glad I came with you. You are much cuter than Ben, I must tell you, and I don't think I'd like his hair on my pillow. Yours, however, is quite welcome."

Samantha giggled and fed him a popcorn shrimp with her chopsticks. *How does she DO that?* He wondered. If he had to survive using those sticks to eat, he'd starve to death.

Marcel paused thoughtfully. "I do wish I'd been able to go to the meeting before I left," he mused.

"What meeting?"

"It's a black awareness group, Double Black. Ben got me involved in it when there was that vandalism last month. They're trying to generate awareness about racism and bigotry on campus."

"I've heard of them," said Samantha. "Didn't they have an article in the school paper?"

"Yeah, they sent pictures to some of the news services, too. We're still waiting for an official statement from the university."

"I can't believe some idiot would make such a racist statement in the first place! I mean, for God's sake, I think we've made some progress since the 1960s. It must have been an isolated incident, just some loser."

"That's what I thought when it first happened, but now I'm not so sure. Double Black was having another meeting about the university's response, dragging their heels, I mean, and I couldn't make it. I've just been so wrapped up in dance rehearsal, with finals week and planning the spring show."

"Are you going to be okay going without dancing for two weeks? Do you need to keep practicing?"

"I can at least do some stretching and exercises every day. If we see any dance studios, let's see if they'll let me come in for a couple of hours."

***

That evening they lay in Shelby's bed, wrapped around each other after making love. They were tired after a long day of travel, but too excited to sleep.

"Marcel, how did you become a dancer?" The words drifted through the night air, amidst the honking and revving of engines on the streets below. A dog barked, glass shattered. Someone cursed loudly—at the barking dog? The broken bottle? Who could tell? Marcel was imagining this night serenade every night, every week, every month. This would be his life when he lived here.

How did I become a dancer? He smiled and shifted gears to a small boy on a Caribbean island years before.

"Have you ever seen the movie White Nights?" he asked Samantha, stroking the soft hair which lay tangled over his shoulder. "It's an old movie from 1985, but the dancing is spectacular."

"No, I never saw it. Wasn't Mikhail Baryshnikov in it?"

"Yes." Marcel thought of Baryshnikov and the incredible opening scene of the movie. Baryshnikov danced like he'd never seen before in his life. He had never forgotten.

"In my village when I was growing up, hardly anyone had a television or a DVD player (let alone Blu-Ray). But there was one at the Don't Mind Your Wife Bar, and—"

"'Don't Mind Your Wife?' That's the *name* of the place?" asked Samantha. Marcel smiled. "Yes. This guy called Pistol Pete owned it, and he'd gone through two or three wives by the time I saw White Nights at his place. Anyway, he would set up his TV and DVD in a window at the bar, and everybody gathered around outside to watch. I must have been about eight or nine years old then.

"Most of the movies we saw were cop movies or war movies, with lots of fighting and guns and all of that. I was pretty old before I realized that not everyone in America runs around shooting up stores with big windows and smashing up police cars."

"Oh, my God."

"I've seen Terminator 4 about six times! But one time, for some reason we ended up with White Nights. I don't know where Pete found it, but there it was. And the opening scene just blew me away—Baryshnikov did this amazing dance called "The Young Man and Death." He was so powerful and expressive, but so in control. I was completely hooked."

"What was the story about?"

"Baryshnikov is this famous Russian dancer ..." began Marcel. "Duh." Marcel laughed and poked her. "Shut up! Do you want to hear this or not?"

Samantha giggled. "Sorry. I'll be quiet."

"Okay, so Baryshnikov has defected to the United States, but he's on a plane that makes an emergency landing in Siberia. He tries to disguise his identity, but it doesn't work, and the KGB, the intelligence service, takes him prisoner. They want him to dance again at the Kirov Ballet in Leningrad, but he, of course, wants to get out of the USSR, the Soviet Union, as fast as he can.

"Enter Gregory Hines, another phenomenal dancer. He's Black and American but defected to the USSR, and he's married to his Russian interpreter. Who, by the way, is extremely cute."

"So you were able to notice something else besides the dancing?"

"Dance and women—what more is there to life? So anyway, the KGB assigns Gregory Hines to Baryshnikov, thinking that since he's also a dancer he'll be able to convince him to dance for the mother country again. Actually, Hines is threatened with being sent to break rocks in the mines if he doesn't do this. So we have these two incredible dancers, one Black, one White, and they don't like each other at first, but dance brings them together. I couldn't believe their skill, their moves."

Marcel was transported to a warm, tropical night, sitting cross-legged on the ground with dozens of other kids. He'd been one child in a sea of bobbing round heads, elbows and arms draped across shoulders, sniffly noses, and poking each other in the ribs. Perhaps he'd been the only one really watching the film; the other kids started to get restive when there weren't guns and car chases right away. A girl next to Marcel had sneezed constantly in his ear, one behind him had bonked him several times in the head with her elbow, and a naked toddler had urinated on his back. But Marcel hadn't noticed; he'd been completely absorbed in the power and grace of the two dancers, at first fighting each other and then fighting their common enemy, the KGB. It also had not been lost on him that the two great dancers ended up with beautiful women in love with them.

"Baryshnikov could do *anything*. Gregory Hines bets him 11 rubles against his tape player that he can't do 11 pirouettes in a row. Even Baryshnikov himself says it's impossible, and then he just goes right ahead and does it without batting an eye. Twirling around and around like it was no effort at all. No one could tell him what to do, no one could tell him how to dance. He was so expressive, but so ... self-contained, so individual. He knew who he was.

"Gregory Hines blew me away—he had such incredible rhythm. After the movie, my brother and I put bottle caps on the soles of our sneakers, pretending to be legendary tap dancers like Gregory Hines." *Maman* had tanned his backside for ruining his sneakers with Fanta bottle caps, but the sound they'd made on an old piece of plywood had been very fine.

"Gregory Hines's character had lost his freedom, and the two of them get it back through their dancing and their cleverness. Baryshnikov refuses to give up; he demands his own freedom and won't cave in when the Russians want him to dance. He refuses to be anyone else but himself, and it shows in his moves. When they make their escape, he uses racism to trick the KGB, but he and Gregory Hines really like and respect each other by then. Dance has transcended all boundaries, and they become like brothers."

Marcel paused, his mind full of those white nights again.

"And you've been dancing ever since?" whispered Samantha. "I guess I have. Back then we only got to see movies about once a month. Pistol Pete's DVD player broke a few times, and the power would cut out, so we went for months without any movies. So my family used to play a little music outside our house after dinner. Neighbors in the village used to come over all the time, singing and drumming while my brothers and I danced. A lot of people from my village moved away, they moved to Big Town, so later on it was pretty much just my family and a few neighbors dancing in the evenings." The demography of Martinique had changed a lot in Marcel's lifetime. With increasing urban migration, more and more people on Martinique were being raised in cities rather than in rural areas. **Demography** is the scientific study of the size, composition, and growth or decline of populations. Demography is concerned with patterns of birth (fertility), of death (mortality), and population movement (migration), which shape the size, composition, and growth or decline of population. Urban migration is the movement of people from rural areas to cities, often to find work. Urban migration is a common pattern in many less-developed countries, including Martinique.

"I don't know when it happened, but when we were singing and dancing in the evenings, I became the only one dancing. My brothers were happy to keep drumming. They just kind of messed around because it was fun, but I kept on. I danced all the time, on my way home from school, out on the beach. I danced when I was supposed to be picking pumpkins." He laughed. "I used to rub coconut oil on my feet, pretending it was rosin.

"My *grand-mère* did a lot of the singing; she has the most beautiful voice. When I was about 13 or so, she took me to see the Obeahman. My *maman* didn't know—she's Catholic and she doesn't believe in that island voodoo anymore. But

Grand-mère does, and she wanted the Obeahman to bless me, and he did. He told me I was going to become a great dancer."

"The Obeahman? What is that?"

"Oh, like a priest. A witch doctor. Just hocus-pocus; the old island people still believe in it, but it's just superstition."

"What do people go see a witch doctor for?"

"Depends. Women go because they can't have babies, or they have babies but they want more. I heard a story about a woman in Macouba who already had 14 children, but she wanted the Obeahman to help her get twins. She thought twins were good luck. We got a high fertility rate on Martinique; there are babies everywhere. I think that woman would have kept having babies forever if she hadn't gotten a fever and died. Sometimes people go because they are afraid of their children dyin'. They see the high mortality rate of da young babies and they want protection for der own." **Fertility rate** is the average number of births per woman in a specific society. It is not uncommon in Marcel's Martinique society for women to have numerous children; thus, Martinique has a high fertility rate. **Mortality rate** is the rate of deaths within a population.

"Did she get her twins?" asked Samantha. "No, she didn't. Maybe she *did* need their good luck."

Samantha was silent for a moment. The cars and dogs outside still kept up their abrasive symphony.

"Marcel, I want to go to Martinique. I want to meet the Obeahman. And I want to eat a papaya."

Marcel smiled and pulled her closer. "Okay, Miss Samantha." She loved how he pronounced her name: *Saman*-ta. He never said th. "Someday, we'll go to Martinique."

Marcel wondered how Samantha would adjust to being in rural Martinique, which, consistent with **demographic transition theory**, is characterized by large families. This is a theory that describes how industrialization affects population growth. In traditional agricultural societies with high birth and death rates, population size is stable. As a society becomes industrialized, declining death rates (as a result of improved health and sanitation) and continuing high birth rates lead to rapid population growth. With advanced industrialization, the increased survival rate of infants and children (along with their declining economic value) leads to a decline in birth rates, and population growth stabilizes once again. Marcel's society is in the second stage of demographic transition, with large families and a falling death rate.

"No, I mean soon, like spring break," she replied. "My grandparents usually give me some money for Christmas, and I have frequent flier miles. We should go in March." Marcel was silent, listening to the street noise and breathing in the jasmine fragrance of Samantha's hair on the pillow. Martinique in March? Was that possible? He pictured taking her to Toussaint, to his family and his village. It was an interesting idea, but the money. ... How could she spend such money, just like that?

A sudden pang gripped his heart as he realized how much he missed his family. He'd been trying to keep a lid on his homesickness, knowing he wouldn't be going back for four years, and in his heart he'd said goodbye to his *grand-mère*. She was an old lady and probably wouldn't be around in another four years. But to see her one more time, to hear her sing again in the warm, tropical night ...

"We'll see," he whispered.

"I love seeing favorite movies like that, over and over again," said Samantha. "How many times did you see White Nights?"

"Just the one time," he answered and closed his eyes

***

Christmas Day was difficult. Samantha called both her mother and father and became quiet and teary-eyed afterward. Each parent had tried to trash the other while on the phone, and she felt guilty but secretly glad that she hadn't gone home for the holidays. After thinking about it for a long time, she finally told Marcel she'd decided she had to back way off from her parents' problems for a while. The whole divorce was eating her up, and she was going to have to put some distance between her and the situation if she was to keep her sanity.

Marcel tried to cheer her up and cooked the only meal he knew how in Shelby's tiny little kitchen: fish balls and fried plantains. Only he couldn't find real plantains and used bananas instead, and they turned gray and mushy when he fried them. The fish balls weren't quite as bad, but without fresh coconut milk and coriander, they were bland and tasteless.

"On Martinique the plantains are brown and crispy when you fry them," he told Samantha as she picked at the food and tried to look enthusiastic. The fried bananas looked like dead gym socks. Finally, he took the plates away.

"I have an idea," said Marcel. "Let's go to Manhattan and find a salad bar instead. Maybe it will snow!" It hadn't yet snowed in their five days in New York City, and he was dying to see it.

Samantha smiled. "Okay, but let's do our presents first." She took him by the hand and pulled him into the little living room. Sitting him down on the couch, she placed a brightly colored box in his lap. Grinning, Marcel pulled the ribbon off and opened it. Inside was another, smaller box.

"It's another box. I'm Master of the Obvious." Samantha giggled, watching his face expectantly.

There was yet another box inside this one, and finally Marcel pulled out a plain white envelope. Inside it were two tickets to a Broadway show for the next evening.

Marcel held them up and read the title of the show. "Bring in 'Da Noise, Bring in 'Da Funk. Hey, this is Savion Glover's show!"

"Have you ever seen him?" asked Samantha.

"No, I never have, but I've heard of him. He's supposed to be a great tap dancer, and he's worked with Gregory Hines. Thank you, Miss Saman-ta!" Marcel kissed her and handed her a small box.

"I'll tell you now, there's only the one box," he said.

Samantha opened it and held up a pretty gold pin. It was a palm tree, with little silver coconuts on it. Each coconut had a tiny little jewel on it, one red, one white, and one green.

"This is beautiful!"

"They're not real," said Marcel, a little abashed. Although he'd thought it was expensive when he'd bought it, it had been a fraction of the cost of the tickets for the Broadway show.

"What, the coconuts? They're *lovely*. Help me put it on." Samantha kissed him long and slow. "Merry Christmas, Dancer-Man," she whispered in his ear, and they forgot about going out.

***

The next day they took the subway to Manhattan and spent most of the day there, exploring Chinatown, Central Park, and then Greenwich Village before heading to Broadway for the show.

Marcel was amazed at the salad bars, tucked away in little corner convenience stores and grocery stores, each one trying to outdo the last, some boasting 250 different items.

"Look here, Sam," Marcel said, as he hovered around the salad bar at Sid's Grocery like a bee at a picnic. "Fresh asparagus. Fried shrimp. Baby carrots. Lingwee-nee! Chocolate pudding!" Samantha laughed. "I can see that! Go ahead, put the chocolate pudding on the linguine. Knock yourself out."

Marcel put the pudding in a little dish by itself, but he crammed as much of everything else as he could get onto the rest of the plate. So many *choices*. In America you can eat anything you want, go anywhere you want, be anything you want. Marcel noticed everything wherever he went. Putting so many countless different cultures together had produced a harmonic mix of restaurants, groceries, and unique stores.

In Greenwich Village, Samantha wanted to take him to a place called the Jekyll and Hyde Club for dinner. "It doesn't have a salad bar, but there's plenty of other good stuff, and they have monsters and dinosaurs."

"Monsters and dinosaurs?"

"You'll see!"

As they emerged from the subway and crossed the street to the club, Marcel looked up to see an unusual billboard. It was an ad for a travel agency, urging you to get away for a romantic vacation, showing a loving couple on the deck of a cruise ship, silhouetted against a magnificent ocean sunset. The couple rested their cheeks together, smiling, their arms wrapped around each other. They were obviously in love, and this vacation was just the thing for a romantic getaway.

Both members of the couple were men. Marcel was so surprised he stopped in the middle of the sidewalk to stare. "Sam, look at this. They're *men*."

She looked up at the billboard. "What, gay couples don't go on cruises in the Caribbean?"

"Well, I don't think so, at least not like—not so ..."

"Not so obvious?"

"No! I can't believe they'd put up a billboard like that!"

"Why not?"

"Well because, because now they're only going to get gay clients, aren't they? Who else would go through this travel agent?"

Samantha laughed. "Oh, come on, Marcel. You wouldn't want to call this travel agent because they'd think you're gay? I'd call them! And I'm sure you have plenty of gay friends who'd like to go on a trip like this."

"I don't have any gay friends."

"Yes, you do."

"I do not!"

"Marcel, you do have gay friends! Don't be so uptight. I guess the social change taking place here hasn't quite made it to Martinique. As the Caribbean moves toward urbanization, you'll probably discover lots of gay people you never knew were gay. Look, here's Jekyll and Hyde." **Social change** is the alteration or transformation of culture, social institutions, or public policy over time. An example of social change is the increased acceptance of homosexuality in US culture in recent decades. Urbanization is the increasing proportion of a population who live in urban areas. **Urbanization** generally leads to greater diversity, and lifestyles previously considered "alternate" or "deviant" may be more apparent and accepted, as Samantha predicts for gays on Martinique.

They entered the lobby of the restaurant, and Marcel found himself surrounded by dinosaur bones, old car parts, suits of armor with moving arms done up with

Christmas lights, several TV screens mounted on the walls, each playing a different classic horror movie, and monsters everywhere.

"Isn't this place cool?" Samantha whispered to him as they were led to a table.

"I do not have any gay friends," he answered.

They sat down.

"Marcel, I know you have gay friends. Connor and Drew from your dance class, for example. Why does this bother you so much?"

"It doesn't bother me. I just, we don't—there aren't any gay people on Martinique, I'm just not used to it."

Samantha laughed. "Sure there are. There are gay people everywhere; it's just a fact of life. I guarantee you there are gays and lesbians on Martinique, they probably just don't feel comfortable being out if it's a hostile atmosphere."

A hostile atmosphere. Hadn't someone else just mentioned this? In a meeting of Double Black?

Marcel considered this. "Connor and Drew, huh?"

"Yup. They like each other, they're both boys, no problem. Right?" Samantha's eyes twinkled.

Marcel smiled back at her. *Right, I guess. Well, what is the problem? Is there a problem?* The image of the gay couple on the billboard filled his head. He couldn't come up with a single good reason why this should be a problem, now that he thought about it. Where he came from nobody ever thought about it, or even really talked about it; everyone just assumed it was wrong and unnatural. Connor and Drew? Were they wrong?

"Sam, do you know where the restroom is?"

"Over there, down that hallway," she answered, smirking. She'd been here before and she knew very well the bathrooms were hidden.

In a few minutes Marcel found himself completely lost. There were strange little hallways and rooms, and cryptic signs on the wall. Bookshelves lined the hallway

Sam had pointed him to, but there were no doors and no signs. Marcel folded his arms and leaned back against a bookcase.

And nearly fell into the women's room. It was a trick door.

"Sorry! Excuse me!" he exclaimed, mortified.

One of the women, applying lipstick at the mirror, smiled at him. "The men's room is across the hall."

He felt along the other bookcases and found another trick door, this time opening into the men's room. *Thank God. Why does this have to be so confusing!*

Back at the table with Samantha, Marcel was about to speak when a commotion erupted on a nearby wall. Blue lights flashed and a large shelf emerged from behind a panel, revealing a huge gargoyle, like the ones found guarding medieval churches. It was hideously ugly, with jagged horns, claw feet, and leathery-looking wings. Its eyes glowed red; it swiveled its head slowly back and forth, and steam escaped from flared nostrils. It began to speak.

"Yo, Rasta-man! Where'd you get the locks, mon? Didja stick your head into a blender?"

Marcel realized with a jolt that the creature was speaking to him! Where the heck had he landed? Talking monsters, two men on a romantic billboard, broadcast for the whole world to see, eating dinner with little sticks ... Every time he thought he was getting the hang of American society, he suddenly found himself in the deep end again.

Samantha clapped her hands and shrieked with laughter.

Grinning, he shook his head. "I guess we don't have anything like this on Martinique either!"

***

On the way to the theater after dinner, it finally started to snow. What amazed Marcel is that nobody else seemed to notice. People didn't stop to look, they didn't pull their collars up or tighten their scarves; they just hurried along as usual, heads down, hardly speaking to anyone. It was strange; everyone seemed so self-contained in his or her own private little world, even though they were in large throngs of people. This collective behavior was so different from Martinique, where everyone was connected and interacting with each other. **Collective behavior** is activity that is engaged in by a large number of people, often taking an unstructured, spontaneous, and emotional form; examples include fads (such as body piercing), riots (such as the Cincinnati race riots), and social movements (such as the gay liberation movement). Collective behavior can also be seen on a more day-to-day basis as Marcel notices with the silent, hurried crowds of Manhattan.

Samantha stopped at a convenience store to buy some ChapStick. She was always buying something! Marcel waited for her outside on the sidewalk.

He watched the snow falling and glittering in the lights along Broadway, enchanted, lost in the moment. Excitement and anticipation filled his heart; he'd never been here in his life, but it seemed somehow familiar. The night sky remained soft and dense, reflecting the busyness and glow of the pulsing city below, the snowflakes silently drifting down into the noise and hustle. They gathered and created tidy little drifts in the lee of a curb, perched atop a streetlight, in the doorframe of a mailbox. Snowflakes pirouetted through the traffic to alight on taxicabs, buses, and limos and on the soft velvet muzzle of a carriage horse standing by the curb, the snow turning instantly to water by its steaming breath. *Are they raindrops now, on the horse's whiskers?* He had had no idea frozen raindrops would turn out to be so ... stunning. Marcel rested a hand on the horse's neck. He was surprised to find it rock solid under a dense, plush coat of mink brown.

Snowflakes everywhere. Floating, dancing, coming to rest unobtrusively on a red knit cap bobbing along in a throng of pedestrians, on a stack of newspapers, on the yellow-striped umbrella of a hot-dog stand, on a cast-iron railing of a stairway leading down to a garden apartment (who lives there? In a little cement burrow next to the busy street? *It will be me; someday I will live here.*). He tilted his head up and let the drifting, silent snowflakes land on his face, soft as a moth's wing against the night sky. The only way he knew they were there on his skin was a tiny sensation of cool, and then they disappeared into minuscule drops of water, just like on the horse's muzzle.

"Do you like it?" Samantha was standing next to him again. "Snowflakes on your face?"

Marcel grinned at her, his eyes sparkling.

"Look!" She said, and stuck out her tongue. Marcel watched, mesmerized, as a snowflake landed on its pink, moist tip, and then she turned and kissed him. He could feel her tongue inside his lips; she had just given him a melted snowflake.

"Come on!" said Samantha, laughing. She took him by the hand and dragged him down the sidewalk. "We don't want to be late!"

***

Bring in 'Da Noise, Bring in 'Da Funk. *Unusual name for a show*, thought Marcel as he leafed through the program, seated in the Ambassador Theatre. A subtitle for the show read A Tap/Rap Discourse on the Staying Power of the Beat. *I like it.* Snowflakes still danced in his head. He imagined he could still feel their tiny cool footprints on his face. The hum and throng of people in the theater gave him a pleasant sense of anticipation, and his mind wandered as they waited for the show to begin.

Nothing could have prepared him for Savion Glover. Marcel's first impression of the lanky, graceful man on stage, with his easy manner and mop of dreadlocks, was *He looks like me*. There was something so familiar about him, as if they'd known each other in another life, that Marcel felt as though there was no one else in the theater with them. This was dance like he'd never seen before, dance of a purity and energy so fine he wanted to be part of it. He wanted to be on stage with Savion Glover and the rest of the incredible cast and let their rhythm and joy and creative power wash over him, igniting his soul with a flame he'd hardly known he'd been searching for.

What moves! Savion's feet and body played the stage and the audience with perfect ease, a consummate professional, yet with warmth and a touch of cockiness, as if inviting the audience to get down with him and then saying, *You ain't seen nothin' yet*!

Savion's feet, a staggering size 12-½, moved at warp speed across the floor, telling the story of racism in America. Streetwise and savvy, bittersweet and hopeful, Marcel watched the slave ships arriving in America, the exploitation of African Americans in factories, the in-your-face Harlem high society, and hip-hop street life. Marcel felt the enduring Black spirit pounded out in an evolution of rhythm— exuberant, defiant, innovative. It was historical, and it was personal, especially during a scene when Savion performs an eloquent tribute to his heroes, the old masters of tap. He danced in front of a set of mirrors, and the effect of seeing him move from different angles, with his voiceover describing how the great dancers had helped him find himself, was electrifying.

At the end of the show, Marcel's heart was pounding, his throat dry. Images of the performance resonated through him: drummers with pots and pans tied all over their bodies, pounding away on each other and loving it; young Black men trying to flag down taxis who refused to stop for them in a clever dance called "Taxi"; Uncle Huck-a-Buck and his old-timey *dancin' for the White folks*; the beating of drumsticks on the bottom of Savion's shoes in a factory ... and the slave dancing. A lasting image burned in his mind of Savion using his feet to speak for the slaves, forbidden the drums and musical instruments of their homelands, the music of their ancestors and their souls. Marcel felt the great pain and sorrow with the hope and defiance of Savion's powerful dance.

Marcel sat unmoving in his seat as the lights came up, the remnants of thunderous applause still echoing through the theater. He felt as if he'd been run over by a freight train. He would never be the same.

Samantha, turning to see the look on his face and a tear in his eye, asked, "Didn't you like the show?"

***

Chapter 7 Study Questions
POPULATION AND SOCIAL CHANGE

1. What makes New York City a **megalopolis**?
2. Explain how industrialization affects population growth (according to **demographic transition theory**).
3. How do you think the **fertility** and **mortality** rates in the United States compare with those on Martinique?
4. How might **urbanization** influence the way homosexuals are treated on Martinique?
5. Give an example of **collective behavior**.

Kingdom of Love

Religion

SAMANTHA KNOCKED ON the door to Professor Rourke's office. She could hardly believe they were three weeks into the spring semester; Christmas seemed like ages ago. Memories from their trip to New York still popped up with pleasant frequency; the noise and flickering lights of the subway trains, Shelby's rickety stove with the broken knobs. Cappuccino at Sal's around the corner, Marcel eating an ice cream cone even though it was only 40 degrees out and then moaning about being cold. Marcel with headphones on over his dreadlocks listening to CDs, Marcel taking a bath in Shelby's old tub, with his big feet sticking out and dripping water on the floor. But the memories were getting hazier every day, especially with the new semester's schedule. She was busier than she'd ever been in her life and felt like it was all she could do to keep up. Marcel was kept busy with his dancing and his classes, and she wished they could see each other more often.

"Ah, Samantha, come in," said Professor Rourke. "Sit down, sit down." Samantha cleared a spot on one of two chairs near the desk; both were piled with periodicals and journal articles. She hoped she wasn't disrupting his filing system.

"Hi, Professor," she started, "I wanted to talk to you about my term project." Guy Rourke leaned back in his chair, his hands behind his head. "You have a nice Christmas, Samantha?" She smiled. "Yes, I did, thank you. I spent it in New York City with my boyfriend."

"Is that where your family is? New York?"

"No, they're in New Hampshire. I didn't see them over the holidays."

He nodded, considering this. "And how are your classes going this semester? Okay?"

"They're okay. Busy. I'm having a hard time getting to the shelter to continue my research and make it to the courthouse." Samantha was continuing her case study of the Miller Street Shelter, changing the focus a little and building on the paper she'd written last term.

"Which one do you want to give up?" asked Professor Rourke. "Oh, neither," she answered quickly, and then reconsidered. "Well, the cases at the courthouse, I just get a little frustrated sometimes ..."

"Go on."

"Well, you know I want to go to law school." He nodded. "I always thought it would be the best way of helping people, you know, fighting for their rights. Making sure the people who can't defend themselves are treated fairly, making sure they get what they need. You know?"

"Is that what your father does? Isn't he an attorney?"

"He's an attorney. But he does mostly corporate work. Lots of suits arm-wrestling each other for how much money they can squeeze out of the corporations."

He smiled. "And that's not helping people?"

"Well, it's just so removed, so ... clinical. I thought by sitting in on the civil cases I'd get a better taste of the frontlines, you know, the people who are really suffering who need someone to fight for them. But what I'm seeing is more suits, arm-wrestling each other for position. They seem to be more concerned about winning their cases than what their clients really need."

"What do their clients really need?"

"Well, they need someone to listen to them. They need help with their problems, with their lives. I guess the attorneys are helping them by trying to win their cases, but they get vicious about it. They don't seem to care about how painful it must be for people up on the stand to have to talk about personal things."

"Maybe they have to do it. That's part of their job."

"I know, but it seems so ... cruel. I think sometimes they ... enjoy it. It makes them feel ... powerful." Her voice had dropped to a whisper.

Professor Rourke leaned forward. "Samantha? You okay?"

She didn't answer, just kept looking down at her lap, her face hot and red, mortified that she seemed to be falling to pieces in front of this good man, someone she respected and wanted to impress.

"Everything okay with your folks?" He asked quietly. Samantha suddenly looked up, her expression fierce. "That's just it! They're going to court, my mother's suing my father for divorce, and the attorneys, they're going to tear apart their marriage, like—like a pack of hyenas! She's told her attorney all kinds of things about my dad, about his drinking, when she ... well, she wants me to testify, and I can't do it! I can't choose sides like that. Whatever I say the lawyers will jump on and twist around, to make it sound different—worse—like I want my dad to suffer. That's what they do!" Tears rolled down her cheeks, and she struggled to catch her breath.

Professor Rourke started looking around, apparently helpless to find anything in his own office, opening drawers and looking under stacks of papers. Finally, he found a box of tissues and handed it to her, his expression kind.

"They're not really interested in helping, are they?" Samantha asked him, blowing her nose. "Well, Samantha, I don't know about all attorneys. Certainly, there are some who thrive on going in for the kill. But maybe they accomplish things no one else can. That doesn't mean you have to be that kind of lawyer. You just have to decide what it is you can do that will help people the way you want to."

"What about ... some kind of social work? Mr. Stroud at the shelter seems to really be doing something there. He's set up programs for adult education and gotten funding for substance abuse counseling, and he even found a company to donate insulin for homeless people who are diabetic. They keep it in a special refrigerator at the shelter. What if I didn't go into law and focused more on sociology or social work?"

"Well, there are a number of paths you can take. A degree in either sociology or social work can lead to a variety of jobs. Sociology is a much broader field than social work. Social workers are often involved with delivering services, such as connecting clients with services, working in hospitals, dealing with domestic and child abuse. Sociology undergraduates often work as court counselors, police officers, criminal investigators, court administrators, parole or probation officers, things like that. A PhD prepares you to be a college professor."

Samantha looked thoughtful. "How about other positions, where you're more involved with people?"

"Oh, there's a whole spectrum of human services careers. Social work case managers, human resources placement specialists, coordinator for county group homes, youth leadership agencies—it's quite a list." The professor leaned forward and folded his hands on the desk. "But for the moment, why don't you focus on the Miller Street project and look for what it really means to you? You don't have to make any big career choices now, and once you find a path that really speaks to you, something you know you can enjoy and make a difference in, your career direction will become clearer."

Samantha nodded and blew her nose again.

"Isn't your dad expecting you to join his firm when you're finished with law school?"

She shrugged. "He's been wanting me to do that forever. I used to think it was a good idea, but now ... I don't even feel like talking to him on the phone. He's sort of ... become someone I don't know anymore. I think it would drive me crazy to be in the same firm with him."

Professor Rourke smiled. "You know, Samantha, going through a divorce does not bring out the best in people. While your parents are in the middle of this, it will be pretty much impossible for them to act like the parents you grew up with. If you can, it will help everyone to try cutting them some slack, and don't let this push you into making big decisions. Your career choice should come from your heart, not in reaction to what's going on around you."

Samantha looked up and met his gaze. The look of concern on his face made her want to cry. "Thanks, Professor," she said hastily, and was out the door before she made a fool of herself again.

***

Jill Hathaway and Samantha sat at a table just inside the entrance of the cafeteria. It was just before noon and they were hoping to catch the lunchtime crowd for their sociology survey. Every time someone came in, a gust of cold January air ruffled the questionnaires neatly stacked on the corner of the table. They had spent an afternoon downtown the week before surveying working people, and now they were giving out their questionnaires to students.

"Couldn't we move the table a little?" asked Samantha. "We're right in the middle of a polar cold front here." Jill rolled her eyes but got up and took one side of the table. "What a wiener you are, Sam! Letting a little breeze interfere with our work—we're on the cutting edge of sociology! We're about to delve into the very fabric of society. We're going to figure out the causes of the modern blight on social consciousness and fix it!" They set the table back down, farther away from the door. "That is, we were until Samantha got cold feet."

"Well, we won't be able to save the world if we freeze to death first, now will we?"

"Hey, Ms. Saman-ta." Samantha looked up to see a familiar shaggy head. "Marcel!" She gave him a peck on the cheek, and then turned to her friend Jill. "You remember Jill Hathaway, don't you?"

"How are you, Jill? I would like to introduce my friend, Ben Williamson."

Samantha smiled; he was so polite. Most of her male friends would have just grunted "yo" or something.

"Hi, Ben," she said and held her hand out. "*Mademoiselle*," answered the big man and kissed her hand like a Frenchman. She and Jill exchanged glances. "I can see you've been hanging around with Marcel," laughed Samantha.

Ben stepped back to look at the sign hanging on the front of their table. "What are you ladies up to here?"

"It's a survey on social values," said Jill. "It's for our sociology class, and we're getting opinions on homelessness. Here, would you like to participate?" she asked, handing him a questionnaire.

"You go ahead, Ben," Marcel told him. "I've already done it. I'm going to go get in line."

Ben pulled up a chair and sat with the two women. "Let's see here," and he began to read the questions out loud. "'Why do you think people become homeless? Rank order the following six answers from 1 to 6, with '1' being the most common reason and '6' the least common: they have a mental illness; they have drug and alcohol addictions; they are lazy; they don't have the opportunities other people have because they lack education; they are unemployed; they are escaping an abusive home and have nowhere to go. Do you think the government should provide food and shelter for homeless people? Yes, under all circumstances; yes, but only for limited periods of time; yes, but only if the homeless people are willing to work; no.'" He grinned at Jill and Samantha. "Did you all write this? It's pretty good." He continued, "'If a homeless person asked you for money, would you give it? Yes, under all circumstances; yes, if he/she looked infirm; no, but I would give him/her food; no.'"

Ben looked up, his eyes twinkling. "Black or White?"

"Excuse me?" asked Jill.

"I mean, it makes a difference if the homeless person doing the asking is Black or White. If a White person is asked for money, it matters if the homeless person is Black or White. If a Black person is asked for money, it matters if the homeless person is Black or White."

"Oh," said Samantha. She looked at Jill. "Well, we didn't want to make this into a racial issue; we're just interested in the social aspects of homelessness."

Ben smiled. "Racial issues are social aspects, maybe the most important ones, since homelessness, drug abuse, and lack of education are all higher in the Black population. Doesn't seem like a very complete picture if you're looking at social problems and you don't consider race, does it?"

Samantha looked at him. "You're right. It does make a difference." She turned to Jill. "But we can't change it now, after we've gotten lots of completed questionnaires without race included. I guess we go to college to learn from our mistakes. I hope this doesn't hurt our grades."

Jill turned to Ben. "Ben, would you mind taking this with you and maybe filling in what you think is missing in the questions and possible answers? We'd be interested in how you think race should be addressed."

He stood up. "Sure, I wouldn't mind. In fact, I'm in a racism awareness group that meets tomorrow. I'll show it to them too." He picked up his backpack. "I'd better get to the food line before Marcel eats everything. I'm likely to waste away," he patted his spare tire with good humor. "Nice meeting you all—good luck with your survey."

"Thanks, Ben," they called after him.

Jill turned to Samantha after he was gone. "Yes, it will throw the results off if we change the questionnaire after we've already gotten started. But he's right about the racial issues, and we want to make this a complete study."

"I can make another appointment to talk to Professor Rourke," Samantha answered. "Maybe we should discount the results we've already gotten, or include them in a separate section or something."

Jill picked up the stack of questionnaires and put them away. "Let's not hand any more out until we decide how to proceed. Why don't we eat and then get over to Miller Street? Do you mind if I drive? I have to pick up my kids from the babysitter afterward."

***

Marcel pulled off his sweatshirt and turtleneck but kept on the black T-shirt underneath. These days it was a little too cold in the dance studio to go bare-chested. Right before he began his stretching and warmup, he glanced over at the window well, a little ritual he'd fallen into. Of course, she wasn't there, but the act of looking provided a pleasant glow, and he thought of Samantha sitting in the leaves there, a piece of paper in her hand, her lips warm and inviting as he kissed her. This was now mixed with other memories: a snowy kiss on Broadway; Samantha cooking an omelet with artichoke hearts (which he'd never eaten before) in the tiny kitchen in Queens, where the refrigerator and oven doors could not both be opened at once; Samantha walking up the steps of the Museum of Art; how fine she looked in her leather boots and tight jeans. "Hey, Marcel," called another dancer as he took off his backpack and sat down on the floor.

"Hey, Drew," Marcel answered and watched him as he began his warmup. Connor approached Drew, who was taking his running shoes off and rubbing his feet. Connor leaned over him and said something that made Drew smile, and he touched him lightly on the shoulder, like a caress. It was a small gesture, but affectionate, intimate, something Marcel would never do to another man. Feeling his face flush, he turned and stared at the wall as he stretched, expelling his breath in irritated bursts.

"Hi, Marcel." He looked up. Connor was standing in front him, holding his hand out. *Oh, God, please don't touch me, I don't want you to touch me.*

"This is the music I told you about." Connor said as he showed Marcel his phone. "It's Mumford & Sons; I'll send you the playlist. I thought you might like to check it out. You know, for the showcase piece."

"Oh. Thanks, Connor. I'll listen to it tonight."

"No problem," he replied. "I hope you knock 'em dead!"

Marcel hadn't said anything to the other students, but rumor had spread quickly about his solo in the spring dance showcase. He didn't know if anyone knew about the Juilliard instructor who was coming, but in this place it wouldn't take long for that to become common knowledge.

He stood and started doing a few pirouettes, loosening up his joints and letting the fragmented energy start flowing through him. At the beginning, when the professor had first told him about the solo piece, he'd felt so together, so focused. But now, three months later, he felt that he wasn't any closer to a solid plan than when he'd gotten off the plane. In his mind he went over a hundred moves a day and as many music clips. Professor Cady had been great, giving suggestions, advice, and encouragement, but always stopping short of telling him exactly what to do. This had to come from him, and they both knew it.

He was taking jazz, ballet, and tap this semester, and the rehearsal schedule was formidable. He had to keep up in his other classes: English composition, humanities, and French; if his grade point average fell too far, he would lose his scholarship. But it was hard to pull his attention away from the dance showcase piece; planning for it hardly ever left his mind. He and Samantha hung out in her room or the library or the Emerson lobby listening to music, and he'd chosen a couple of pieces so far, but something was still missing. The cold, gray days of late January seemed to sap the strength from him, and he longed for the bright sun and sultry salt air of the Caribbean to wake him up again.

"Nice, Jamaica, let me see that again." Professor Cady had suddenly appeared, as if she never really left the dance studio but only made herself visible and invisible. Marcel swiveled his head back and forth, rooting out the tension in his neck, took a deep breath, and repeated the groove he'd been working on.

"No, the way you did it before. About five minutes ago. You were rushing this time," Esther Cady announced.

Marcel nodded and tried it again. Looking at the professor's face when he finished, he could see he hadn't made any progress.

"Sorry, Professor," he said. "It's just not coming like it should. I've worked on that sequence for two weeks and it's not going anywhere."

"Then you need to scrap it and start over. But I think you're going about it the wrong way."

Marcel folded his arms across his chest and waited. There was a barely perceptible tightening in his throat; he wondered if Professor Cady was regretting her decision to have him perform solo. She had invited her friend from Juilliard to come all this way.

"You're working too hard, Jamaica." She smiled at the look of surprise on his face. "Never thought you'd hear me say that, did you? I don't mean the hours you are practicing—they are necessary. I mean your attitude, the way you're going about it. You're after perfection, and it's unbalancing you. If you think about an acrobat on a tightrope, he doesn't try to hold tightly to perfect balance. If he lets his balance shift back and forth, he keeps finding a new equilibrium. If you keep holding tightly to an idea of perfection, you get in the way of your own equilibrium: you strive for perfection, you get dissatisfied, and it shows in your moves. When you strive for excellence, there's always a higher place to find, and the joy of finding it releases you. I've seen this in you. There's always a new place to find, and it builds on the place you've found before. Remember, Marcel, there is a difference between perfection and excellence."

***

After dance class Marcel walked to Emerson Hall to meet Samantha and Dash for dinner. They'd been planning on driving downtown for Thai food at the Golden Rose but had finally decided they were all too busy so they'd just go over to the cafeteria instead. Marcel wanted to get back to the dance studio that evening, Samantha was rewriting her sociology questionnaire, and Dash had a paper due the next day.

Marcel knocked on the door of 306, and Samantha flung her arms around him when he entered. "Marcel! You would not *believe* the day I've had!"

"What happened? Did the Vampire Weekend break up? Hey, Dash."

"Hey, Marcel." Dash was filing her fingernails to a point and painting them black. "No, the Vampire Weekend are still together—that would be a disaster of biblical proportions. Samantha must have been abducted by aliens."

"Oh, you *guys*," Samantha dropped onto her bed and lay back as if exhausted. "There was this woman at the shelter, she started having a seizure. She came out of it when Mr. Stroud gave her some orange juice. She's diabetic and has a problem with low blood sugar." She sat back up to properly regale the others with her story. "He drove her to the hospital, and Jill and I stayed with her while she got some tests. She was supposed to go in for a whole set of blood tests a month ago, but she wouldn't do it. It turns out she can't stand getting blood drawn, even though she has to have insulin shots every day. She was in such a state! She puked on the floor and yelled at all the nurses and wouldn't let anyone touch her until Jill and I both rolled up our sleeves and agreed to get our blood taken, too! See?" She showed them a Band-Aid on the inside of her right elbow.

"What tests are *you* having done?" asked Marcel.

"None! Our blood was just tossed after they finally got Rosie's!"

"I would have asked for a Smurf Band-Aid," said Dash.

"Oh, brother!" said Samantha and fell backwards onto the bed again. "I'm giving blood, sweat, and tears for my fellow human, and I get no sympathy."

"Hey, it's hard to feel a lot of sympathy for someone who's going to the Caribbean for spring break in a few weeks!" retorted Dash. "I'll be slinging my tits over a hot stove in New Jersey while you're worshipping the sun in Martinique!" Dash usually worked in her uncle's restaurant on breaks from school.

"You'll be *what*?" Marcel asked Dash. "Oh, yeah!" said Samantha with a grin. "Sun, sand, and surf. I'm bringing three bathing suits so I don't end up with tan lines!"

A fist pounded on their door. "Coming, coming, keep your pants on," said Samantha. She opened the door.

"Samantha." It was Daly Brown.

"Yes, Daly, that is my name," she smiled at him.

"You have to come with me. You have to help me rescue Kevin."

Samantha frowned; Daly seemed a little distraught. "Uh, why don't you come in, Daly?"

Inside, he told the three of them about his roommate, also known as Brother Tree.

"He's been gone for a week. He got involved in some kinda weird religion thing. I've tried to get him to come back, but he won't listen. He just lies around at this place smoking weed and says he's ascending to a higher level of consciousness." **Religion** is a system of beliefs, symbols, and rituals involving the sacred or supernatural realm. Religion provides meaning to life, guides behavior, and unites followers.

"Wait, wait, what place? Where is he?" asked Dash.

"The Kingdom of Love. It's about an hour from here; it's the center for the Truth of Love Warriors. Raj Ramahatrian started it up out there in response to the materialism and secularization of our society. It's supposed to be a haven of sacred truth and love in a profane world." **Secularization** is the decline in the importance of religion for society and its members. The Kingdom of Love was created as an attempt to return to religious values. **Sacred** refers to those things that members of society view as holy and worthy of respect, honor, and worship. The members of the Kingdom of Love view love as sacred. **Profane**, on the other hand, is the everyday worldly aspects of life. Raj Ramahatrian believes that truth and love (sacred ideals) cannot be found in the everyday, materialistic world, so he has created the Kingdom of Love.

"Aren't you one of the Warriors?" asked Samantha.

"Nah, I found out it was all a load of horse manure. Raj Ramahatrian preaches all this crap about peace and sacred love and sharing and all that, but what he really wants is for you to share your money with him. We have to support him in the material world while he helps us transcend it to a place of higher consciousness. It was kind of entertaining for a while until he started hitting us up for money, so I split. He had some great weed, though."

"What about Kevin?" asked Dash.

"Well, I told him I thought this guy was full of hot air and I was finished with him and his cult, but Kevin just kept going back. It wasn't too bad last semester, but now he's stopped going to his classes. He's about to flunk out, and now he's giving this jerk all of his money. I don't even think he's eating out there, just smoking his eyeballs out." A **cult** is a relatively small religious group that is considered to be extremist or fake and is usually started by a highly charismatic leader. Cults have beliefs, teachings, and behaviors that differ from the mainstream culture. Kevin has been consumed by the new cult, "Kingdom of Love," and virtually dropped out of mainstream society in terms of attending classes, staying in the dorm, etc.

"Can't you talk to him?" Samantha wanted to know.

"What do you think I've been doing all week? I've been out there three times since Saturday trying to get him to come back. First he told me everyone has their own religion and to leave him alone. Now he thinks I'm a subversive and I've come to plant bugs in everyone's craniums."

"Well, are you?" asked Dash.

"Look, are you gonna help me or not?" demanded Daly.

"Why don't you call his parents?" suggested Samantha. "Or the RA? They would probably know what to do."

"He'll just see that as a threat. His parents will kill him if they find out he hasn't been going to classes." Daly looked Samantha directly in the eye. "I need you to go out and talk to him."

"Me? Why me?" She was taken aback. She was already thinking of all the things she still had to do tonight after they had dinner at the cafeteria.

Marcel spoke for the first time. "Kevin might not be listening to Daly," he said. "But he will listen to you."

Samantha looked at him helplessly. She had so much to do, she had to get to the library tonight, she was meeting with Professor Rourke in the morning, and why *her*?

"Well, I, I hardly know Kevin; I don't really know what I'd say to him ..." Even as she uttered the words, they sounded lame.

Marcel picked up Samantha's coat and handed it to her. "Sam, this is how you save the world. One friend at a time."

***

The Kingdom of Love was a ramshackle old farmhouse at the end of a muddy dirt road. Patches of dead grass interspersed with mud gave the lawn a moth-eaten appearance, and one shutter hung at a crazy angle from a front window. A hand-painted sign on the porch announced that all who entered the Kingdom of Love would find their True Destiny.

On the front porch Daly turned to Samantha, Marcel, and Dash. "There's a guy inside who's kinda like a bouncer. Just let me talk to him."

The guy inside was about six foot three, wearing sweat pants and a large, flowing white tunic. He recognized Daly but looked suspiciously at the other three.

"Brother Peace," Daly greeted him. "I wish you the blessings of purest love."

"Brother Destiny," replied the man, "I wish you the joy of an open heart. But I don't think I know your friends."

"They come in peace, my brother. They, uh, they wish to join us on the journey to love and freedom, they seek to unchain their hearts from the toils of commercialism and greed." Daly took Samantha by the arm and pulled her up next to him. "Meet Sister Circle, Brother Rasta, and um ..." he looked at Dash, who was wearing eyeball earrings and bright lavender eye shadow, "Sister Clear Vision."

Brother Peace nodded and belched. "Wait here."

Standing in the foyer, they peppered Daly with questions.

"We're not here to join up!" Samantha stage-whispered. "Aren't we gonna just get Kevin and get out of here?"

"I'm not a Rasta," said Marcel.

"If I'm Sister Clear Vision, can I shorten that to 'Visine?'"

"Listen, everybody just shut up for a minute!" said Daly. "We'll have to see Raj Ramahatrian before we can talk to Kevin. Just tell him we want to see Brother Tree and bring him the love in our hearts. Kevin can leave if he wants to, we just have to convince him that he wants to."

Brother Peace returned. "Come with me."

They followed him into the house, which was minimally furnished with old rugs, a few battered couches with their springs showing, and some rickety old chairs. A few people were sleeping on the couches, and flute music and incense hung in the air like a shroud.

"Don't let this fool you," Daly whispered to the others as they passed through a kitchen with cracked counters, peeling wallpaper, and a leaky refrigerator. "Raj himself has a king-size bed and a Jacuzzi in his quarters."

"What kind of religion is this?" whispered Samantha.

"I'll bet he's getting ready to become a televangelist," said Dash.

Brother Peace stopped them in front of a door painted with a flaming heart and sword.

"Not you," he said to Daly. "Just them." He opened the door and ushered Samantha, Marcel, and Dash inside and closed the door. It was dark inside, lit by candles at the far end of the room. A figure knelt by an altar of red and black velvet with a painting of a large heart and two crossed swords. The man stood and addressed them.

"Do you come in peace?" The three looked at each other. Dash spoke up. "We come in peace. We've come to see Brother Tree."

"I see," replied Raj Ramahatrian. He was really a stockbroker named Marvin Sanborn, who'd had a vision on some particularly fine hash one day, so he'd changed his name, moved to the country, and started up the Truth of Love Warriors. "Brother Tree is well on his way to a higher level of consciousness. You wouldn't want to do anything that would compromise his state of being, would you?"

Marcel stepped forward in order to better see him, the King of the Love Warriors. "We only want to bring him the love in our hearts," he said. Raj Ramahatrian had bloodshot eyes and a paunch and a salt-and-pepper beard covering a weak chin. "We want to see him follow the path that is right for him."

Raj Ramahatrian approached Marcel and looked him in the eye. "What is your path, Brother Rasta? What is it you desire most in this world?"

Marcel returned his aggressive gaze. The flickering candlelight gave the man's face a strange glow, as if he were a vision in a dream. He thought he could hear Dash and Samantha breathing behind him, waiting for his answer. "A new system of essentially humane values," he finally said, his eyes never leaving those of the Love King. The words were not his own, but those of Aimé Césaire 50 years earlier, the Martinican mayor and poet who had helped start the Negritude movement. This is a movement that began in the 1930s, designed to raise and cultivate "Black Consciousness" in an effort to disavow Colonialism.

Raj Ramahatrian looked at Marcel long and hard and then nodded. "Go. He's in the sun room."

Daly was waiting for them outside Raj's receiving room, his face anxious. "How did it go?"

"He's in the sun room," replied Dash. "Do you know where it is?"

"Yeah, come with me," and Daly led them to a room at the back of the house. There they found more Love Warriors in various states of repose on the floor and couch. Kevin was slouched in a corner, his eyes half-closed. He was wearing the same clothes he'd had on a week ago, jeans and an old sweater. His hair—and for that matter the rest of him—was unwashed, and he was barefoot. Most of the rest of the cult members were in similar states.

"I'd better stay back here," said Daly. "He didn't respond too well to me when I was here before."

Marcel thought for a moment. He knew Kevin didn't like him much because of Samantha. "I'll stay here with you," he said to Daly.

"Looks like it's you and me," Dash said to Samantha, and they approached the supine and odiferous form.

"Hey, Kevin," said Dash, kneeling on the floor. "Brother Tree," said Samantha quickly, shooting a glance at Dash. "Oh, yeah," Dash mouthed back at her.

Kevin opened his eyes a little wider. They were bloodshot with little crusts in the corners. "How you doing?" asked Samantha. "We came to see you. Dash and I." Kevin looked back and forth at the two of them. "Samantha? You're not here. Can't be." He hadn't brushed his teeth in a week.

"Well, yeah, Kevin—Brother Tree—I'm here. So is Dash." Kevin shook his head, the greasy lock of hair barely moving on his forehead. "No, Samantha's in Wichita. I saw her there."

Samantha looked up at Dash helplessly. What should they do? What should they say?

"Dash," she whispered. "See if you can find his shoes and a coat or something." Dash nodded and started looking around the room, picking through piles of trash and debris. She saw part of a Taco Bell wrapper; *well, at least they're eating something.*

Samantha was still crouched next to Kevin, talking softly to him, when Dash returned with a pair of grubby sneakers and a jacket.

"I don't know whose these are," she told Samantha, "but they're now being donated to Kevin." She and Samantha wrestled his feet into the sneakers, and got his arms into the jacket sleeves.

"Come on, Brother Tree, stand up," said Samantha. She and Dash each took an arm and pulled him up. Kevin was silent as they herded him out of the sunroom and into the kitchen. Marcel and Daly had been waiting in the doorway, watching the two women with him but unable to hear what was being said.

"Got your car keys ready?" Samantha asked Daly. "We're going." Suddenly she was apprehensive as the four of them walked back through the house to the front door. What if someone—that big guy, Brother Peace—tried to stop them? What if Kevin decided to create a fuss? Would they have to call the police? What if they couldn't even get out of the house? She shot an anxious glance at Marcel, who was right behind her. He placed a hand on the small of her back.

Brother Peace was back at his post inside the front door. Marcel whispered to Daly, "Keep going and get in the car; I'll come in a minute." And he left the little group to approach Brother Peace.

Samantha and Dash kept a steady grip on Kevin's elbows as they kept him moving toward the front door, opened by Daly, and outside. She glanced back at Marcel, who was talking with Brother Peace.

They got Kevin into the back seat of Daly's car, sitting him between Dash and Samantha. Daly started the engine. Marcel still hadn't emerged from the house.

"Come on, Marcel, let's get moving," murmured Daly in the driver's seat, staring at the door of the farmhouse.

Kevin, quiet until then, started getting agitated. "What's the matter, Kevin?" Dash asked him.

"My cell phone, I forgot my cell phone ..."

"Maybe it's in your pocket," suggested Samantha.

Kevin fumbled around in his pockets and produced the cell phone, and started pushing on the buttons. "It's dead, the phone is dead!" he cried, and burst into tears.

Marcel finally showed up and got into the passenger seat. "Let's get outta here!" Daly revved the engine and he spun the car around, shooting off down the driveway.

"Be careful, the road's muddy!"

"Marcel, what were you doing in there?"

"Kevin, it's all right, we can charge it up when we get home."

The car flew down the driveway and onto the main road, another pitted dirt road.

"I was talking to Brother Peace," Marcel said to no one in particular. "I asked him if they had any pamphlets about the Truth of Love Warriors. I was buying time."

"Daly, watch out!" yelled Dash, but it was too late. The car hit a muddy patch and slid, coming to rest at the side of the road. When Daly stepped gingerly on the accelerator, the wheels just spun, revolving helplessly in a slick, butter-like goo.

Groaning, they all got out to push. Kevin kept wandering off, insisting that he had to go recharge his cell phone, that he'd left the charging chord in Wichita. Samantha stayed with him, herding him repeatedly back toward the car, where Dash steered as Marcel and Daly pushed, slipping and sliding in the mud. Each time Dash revved the engine, the wheels spun again, splattering the two men with muck.

It took an hour and a half to get the car out of the mud after pushing, revving, digging, and arranging sticks and stones in front of the wheels. Exhausted and filthy, they piled back into the car and started the journey back.

Kevin continued to sob, moaning about his cell phone, the lack of love in the world, bombings in Syria, and a flickering light behind his eyes. He was so miserable that Dash pulled him down to rest his head in her lap and then exclaimed, "Ow! Hey! He *bit* me! Daly!"

Daly pulled into a gas station and they all got out of the car, leaving Kevin huddled in the back seat. It was one o'clock in the morning, they were covered with mud, and Dash was pulling her jeans down to look at her thigh. Samantha leaned over and inspected a faint red mark.

"Doesn't look like the skin is broken," she told Dash. "Good thing you were wearing heavy jeans."

"Well, what are we going to *do* with this guy? I don't want to get back in the car with him!" declared Dash. They all looked at each other, tired and frustrated.

Marcel took out his cell phone. "Let's call someone."

"Daly, can you keep the car doors locked? Watch him," said Samantha, and hurried over to Marcel. "Who are you calling?"

He was flipping through a fat telephone book. "I want to see if I can find Marjorie Trask. She's the counselor at school, she might know what to do." But there was no listing, and he didn't have her card with him.

"We could call the police," suggested Samantha.

"Well, let me try Marjorie Trask first; she's always been willing to help when I've talked to her." He found the number and dialed.

A sleepy voice answered. Marcel cleared his throat. "Good evening, this is Marcel Devereaux. Is this Marjorie Trask?"

"Marcel! Are you all right?"

"I'm fine, thank you. I'm calling about a friend. Do you know Kevin Bittner? He lives in Emerson Hall?"

"Kevin ... Yes, I know Kevin. What's the matter?"

"Well, we just picked him up from this place, this cult kind of thing, and he seems kind of, well, hysterical. He bit my roommate. We don't really know what to do with him."

There were a few moments of silence. Then, "Do you have a car? Where are you?"

"Yes, we're in Daly's car. I guess we're a few miles outside of town."

"Get him to the emergency room at the hospital downtown, and I'll call his parents to meet you there."

"All right, we'll do that. Thank you, Marjorie."

Marcel hung up, and they returned to the car. "We're supposed to take him to the hospital. Sam, can you sit in the back with Kevin and me? Dash, why don't you sit in the front seat?" They carefully got back into the car, and Kevin turned to look at Marcel, who slid in next to him. Kevin grimaced and said, "You just better watch your step." But he didn't seem as agitated. Daly suggested singing Christmas carols as they drove into town. Kevin remained in a stupor and just sniffled while they sang. Samantha wondered if Kevin would be put in a total institution.

At the hospital where Samantha had just been that afternoon, a nurse asked them questions while Kevin sat with an orderly in a room. Was he taking any drugs? Did he have any preexisting medical conditions? Had he ever had any psychotic episodes before? Daly, who knew him best, answered most of the questions, while Samantha found Kevin's mother in the hallway. Apparently, this wasn't the first time Kevin had ended up in the hospital with similar problems. He was supposed to be on medication and had stopped taking it.

Finally, Marcel, Samantha, Dash, and Daly dragged themselves out to the car and got in. Daly started the engine but then turned around to address Samantha in the backseat; she was leaning her head on Marcel's shoulder.

"What did you say to Kevin, anyway? I've been trying to get him to come with me for a week!" All three of them looked at Samantha expectantly. "I just asked him if he wanted to go out for a pizza. He was hungry."

***

Marcel sat at a carrel in the library with a stack of books. He was still tired from their big adventure the night before, but he had to get some work done on a paper for English comp. He'd been looking up civil rights, slavery, dance, and the old tap masters and had found a real treasure: an autobiography of Savion Glover. He also read about W. E. B. Du Bois, Léopold Senghor, Aimé Césaire, Hosea Williams, and Malcolm X.

Everything he read seemed to lead to something else. He knew there was some way to tie it together, to make sense of it all; he had only to keep looking and thinking. He reread passages in Savion Glover's book, impressed by his ability to make a connection between the historical and the personal, taking responsibility to carry on where these great men had left off. It wasn't just about dance, it wasn't just about history, race, and culture—what Marcel wanted to write about encompassed all of it.

The enormity of the task settled in on him as he read passage after passage about how the enslaved Africans were forbidden to practice their religion. Drumming—integral to the religious rituals—was expressly forbidden. It wasn't a great leap to suggest that they would have found ways to express themselves and the drums of their ancestors through clapping and dancing, tapping on the floorboards. Marcel was still haunted by an image of Savion's feet tapping out the heart and pain of the slaves, just arrived from their crossing on the Middle Passage. Once in the New World, there were digging songs and work songs on the farms and plantations, enabling the slaves to communicate while under the watchful eyes of the overseer and helping to lighten the work. And the drums of Africa kept finding their way out of exile, as tap and new dance and music evolved, merging and blending with European, American, and Caribbean stories. Dance was life; dance was history.

He read a passage from the University of the West Indies in Jamaica: "In the face of what many call cultural colonization by the U.S. and others, it is becoming increasingly important to record and preserve our folkloric traditions." Tapping his pen on his chin for a moment, he wrote a title at the top of a blank sheet of paper: "The Power of Rhythm: Dance in America as Individual and Cultural Expression."

He dug through his stack of books, wanting to go back to the beginnings of dance and drumming as cultural expression: African traditional religion. He wanted to trace its expression and transformation through dance in the New World and show how certain dance forms could act as a traditional record, changing as powerful individuals and events left their mark but still coming from the heart and soul of a people.

Marcel found a section on African traditional religions and its manifestations in West Indian culture. Traditional Africans had modified mainline Christian religions by forming sects that permitted tribal custom to merge into new world beliefs. A **sect** is a religious group that has separated from a large, established religious organization. The Kingdom of Love is not a sect because it did not break away from a conventional religious organization.

He read about how many people use the advice and guidance of mediums to overcome their problems, finding themselves in situations beyond their comprehension. Some believe that when a medium is in a trance, a certain spirit communicates through them and offers guidance to those seeking help. Others believe that the trance state is the work of the subconscious mind, which surfaces and takes over the conscious mind.

You just better watch your step, Kevin had told him in the car on the way to the hospital. He had seemed lucid and clear then, as if for a moment he knew exactly what he was talking about. In another place and time, they might have been taking him to a witch doctor, someone who specialized in maladies of the spirit. Some might even have thought that Kevin wasn't ill at all but merely passing on the wisdom of the spirits through a mind too young and naive to handle it well. But here in America you ended up in a hospital with tests and drugs. Marcel read on: "In times of sickness when medical help is apparently ineffective, some people may become desperate and turn anywhere to seek solace. At such times, mediums are often consulted."

The words on the page suddenly blurred, and Marcel felt as if he'd been struck by lightning. A memory so clear came to him as if it had happened last week, something he'd forgotten for years and years until just now.

"I told her *Grand-mère* had taken me to Obeah when I was 13," he murmured out loud. "Dat were no be de firs' time, no de firs' time a-tall."

Marcel himself had been taken to a spirit medium, the Obeahman, when he was about five years old by his grandmother who had feared for his life. It had to be done in secret; Marcel's parents were devout Christians and wanted no part of the old island folklore. But Dule, Marcel's older brother, had recently died of strep throat, and Marcel had fallen ill a few months later.

Marcel could barely remember his brother, but now he could see him lying in bed with a white rag laid on his neck. He remembered the funeral, where the women had wailed and cried for days, mourning the loss of a life so young and full of promise. Dule had been seven years old, and three trips to the medical clinic hadn't helped him. They'd had only aspirin to give him when he'd needed antibiotics.

Terrified that the same fate would befall Marcel, *Grand-mère* had spirited him away in the middle of the night to see the Obeahman. She was convinced that Dule had died of a hex, and no one had ever paid the Obeahman to have it removed. Now it had passed on to Dule's little brother, Marcel.

Isn't it all about control? thought Marcel. *One group of people trying to force their views and their way of life on another?* He had seen this in his own family. According to his *grand-mère*, Christianity had killed Dule because it had prevented him from getting the Obeahman's ministrations and counter-hex. And obviously the Christian God hadn't been strong enough to overcome the Obeahman or the hex. Christianity—a White man's religion.

And then, a few months after Dule's death, Marcel had taken ill with a sore throat. The family was in a panic, using every remedy and medicine they could find. He had to gargle with shark liver oil, he slept with warm rags dipped in Epsom salts wrapped around his neck, and they burned little pots of palm oil and herbs in the room day and night to clear his lungs. The priest from the church came to pray for him, and precious money had been spent on a crucifix to hang over his bed. A broken-down taxi was hastily resurrected and dispatched to Big Town to buy medicine.

But by this time, *Grand-mère* knew better and took Marcel to the Obeahman. Marcel's breath came in shallow gasps as he remembered that long-ago night, his throat on fire and his *grand-mère* holding him still as the Obeahman had anointed his eyes, nose, and mouth with a strange liquid. The old man, with his piercing brown eyes and a mole on his bulbous nose, had chanted and sung to him, spitting white rum over Marcel and his grand-mère and making him drink a hot tea that tasted like burned rubber. Drums had beat an insistent rhythm into him as he coughed and spluttered, drums rattling and pulsing in the firelight like the dancing of unseen beings.

Memories and voices swirled in his head like a kaleidoscope: Bones, the King of Death, the crooked path. De crooked path o' knowledge. *Grimorium Verum,* the *grimoire* of the Obeahman. *Maman Brigitte,* the Black One. *Only a taste for truthful eyes to become even wiser.* He had no idea what it all meant.

And the blood. The blood had frightened him, there was so much of it. It had splattered on his arms and face, and he'd cried and tried to rub it off. *Grand-mère* had started wailing and scared the five-year-old Marcel even more, thinking the Obeahman had somehow hurt her, and now she was bleeding on him. He'd been too upset to notice the soggy bundle of feathers in the Obeahman's hands, waved back and forth over him: a freshly killed chicken brought as a sacrifice by *Grand-mère*.

And Marcel had lived.

***

The book made a solid *thwack* as Marcel dropped it on the table in front of the others. Double Black was once again in session in its usual cafeteria venue, and Marcel had reappeared after a long hiatus.

Ben, Michelle, Raymond, and Cliff studied the book's title: Modernism and Negritude by Aimé Césaire. It was a book of poetry. "Aimé Césaire was a native of Martinique," said Marcel, pulling his backpack off and sitting down. "He was a mayor of Fort-de-France, and he was one of the founders of the Negritude movement; he and Léopold Senghor of Senegal and Léon Damas of French Guiana. Three men in different parts of the world using literature and philosophy to resurrect Black pride, which was completely denied by French education."

Cliff picked up the book and looked at Marcel appraisingly. "Negritude was a student movement, you know. Black students from Africa and the Caribbean in Paris took the writings of these men and used it to attack White superiority."

"Yes, students back then brought Black consciousness into the academic arena through the arts and literature, and we can do the same." Marcel unfolded a piece of notebook paper and laid it on the table. "I'm writing an article on dance as cultural expression for the school newspaper." He took a deep breath. "I'd like to include it as part of our reply to the university's response on racism."

He looked around the table at the four Black faces. The university had finally printed an announcement in the school newspaper addressing the racist vandalism, warning that whoever was involved in such an act would be prosecuted and summarily dismissed from the school. No further incidents had occurred.

Ben regarded Marcel with a grin. "So, did you wake up this morning and smell the coffee?"

"Yeah, what coffee did you smell?" joked Raymond.

"What?" asked Marcel, bewildered. "I don't drink coffee!"

***

Chapter 8 Study Questions

RELIGION

1. Give an example of US society that could be described as **profane**.
2. Is the Kingdom of Love a **cult** or a **sect**? Explain.
3. Are the practices of the Kingdom of Love and Obeah both **religions**? Why or why not?
4. Marcel's parents rejected belief in the traditional Obeah and turned to Christianity. Is this an example of **secularization**? Why or why not?
5. Would the practice of Obeah be considered a cult back in the time of Marcel's grandmother? How about now, during Marcel's time?

The Mahogany Bird

The Family

Tʜᴇ ɪꜱʟᴀɴᴅ ᴏꜰ Martinique rose majestically from the blue-green ocean as the aircraft traced a mammoth circle in the air above it. Samantha, in the window seat, drew in her breath at the sheer physical beauty of it, now a living, three-dimensional island instead of a speck on a map. Its mountains were thickly carpeted in a thousand shades of chlorophyll, and the Caribbean Sea created a meandering, shifting border along its coastline, white sand against turquoise, dark volcanic rock against aquamarine. From this height the differences in depth showed clearly as a patchwork of light azure, robin's-egg blue, and deep midnight blue. The Caribbean seemed to have invented the color blue.

"It's so beautiful," she whispered to Marcel, who was leaning over her to look out the window. "If I lived here, I'd never want to leave."

Marcel's heart quickened as he gazed upon the island of his birth. He'd flown out at night back in September, so this was the first time he'd really seen it from the air.

"Where do you live?" asked Samantha, her eyes shining.

"You can't see it from here," he answered. "Toussaint is on the northern tip of the island, over those mountains. Look there, see that rock jutting out of the ocean? That's *Le Rocher du Diamant*. Diamond Rock, the Gibraltar of the Caribbean. There was a garrison there in the early 1800s; it held out against a British invasion for 18 months."

"Wasn't Martinique a French colony?"

"Oh yeah, but there was a lot of wrestling for these Caribbean islands between the English, the Dutch, and the French in those days."

"And now Martinique is a … *département et région d'outre-mer*?"

Marcel laughed. "I can see you've been reading your guidebook! We're actually a region of France, not an overseas department, and we have the same benefits as French citizens. But don't worry about the language; I've warned my family that they have to speak English while you're here." A **family** is a group of two or more persons related by blood, marriage, or adoption. Broader definitions of family include individuals who live together who are emotionally and economically interdependent. Marcel's family members are related by marriage and by blood.

Samantha grinned at him. "I could handle a little Spanish, if someone wanted to know how much are the peppers at the market or where my mother's from. That's about it, I'm afraid. I've never been very good with languages."

"I've noticed that in America," commented Marcel. "I was surprised to meet many people who speak only English, no other languages. Why is that?"

"Oh, you know—we ethnocentric Americans are the pinnacle of civilization. We couldn't possibly have anything to learn from anyone else!"

***

The first thing Samantha noticed when she got off the plane was the air, how thick and warm and pungent it was, how different it felt to breathe in. In a minute there was so much else to think about that she forgot about the spongy air, but she remembered it again every morning upon waking.

"*Mon Dieu*," murmured Marcel, looking off in the distance. "It looks like half the village has come to meet us. I haven't seen some of these people since my sister's marriage two years ago." Marriage is a social arrangement that unites people economically, socially, and sexually and that involves certain rights and responsibilities. In the United States, marriage involves a legal contract between two people, including same-sex couples, and the state in which they apply for a marriage license.

Samantha followed his gaze and saw a large crowd of people just outside a chainlink fence next to the terminal building. She couldn't tell which people were there for her and Marcel; they all seemed to be shouting and waving at people getting off the plane.

I hope I'm ready for this, she thought as they walked across the hot tarmac to the Arrivals building. After half an hour of Customs, Immigration, filling out forms, and picking up their luggage, she and Marcel pushed their way out of the terminal to the fenced-off receiving area. People shrieked and hugged each other, pushing and jostling, and before she knew it, she and Marcel were enveloped in a sea of smiling Black faces, several topped by dreadlocks, all clamoring to embrace them and shake their hands.

Marcel tried to keep up with introductions as Samantha was embraced and kissed and her hand gripped and pumped again and again, but she promptly forgot who was who. A large woman in a shiny magenta dress and a fake fur hat threw her arms around Marcel and kissed him on the cheeks repeatedly, leaving tracks of lipstick. Marcel extracted himself with difficulty and turned to Samantha, grinning.

"Samantha, meet my *Maman*."

Thielda Devereaux exclaimed, "You are Saman-ta!" and enveloped her in a perfumed taffeta embrace.

Samantha took a deep breath (having been unable to breathe during the enthusiastic embrace) and managed to get out a greeting in French. "*Horreur de faire votre connaissance*." She'd been studying it in her guidebook and hoped she was saying "I am happy to make your acquaintance," but when the crowd burst out in good-natured laughter, she whispered to Marcel, "What did I just say?"

"'I am horrified to meet you!'" He laughed and put his arm around her shoulders when she looked crestfallen. "It is okay!" assured *Maman* Devereaux. "We are speaking English!"

Somehow the whole crowd made its way to two small white cars, and she wondered how they would ever all fit. Samantha wondered if they all were members of the same **household**. This is one or more individuals who occupy a housing unit, such as a house, apartment, or condominium. In a **nonfamily household**, there is either one occupant or the occupants are not related by marriage, blood, or adoption (e.g., college students in a dorm room or apartment). In a family household, the occupants are related to each other. Samantha wondered how many people would be living in Marcel's household.

A young girl took Samantha by the hand and smiled shyly at her, presenting her with a pretty red hibiscus flower. Was this Marcel's younger sister? Daphne?

"We're going to stop by my aunt Cécile's before we go home," explained Marcel as they both crammed into the passenger seat of one of the cars. *Maman* and Papa

Devereaux and a sister or two sat in the backseat, and one of the brothers (Loicq) drove the car. The atmosphere in the little car was stifling, even with the windows open, and Samantha realized that using deodorant wasn't too popular here. Marcel's family chattered to him in French, occasionally directing a comment her way in English.

"Saman-ta, we are cooking *ragout* for you. You will love it."

"Not too spicy, Mariette!" warned Marcel. He thought it best not to mention that this was squid stew.

"Look, Sam," Marcel told her, "You can see some of the city on the way. See that church there? It's been rebuilt seven times since 1895. There's the library ..."

Samantha was surprised at how chic and modern Fort-de-France looked. She had expected a sleepy little town, but this was a major urban center, an interesting combination of commerce and tropical beauty. A cruise ship was docked in the harbor. This one was part of the Norwegian cruise fleet.

"Marcel, look!" She pointed out the window. "Why is there no head on that statue?"

"Oh, that's Empress Josephine; she was born here. She was Napoleon's wife and she used to be the pride of Martinique. Then someone read in a guidebook that she had encouraged Napoleon to reintroduce slavery for the benefit of her family's plantation, so her statue was beheaded in 1991."

Maman Devereaux leaned forward with a rustle of taffeta. Her hat fit snugly against the roof of the car. "When she born" (it sounded like bahn), "de midwife look at she and declare someday she will be 'more dan a queen!'"

The car, after honking its way through crowded streets with French names, pulled up to a curb and discharged its occupants. "My aunt Cécile's shop," Marcel explained as they got out. It was a dress shop, small and dark, and tucked in among many other shops. It was too small for all of Marcel's family at once, but no one seemed to notice, and there was another round of shrieking and kissing and introductions. With a huge smile, Aunt Cécile presented the newcomer with a dress. There was an approving chorus as she held it up to Samantha's shoulders. Samantha smiled weakly and thanked her, thinking, *I'm expected to wear this thing*? It was shiny and colorful with puffy sleeves and a sash. Everyone else seemed to love it.

Teacups were passed around and Aunt Cécile insisted on pouring Samantha's tea. It was very good, smooth and creamy, and a plate of little pastries made their way around the crowd, making its first stop in front of Samantha, the guest. Finally, goodbyes and thanks were given, and Samantha thanked Aunt Cécile again for the dress, and they piled back into the cars. Now the two cars had things tied to their roofs; a tire, a chair, and a few boxes and baskets.

"What's all that?" Samantha asked Marcel as they got in.

"Oh, my family's just doing a few errands for our neighbors. People who don't get to Big Town very often. Hey, see that sign?" *Les Grands Ballets Martinique*, she saw on a poster.

"I read about that!" she told Marcel. "That's the dance troupe—they've performed in Europe and everything!"

"I used to think that's what I wanted to do when I was growing up," said Marcel, looking out the window. "I wanted to be a dancer in the Martinique Grand Ballet. They do all kinds of dance: traditional Martinican and Caribbean, the mazurka, and of course the *beguine*. Bet you didn't know that the *beguine* was not invented by Cole Porter!"

"But now you're going to dance on Broadway," Samantha smiled at him. "I'd love to see the Grand Ballet while we're here, though." She remembered from the guidebook that this internationally acclaimed group of musicians, dancers, and choreographers toured the island regularly when they weren't in Paris or London, presenting exuberant traditional dances of jealous brides, faithless husbands, demanding overseers, and toiling cane cutters. Island soul. *We ain't in Kansas anymore, Toto.*

A moist blast from a fish market filled the open car window, and Samantha could feel a prickly heat rash breaking out on the back of her neck. Her long hair was loose and now stifling against her neck; she wished she'd thought to tie it up.

***

Marcel watched the city through new eyes as they drove through. In some ways it was as familiar as an old shirt, although he hadn't been here very often, but after an absence of 7 months, he was now just starting to realize how much he'd changed.

Fort Saint-Louis loomed over the harbor, and he thought of the survivors of the Middle Passage huddled in its dungeons, their skin oiled up to make them appear healthier for the auction. There were so many Blacks (imported from Africa because they could stand the tropical climate better than the Europeans) that the few Whites lived in constant fear of rebellion, so they ran their little private kingdoms with an iron fist. Pain and torture, fear and death ... all because people were afraid of each other.

"Samantha, there's the fort; it's over 300 years old," he told her and was about to go on, but she fidgeted, pulling her hair up and twisting around.

"Can you see my neck?" she asked him. "Is there a rash there?"

"It's just the heat," he said. "We can put some aloe on it when we get home."

"Oh, look!" Samantha leaned over him to look out the window. "There are people swimming in the ocean. I can't wait to get to the beach!"

"The water's pretty polluted here," said Marcel. "There are better places." He watched the "swimmers," mostly Frenchmen standing chest-deep in the water smoking cigarettes.

"Can we go swimming in Toussaint?"

"Well, Toussaint is inland a bit. Macouba is on the coast, but the water is pretty rough there. It's on the Atlantic side, right on the tip of the island. We'll have to go to *Sainte-Marie or Anse l'Etang*."

Samantha watched the scenery passing by as they left the city and drove north. Banana plantations, coconut trees, and pineapple and sugar cane fields were interspersed with little shops and houses along the road. Marcel and his family of origin continued their rapid-fire conversations in French; Marcel couldn't afford to call very often, so they had a lot to talk about, and they all wanted to know about Mademoiselle, his American girlfriend. The **family of origin** (also referred to as the **family of orientation**) is the family in which an individual is born or reared. Marcel is in the car with both his parents and a couple of siblings; they are members of his family of origin.

They'd been driving for a long time when they approached the town of *Ajou-pa-Bouillon*. Samantha had never seen so many beautiful flowers in her life. They were everywhere, growing wild and abundant along the roads and occasionally spilling over, littering the tarmac with confetti-like petals.

"Look at this, it's incredible!" She exclaimed to Marcel. "*Ajoupa-Bouillon*, they call this *ville florale*, town of flowers. See that little road over there? There's a trail that leads up through the rainforest to a swimming hole. My brothers and I used to go play in the waterfall there."

"A waterfall! I'd love to see it. Do you know what all these flowers are?"

Marcel spoke to his parents in French for a moment. "I think the English names are anthurium, wild begonia, and croutons—no, crotons—and those over there are shrimp plants." He spoke to his brother in French, the one driving, who obligingly pulled the car off the road so Samantha could get out and look at the flowers. Everyone piled out of the two cars and insisted on having their pictures taken with the American *mademoiselle*.

They continued their journey, with the little cars chuffing and puffing along the winding mountain road to Macouba, passing through stands of giant bamboo, mountain palms, and chestnut and mahogany trees. As they made their way deeper into the rainforest, the roadsides became thick with ferns, climbing vines, and orchids. Brightly colored birds chattered and flitted everywhere.

"What was that?" asked Samantha, as they drove by a boy by the side of the road holding something brown and furry. "An agouti. They catch them in the forest and sell them. We can go back and buy it if you want; my sisters make a great agouti stew," Marcel said with a smile. "Stew? It looks like a big guinea pig or a rat or something! I think I'll pass. But I still want to eat a papaya."

She hadn't expected the town of Macouba to be so lovely, majestically perched atop a cliff overlooking the Atlantic Ocean. After a stop to meet more people, friends, and relatives who ran businesses in town and to pick up mail for half the residents of Toussaint, they finally set off down the rutted, dusty track inland for Marcel's home. It was nearly dark when they finally arrived, and Samantha just wanted a bath and a bed, but there was another slew of introductions as she met the rest of the Devereaux family household, more smiling faces, cheek-kissing, and hand-clasping and promptly forgotten names.

At first Samantha thought Marcel's family of origin must be a blended family because it was so large, but she later realized that this was not the case, it was just a large extended family. A **blended family** (also known as a **stepfamily**) is a family created when two individuals marry and at least one of them brings children from a previous marriage or relationship into the new marriage. Blended families are common in societies with high divorce and remarriage rates. The **extended family** consists of one or both parents, children (if any), and other relatives, such as grandparents, aunts, uncles, and cousins. Samantha discovers that extended family households are common on Martinique.

The cacophony of French and patois (dialect) made her feel more and more surreal, as if she were the star of some foreign film with an unknown cast and plot. This was certainly different from her own **nuclear family** (a family household made up of husband, wife, and children). In her exhaustion, she found herself clinging to Marcel. She'd have to get used to a larger, more diverse family if either of her parents decided to remarry after they divorced.

Daria, the oldest sister, had stayed behind cooking dinner while the welcoming party had made the pilgrimage to the airport. She was heavily pregnant ("belly-woman," she had heard in a snippet of conversation) and didn't travel well. The fishy aroma of the ragout did battle with the musky smell of goats and the warm, insidious stench of rotting garbage in a shallow pit not far from the outdoor kitchen. Samantha's appetite, after the air travel and three hours of bumpy, dusty roads, went into hibernation.

Marcel's *grand-mère* had also stayed behind, claiming her bones were too old for the bouncing of the car, and in fact had resisted a trip to the hospital for months now to investigate a gall bladder problem. But now she stood ready to greet her returning grandson and his lady friend, wearing her best dress and a little straw hat adorned with fake roses. Mice had chewed at one edge of the hat and the rumpled roses had been pulled over a bit as camouflage. It was her favorite, and only, hat, and she refused to part with it. On her dress was pinned a large glittery brooch given to her by Marcel for Christmas.

Marcel presented Samantha to her, and she carefully kissed *Grand-mère* on both papery cheeks. She was small and slight, and Samantha was afraid to embrace her, afraid her stick bones would snap like kindling if she squeezed too hard. *Grand-mère* looked her over solemnly with rheumy eyes with their spotted pouches underneath as if to hold a lifetime of tears. She cleared her throat and announced in a reedy voice,

"Dis ol' leddy heppy to see you." And Samantha started as *Grand-mère* tossed something at her feet, something which scattered with a tiny hiss. "*Grand-mère*," said Marcel quickly and spoke to her in French. He didn't sound very happy. He turned to Samantha. "Don't worry, it's only salt. It's for good luck." *Grand-mère*, thought Marcel with exasperation. *Well, at least she doesn't have her bag of bones with her.*

At dinner, Samantha tried to eat the pungent *ragout* by the light of the kerosene lantern with its halo of moths, but finally begged to be excused. She was so tired she thought she would drop if she stayed up one more minute. She bathed in the indoor bathroom, surprised to find no bathtub or shower stall, only a showerhead emerging from an iron pipe in the wall. The shower water meandered over the bathroom floor before slowly making its way down a drain in one corner amidst much choking and gurgling. Samantha couldn't keep her eyes off a large dead spider floating in the water on the floor, and she splashed at it to make it go down the drain. It never did; it just continued floating around in a silent, Brownian death dance, and the thought of it drifting over and touching her feet gave her the incentive to hurry and finish.

Marcel showed her to her room, a small addition on one end of the house with its own door. A couple of his brothers had been relocated to nearby neighbors in anticipation of Samantha's arrival, and it had been scrubbed from top to bottom. Inside the small room was a bed with a newly purchased mosquito net draped over it, a table, a chair, and her suitcase.

"I'll leave the lantern right outside the door," Marcel told her. "You can use it if you want to get up during the night."

"Where will you be?"

"I'm sharing my old room with Loicq. But maybe I'll sneak in sometime when everyone's asleep," he whispered in her ear. "So don't lock the door!" Samantha smiled and kissed him. "Good night. I'll miss you."

Marcel took the lantern outside and gently closed the door. It was still early, and he was eager to rejoin his family and friends. The steady stream of visitors had hardly slowed. As he set the lantern on the ground near the doorframe, he softly cursed in French. He would have to talk to *Grand-mère* again; the doorway had been splashed with chicken blood.

***

Samantha awoke before dawn. She knew instantly she was in a different place because of the springy, salt-and-sweet air, and it took a second to realize she was in

Martinique with Marcel's family. In the pearl-gray darkness of dawn, a smile spread over her face, and she lay under her mosquito net, listening to the roosters crowing. They'd started up hours earlier, about the time something else had left off, some murky forest creature that had choked and rasped and howled like some prehistoric missing link, clambering out of the earth and demanding recognition at two in the morning. Samantha remembered lying awake for part of the night listening; the roaring, gurgling night monsters growing ever larger and more violent in her mind until they were rhinoceros-sized behemoths hovering just outside her bedroom windows, red-rimmed eyes aglow and fangs dripping with venom. She would find out later that this nightly monster chorus came from innocuous little tree frogs no bigger than a thimble, the kind that adorn cute, offbeat greeting cards.

Getting up and standing in the open doorway of her room, she was met by an exquisite fragrance, like an invisible, diaphanous shawl draped over her by unseen fairies. *Jumbies*, Marcel would call them. The aroma was ethereal and delicate, soft as the snowy tufts in a fawn's ears, emanating from clusters of tiny flowers the color of sweet cream on a vine over the doorway. She picked a little bunch and held it under her nose: jasmine. *These are real jasmine flowers.*

Samantha surveyed the village of Toussaint, what she could see of it in the ghost-like morning light filtering through the banana trees. Small houses, cinder-block with corrugated iron roofs like the Devereaux house, were interspersed randomly with stands of banana trees, mahogany, and mango, and chickens scratched and clucked in the reddish volcanic soil. There were no real lawns to speak of, only carefully raked dirt between the trees, thickets, and little gardens near the houses, but this was filled in with wild vegetation farther away from the houses. Two wooden sheds with thatched roofs stood near the Devereaux house; she remembered from last night that one was an outdoor kitchen and the other for storage. Off to the left was the outhouse. The front door of the house would be locked this early in the morning, and since her room had its own outside door, she'd have to knock on the main door and wake someone up to let her in to use the indoor bathroom. She was sure she could manage the outhouse instead.

She took the dying lantern to the outhouse with her, wanting to make sure there were no snakes, spiders, bats, or anything else inside it. It was a little dusty and cobwebby, but she didn't see any major creatures. There was a roll of pink toilet paper hanging from a piece of string, bought specifically in honor of her arrival.

A few minutes later, Samantha came bursting out of the outhouse with a shout, her heart pounding and arms thrashing. Something large and noisy flew out of the outhouse with her, its wings whirring and clicking like some animated mechanical creature.

A boy of about 15 near the door of the house stopped and stared at her in surprise. Samantha felt compelled to explain her crisis to him, since he was the only one around. "That thing! A bat or something! It flew out of the toilet while I was … I was …"

The young man picked up a stick and hurried over to where the flying thing had landed in the dirt and whacked it with an expert flick of the wrist. He watched it twitching in the dust and then grinned at Samantha. "A mahogany bird," he said, in the island's musical lilt. Gingerly, Samantha approached him and looked down at the scene of carnage. *A bird? What was a bird doing down a toilet hole?*

The "mahogany bird" was the biggest cockroach she had ever seen, about 6 inches long, its long curved antennae drooping to the ground, its large, brittle, translucent wings now cracked and crumpled like frozen tissue paper.

"You got to kill dem quick, wit' one blow," explained the boy. "Odderwise you jus' mek him mad." He tapped the stick against the ground for emphasis, and then demonstrated his fast, lethal, mahogany-bird-killing strike again, pulverizing the front half of the thing. Samantha stared at the huge insect, mesmerized, and all she could think of to say was, "Cockroaches can live for nine days without their heads. Then they starve to death."

"I thought I heard you out here," said a familiar voice. "Marcel! *Bonsoir*!" Samantha kissed him on the cheek. He chuckled. "That's 'good night.' You can just say good morning. Was that you screaming and yelling a few minutes ago?"

"There was a mahogany bird. It was in the toilet. He killed it," she gestured to the boy with the stick. Marcel spoke to him in French for a minute, and Samantha thought she recognized *merci*, thank you. The boy handed Marcel two baguettes from a basket on his back.

"Good-bye, American leddy," he said as he started off to continue his deliveries. Samantha hadn't even noticed all the bread he was carrying until he'd given the loaves to Marcel, who stuck them inside the outdoor kitchen. As soon as they walked away from the mangled cockroach, several scrawny hens rushed over to tear it to pieces.

"Come," he said to Samantha, taking her by the hand. "I want to show you something." He led her around the side of the house to a little tree about 8 feet tall. It looked a bit like something out of a Dr. Seuss book, with a slender, tapering trunk and a little canopy of bizarrely shaped leaves at the very top. Several fat, irregular green fruits shaped like giant avocadoes hung precariously from the trunk just under the canopy, dangling like large green breasts on an otherwise skinny girl. In fact, the fruits looked heavy enough to pull the slender tree over in a strong wind.

Samantha stared at them for a moment and then exclaimed, "Papayas! This is a papaya tree!"

"Yes, this is a female. The male trees only have blossoms, no fruit," said Marcel.

"Can I pick one?"

"Wait, there's something I have to get first," said Marcel, and he hurried back into the house. Other family members were up by now, and his mother and little sister and brother came back out with him. Marcel's mother's role in the family was so prominent that Samantha had thought at first that Martinique was a matriarchy, but she soon learned that it was like the United States (and most of the world), a patriarchy. **Matriarchy** is a social system in which women dominate in positions of power and authority. A **matriarchal family** is one in which power and authority are held by the eldest female (the mother or grandmother). While Samantha observed that Marcel's mother was the most verbal, it was his father who seemed to make the decisions and had the power/authority in the family. **Patriarchy** is a social system in which men dominate in positions of power and authority. A patriarchal family is one in which power and authority are held by the eldest male (the father or grandfather). Samantha observes that Marcel's family is a patriarchal family.

Marcel had a camera in his hands, and *Maman* insisted on taking it from him and photographing the two of them together as Samantha picked her first papaya. The fruits were just a little higher than she could reach, so Marcel picked her up around the legs, raising her up. Other family members leaned out of windows and cheered her on, clapping and laughing, while *Maman* took several snaps, most including Lyon and Daphne, who, after a moment's shyness, rushed over to get in the pictures, grinning like little monkeys.

The table in the small living room was laid out with a brightly flowered plastic tablecloth, and Samantha and Marcel sat down for breakfast, brought in from the kitchen by Mariette and Daphne: baguettes, cheese, porridge, fruit, tea, and coffee. The table was too small for the whole family, so Samantha and Marcel ate with Maman and Papa Devereaux and *Grand-mère*, while everyone else sat outside as usual.

Samantha was photographed eating the papaya, now gutted and sliced on a plate in front of her. She hoped she looked enthusiastic, although she found she didn't really like the papaya. It had a slippery, mushy texture and an odd flavor, with a subtle, soapy aftertaste. She surreptitiously slid the plate over to Marcel, who was happy to dig in.

"Saman-ta," said *Maman* with a smile, "how do you find Martinique?"

"It's beautiful, *Madame* Devereaux. I love all the flowers, and everyone has been so nice to me, so friendly."

"Sam has already met some of the island wildlife," said Marcel. "The bread boy killed a mahogany bird from the outhouse this morning."

Papa Devereaux grunted. "I don' know who de mos' danger-ous wildlife, de mahogany bird or dat bread boy." At that moment another member of the island wildlife plopped into Papa's porridge, a bright green lizard that had been making its way across the wall above him and lost its footing. Marcel laughed while Samantha gawked, open-mouthed. *Maman* called for Daphne, and Papa Devereaux stared morosely at his breakfast, the lizard struggling like a buffalo in a tar pit.

Grand-mère, scowling, leaned forward to get a look and muttered something in French. Her head was bare this morning, and little peppercorns of gray hair dotted her head like an ancient doll that has been played with too roughly.

"*Grand-mère*," murmured Marcel, "it is *not* bad luck. It's just a lizard."

Daphne came to take Papa's bowl away and replace it with a new one, her eyes dancing merrily at Samantha and Marcel. Papa grumbled at her in French, which didn't seem to faze her a bit.

Samantha looked questioningly at Marcel. Surely it wasn't Daphne's fault that a lizard had fallen into his breakfast?

Marcel smiled. "Those green ones don't stay on the walls very well, not like the geckos."

"Dose kids, dey supposed to keep de lizards out!" said Papa Devereaux. "De geckos, dey okay, dey stick good and dey eat plenty o' flies. But dem green ones, dey clumsy, dey have to go outside!" He grinned at his son. "Since Marcel gone, nobody know how to do dey work anymore!"

"I don't know how you can get along wit'out me, Papa," he answered. Marcel remembered competitions with his siblings to see who could catch the most lizards in the house. They made a circle of stones outside and tossed the captured lizards into it one by one, betting on which chickens would get them first. If a lizard was quick enough and brave enough to make it outside the stone circle, the kids would chase the chickens away from it and let it scamper to freedom, disappearing into the undergrowth.

Maman Devereaux turned to Samantha and patted her hand, her eyes teary. "We t'ank you for you to he'p Marcel come home. We t'ink we nevah see him for four years." Samantha protested that she was happy to do it, and she thanked *Maman* for having her.

"Weren't no lizard," announced Grand-mère in her raspy, reedy voice. "Dat were Obeah, comin' to check American *mademoiselle*."

***

During the day Marcel was dragged off for a few hours by his brothers to go visit friends, and Samantha spent a cozy afternoon with his three sisters in the outdoor kitchen, learning how to cook. They were making bébélé, sheep tripe and green bananas, and Samantha wondered how she would be able to gracefully get out of eating it at dinner. The sheep stomach had gathered flies for quite a while in a blue plastic basin outside the kitchen, and its tenure in the stew pot didn't seem to be improving its smell. Samantha tried to stay away from it by asking to learn how to grate coconuts.

Daphne was removed from her seat on a funny little wooden stool-like contraption, where she'd been scraping the insides of coconut halves against a serrated metal prong protruding from the front. Smiling, she gave Samantha the coconut she'd been working on and showed her how to place it over the metal prong, pushing and turning the shell as little curls of white coconut meat dropped into a basin underneath. Straddling the little wooden bench, Samantha gripped the coconut shell with both hands, and gave it a try. Nothing happened, and Daphne, Daria, and Mariette laughed as they watched. Daphne placed her small brown hands over Samantha's and pushed down, turning at the same time. Samantha was amazed at the amount of force it took, watching the shavings drop into the bowl. Who would have thought Daphne's skinny little arms could do this for hours? Maman Devereaux brought the camera out and Samantha's dubious help in the kitchen was recorded for posterity.

Daphne, giggling, finally took over again when Samantha's sweating, grunting efforts produced only a paltry little pile of shavings, and she was sent to the table to help Mariette with the christophine au gratin. She peeled and sliced the large, knobby-looking fruits while Mariette rolled them in egg and breadcrumbs and then grilled them in a pan, sprinkling grated cheese on top as they finished cooking. She gave Samantha one to eat, and the crispy fillets with their topping of melted cheese tasted a bit like fried potatoes.

After some initial awkwardness, Samantha and the sisters began chatting like old friends. She learned that Daria was married to Luc (whom she realized she'd been confusing with Loicq, Daria and Marcel's brother), and her family of procreation lived in a little house close by. It had no kitchen and no plumbing, so Daria usually used Maman's kitchen and they ate here with the family. She took buckets of water over to her own house for cleaning and bathing. The **family of procreation** describes the family in which two people (usually married) have or adopt children. Daria and Luc have their own family of procreation, and they live in close proximity to Daria's family of origin. Samantha has no family of procreation yet, since she is unmarried and has no children.

Daria's little son and Mariette's daughter played in the dirt outside the kitchen as they worked, and Daria was expecting her second baby in about 6 weeks. Mariette and her child lived with the family; she'd been in a cohabitation relationship with the child's father, but he had left, so she had returned to her family household. **Cohabitation** is the sharing of a common residence of two adults who are not married to each other and who have an emotional and sexual relationship. Mariette and her child's father had lived together for several years when he moved out and away.

Well, thought Samantha, *with Daria living right next door and children returning to the fold and plenty of grandchildren around, Marcel's mother will certainly never experience the **empty nest** syndrome.* This is the stage of the family life cycle in which children have grown up and left their parents' home. The empty nest syndrome refers to the difficulty some parents experience in adjusting to their children having left home.

Samantha wanted to ask about the other children, those "outside" the marriage, and why *Maman* didn't **divorce** (the legal ending of a valid marriage contract)

Papa Devereaux over this, but it just didn't seem appropriate. She'd thought maybe it was because the man wears the pants in a traditional household in a patriarchal society and a wife wouldn't consider going against her husband's wishes. Samantha wonders if Marcel, having grown up in a patriarchal family, valued egalitarianism. Samantha valued egalitarian relationships and would not stay in a relationship with someone who did not have a similar value. **Egalitarianism** is the belief in and practice of sharing power and authority equally among members of a social group or organization. Egalitarian relationships are relationships in which power and authority are shared equally. Samantha would not consider being in a long-term relationship with anyone, Marcel included, unless their relationship was egalitarian.

Growing bolder and more comfortable with the American *mademoiselle*, the sisters wanted to know all about America. Was it true that everyone carried a gun? And there's a machine for washing dishes? Did women have operations on their breasts to make them large and firm? Didn't that interfere with nursing their babies? Were there very many Black people in America? Did they all have cars? Was going to college very difficult?

"All dat reading," said Mariette, shaking her head. "Too much for my own eyes." She pointed to Daphne with a floury hand. "Dis young miss love de reading, she does. Someday maybe she go to college, like Marcel. Like you."

Daphne smiled and blushed and grated her coconut furiously. "Really?" asked Samantha. "Do you like books? I can send you some from America. Oh! Look at that!"

A little bird had landed in the dirt near Daphne and was bravely darting in to pick up a few little shreds of coconut, which had scattered outside the bowl. It was beautiful, soft brown with a brilliant yellow throat and breast.

"What is it?" Samantha asked, watching the pretty bird. The others laughed good-naturedly; who got excited about a bird? They were everywhere. "Banan-aquit," said Daria, and she said something in French to Daphne. The young girl left her seat and the little bird flew away, but not far. She returned with a little dish of liquid and placed it on a stump, where the babies couldn't get into it. Samantha watched, enthralled, as the little bananaquit and then several of its friends cautiously approached the dish and then started drinking. "Sugar-water," explained Mariette.

The birds scattered upon the return of Marcel and his brothers, bringing with them several friends who were dying to meet the American woman.

***

Dinner was served outside that night so everyone could eat together, including three or four of Marcel's friends, one of whom wanted to take Samantha dancing that night and another who tried to get her to come to the beach with him tomorrow. Marcel chased them off with a laugh and didn't mention to Samantha that he'd been asked more than a few times how they could get an American girlfriend. A rich American girlfriend.

Marcel's family never seemed to tire of hearing about America. "Your favorite t'ing," said Lyon, the youngest brother. "Tell your favorite t'ing about America."

"Salad bars and marshmallows," he replied without hesitation. Samantha laughed.

"I think Marcel would die happy if he could find a salad bar *with* marshmallows," she said, and she glanced up when *Grand-mère* sucked in her breath through her teeth. The old lady muttered something in French, and Marcel quieted her. Samantha looked at him and started to ask what the matter was, but he shrugged his shoulders. He didn't need to tell her about *Grand-mère's* fixation on death, that to mention it casually was to bring it about.

Sebastian, two years older than Marcel with an even shaggier head of dreadlocks, kidded his younger brother about being in college, wondering how anyone with rocks for brains could make it. This led to an outburst of "Big Bwoy" jokes, apparently a favorite of schoolboys on Martinique, and each brother tried to outdo the other. Sebastian jumped up and stood in front of Marcel, his hands on his hips, and said, "Big Bwoy inna composition class, an' di teacha ask he fi mek a sentence wid 'defence, defeat, and detail.' Guess wha Big Bwoy say? 'De dawg jump over de fence and de feet go before de tail!'" There was a roar of laughter; it was clear who he thought Big Bwoy was.

Marcel, grinning, countered with: "One morning Big Bwoy did late fi school so he ride 'im father donkey, 'Gee Gee,' go a school. Him did in such a hurry dat him nevah tie de donkey propaly. Well, guess wha' happen'? In di midst a spelling class, Gee Gee get loose. Big Bwoy frighten so till wen him look out a di window an' see di donkey a gallop wey. Meanwhile, di teacha ask de class, 'Children, how do you spell egg?' Big Bwoy nah listen di teacha, him only waan di donkey fi stop, so him shout out 'EE GEE GEE!'"

The hooting and hollering this generated apparently meant Marcel had told the better joke, but Samantha wondered what was so funny. She could hardly understand the *patois*, and Marcel fell into speaking it more and more. While the Big Bwoy jokes continued, she went into her room and pulled out a secret stash of marshmallows and other goodies and brought them outside to the group of people around the fire.

"Aha!" said Marcel. "I see you have brought me a bag of marshmallows. But I don't know what the rest of you will eat, you don' be getting' dese a-tall!"

"Come on, Marcel," Samantha smiled. "Find some sticks and we'll roast them."

This caused a stir—no one had ever heard of doing such a thing. There was a scramble through the firewood for little sticks, which were soon held poised over the crackling fire, each with its own marshmallow. There was much discussion about how close and how far to the flames to hold them, and dismay when a couple of marshmallows caught fire. Sebastian suddenly became an expert, offering advice and taking the roasting sticks from those less proficient to show them how to do it, and then trying to eat their marshmallows.

"Be careful when you eat them, they're hot!" warned Samantha. She opened the box of graham crackers and a chocolate bar she'd brought and put half of a bar on a graham cracker. Placing a nicely roasted and mushy marshmallow on top of it, she put another cracker over it and pulled the stick out. It made a nice little sandwich, with chocolate-tinged marshmallow goop oozing out the sides. She handed it to Marcel.

"Ta-daaa! Now you have a s'more."

"A *what*? What dis t'ing called? Make me one!" the friends and brothers called out. Samantha looked at Marcel, who was polishing it off with gusto. "Do you like it? Do you want another one?" He nodded, and she said triumphantly, "There! When you eat one of these, all you can say is, 'I want s'more!'"

There was a flurry of crackers and chocolate being passed around, and Daphne insisted on having Samantha make her one. *Grand-mère* ate two. Marcel looked sadly at the empty marshmallow bag; it hadn't lasted long. It was a good thing he had another bag in his luggage, but when he went to get it someone else had beaten him to it. *Not again*! He thought peevishly. His luggage had been gone through several times since he'd arrived. It was a good thing he'd made it clear to everyone that Samantha's bag was off limits.

Loicq wanted to get the drums out and have Marcel dance, but Marcel wanted to take Samantha out instead. For some reason he found himself reluctant to dance for his family, as if it might not be like old times. Of course he'd do it, just not now. Another night.

"Come, Sam, put on your dress and we'll go listen to zouk," he told her. Pictures were taken of her in Aunt Cécile's dress, an outrageous creation of pink and black with its poufy sleeves and ruffled hem, but everyone assured Samantha she looked divine. *Grand-mère* wanted a picture of just her and *Mademoiselle*, and she went inside to get her hat. Later, when Samantha went through these pictures, she would discover that *Grand-mère* still had a bit of chocolate on her chin from the s'mores.

Marcel, Samantha, several brothers and friends, and Mariette walked through the village to a little shack called the New Hangover Hotel. Samantha had wanted to go to the Don't Mind Your Wife bar, but that had closed a few years earlier. The New Hangover had a small dance floor and a few tables, and someone had made a disco ball out of tin foil. It was crowded, and Samantha was the only white face there, but the smiling faces and the lively music made her feel welcome and comfortable. She was herded out to the dance floor with a dozen other people, and the flimsy wooden walls of the New Hangover vibrated with dancing and music until late. Rum flowed freely, people drank it in pineapple juice, Coke, even orange pop and another soft drink that tasted like bubble gum. Samantha had a rum and Coke, but her stomach was already a little unsteady from dinner (she'd hadn't managed to avoid the dreaded bébélé), so she stuck to just Coke after that.

Mariette, resplendent in an orange dress and orange pumps wearing the earrings she'd gotten from Marcel for Christmas, taught Samantha the *beguine*. She was a large woman with full hips, and she moved with the grace of a queen. She told Samantha that the zouk music they were dancing to came from the *beguine*, Afro-French dance music, but then had other Caribbean folk music added in and finally modern electronic music, and the result was *zouk*. It had a compelling, complex beat, and Marcel and Mariette seemed to be able to move several parts of their bodies at once in rhythm to the music, but Samantha suspected she herself just looked like another skinny White girl bouncing around. It was strange; in America Mariette would be considered too heavy and the overstrained orange dress ghastly, but here she was beautiful as she danced, and she knew it. Samantha didn't feel so out of place with her shiny pink and black ruffles.

Tired and sweaty after two hours of dancing, Samantha caught Marcel's eye, and they made their way off the dance floor. They ended up in a room at the back of the hotel where men were crowded around a wooden pen, smoking, drinking rum, and shouting. Marcel started to take Samantha out, but several of the men waved them over. "Let her come! *Bonsoir, Mademoiselle!*"

Samantha found her hand being shaken again and again, and she wound up right next to the wooden pen, which was about waist high and covered over with wire mesh. The activity inside seemed to be generating a lot of commotion among the men, almost as much as her presence did. She looked down into the pen.

A small, brown, weasel-like animal was locked in mortal combat with a green snake, and they rolled around and around in the dirt. Angry squeaks came from the little animal, and the snake's long tail whipped back and forth, stirring up puffs of dust. Blood speckled the ground, but it was impossible to tell which one it came from.

Eyes wide, Samantha glanced at Marcel. "Mongoose fights," he told her. "Looks like it's just a bush snake tonight. It's a little more interesting when they use a *fer-de-lance*, they're very poisonous. The mongoose has to move really fast to avoid getting bitten. Once one of the snakes got out onto the dance floor."

Samantha watched in fascinated horror as the mongoose sank its sharp teeth into the snake's neck, just behind the head. The reptile's green body whipped around but couldn't dislodge the tenacious little creature, who was breathing hard and jerking its head back and forth, trying to break the snake's neck. Apparently, something happened because the snake's body slowed its thrashing and finally stopped moving, the whitish-pink inside of its mouth showing in silent protest, its hooded reptilian eyes unchanged in death.

It was the first time Samantha had ever seen anything die. The crowd of men around the snake pit erupted in a cacophony of French and patois as money exchanged hands and arguments broke out.

"Let's get out of here," Samantha whispered to Marcel, and they left the noisy room.

*** *** ***

Everyone else was asleep when they got home in the early hours, so Marcel slipped into Samantha's room with her, and the damp pink-and-black dress was promptly forgotten on the floor. They made love quietly, fervently, hoping no one would hear, and afterward lay in the glow of romantic love, clothed only in the velvet darkness, with Samantha's hair on Marcel's shoulder the way he liked it.

Samantha wonders how her feelings for Marcel will change over time. Will they stay together? Will their love develop into conjugal love? **Romantic love** is characterized by intense emotions, thoughts, and sexual passion. The love between Marcel and Samantha may be described as romantic love. Conjugal love is characterized by companionship, comfort, calmness, and security. **Conjugal love** is more common among older married couples, whereas romantic love is more common among unmarried and newly married couples.

Although it was the middle of the night, roosters from their various posts around the village began to crow. "Marcel, why do they *do* that? They're supposed to crow at dawn!" Samantha sighed. "Don't they know what time it is?"

"They don't have a clock," he answered. "Hear that one? He's yelling to his friend, Hey, what time is it? Is it time to crow? And his friend yells back, No, we still have an hour. And the other guy yells, you're not just having me on, are you? So you can hustle off with that little brown hen? And another one yells over, shut up about the brown hen! She's mine! And so is the white speckled one! Is it time to crow now? How about now?"

Samantha laughed, and buried her face against his shoulder to muffle the sound. She breathed in his sharp, musky body odor, something that always baffled Marcel—how could she stand it? He'd been dancing at the disco for hours and really needed a shower. But she seemed to like it. He pushed her away; he felt unclean and wanted to get washed up and into bed before he fell asleep and was discovered here in the morning.

Samantha lay awake listening to the roosters crowing, remembering the death throes of the doomed snake.

***

The next day Marcel and his brothers took Samantha on a long hike. They were going to a beach near Macouba for something they called "wind fights." It was shortly after Easter, and every year the boys all made kites and took them to the beaches where there were breezes coming in off the ocean. Samantha wanted to wear her swimsuit, but Marcel said it wasn't a good place for swimming; the water was rough.

Lots of neighborhood kids giggled and shouted when they saw Samantha walking through the village with the Devereaux boys and followed them, chattering in French and sometimes coming up to take her by the hand. By the time they got going on the path down to the ocean, they had an entourage of about a dozen kids, plus a couple of scrawny pups tagging along and a reluctant goat on a string. Before the trail started down to the sea, they followed a high ridge, and when they came out of the trees, a magnificent sight greeted them. Mont Pelée rose in smoky green-gray splendor against the horizon, the clouds touching its summit looking ominously like smoke.

They stopped for pictures. Marcel, Samantha, Loicq, and Lyon posed with Pelée as the backdrop while Sebastian shot the pictures, and the whole crowd of kids joined in, the goat bleating in protest as he was dragged to a place of pride in front of Samantha. She laughed. "Maybe he's camera-shy," she said, looking down at the goat who was now leaning against her legs. The string was wound around its stubby horns, and flies buzzed around its ears.

"Didn't Pelée destroy half the island when it erupted?" Samantha asked Marcel as they continued. Marcel started to answer, but Loicq elbowed him aside. "Don' be listen' to he, he an' knowin' notting," Loicq assured her, taking her by the elbow. "Dat volcano, she getting' ready to blow for weeks, about a hun'red years ago, but de mayor of Saint-Pierre tell de people 'don' worry, she no goin' to blow. She jus' grouchy, she jus' bellyaching.' Dem Obeah people makin' all kind a charms an' hexes, one to quiet de mountain, de nex' for to make she blow. Dey say de mountain got fed up wit' alla dese Obeah people and blew she stack, an' t'irty t'ousan' people got deyselves burned up in one hour."

Amazed, Samantha asked, "30,000 people?"

"All except one," began Marcel, but Loicq took her by the arm and hustled her ahead again.

"Who be tellin' dis, anyway?" he called over his shoulder, and Marcel laughed, shaking his head.

"So," continued Loicq, "dis one man, he in jail for murder—"

"He was not! He was a drunk," pointed out Marcel, who was ignored by his brother.

"So dis murderer, he protected by de brick walls o' de jail, and he de on'y one lef' after she blow, and he goin' blind from alla de smoke and ash. Dey find him t'ree days later, when dey come from Big Town to dig up alla de bodies."

"It wasn't Big Town then."

"An' you know wha' happen' dis guy?" asked Loicq. Samantha shook her head. "He go out on parole, and he join up wit' Barnum an' Bailey circus. He travel all over de place wit' dem, alla de people want to see de one man who survive."

"Why would they parole a murderer?" Marcel asked. "He was just a drunk! Pelée was the best thing that ever happened to him. They say that the explosion was 40 times bigger than the atomic bomb dropped on Hiroshima."

"Ah, Mister College Boy!" said Loicq. "You t'ink you're getting' some kind o' smarts."

The Atlantic Ocean spread out before them like blue glass as they made their descent to the coast. The salt wind picked up as they neared the water, and large sea birds wheeled and called overhead. There were already lots of boys on the beach and a few girls in ruffly white blouses and skirts the colors of rainbow sherbet, and the lines of brightly colored kites crisscrossed in the sea breeze.

"Marcel, look at the sand! It's black!" Samantha remembered that the beaches of the northern part of the island tended to be dark and volcanic rather than the white sand of the south, but she hadn't been expecting this sparkling, dusky carpet tracing the frothy water's edge.

Samantha took picture after picture of the boys and their kites. The boys were delighted to mug for the camera and show off for her, each claiming to have a bigger and faster kite than the next. Several kids without kites tumbled and posed in the black sand until she had dozens of pictures of grinning faces, many with teeth missing or just sprouting, sand being thrown at each other, and a tangle of arms wrapped around each other's shoulders.

Three little boys over near some strange *pandanus* palms, with their odd, floppy fronds, had taken their clothes off and were rolling around naked in the sand. Samantha hoped the presence of the camera wouldn't make them shy, but it didn't seem to bother them. Whooping their war cries, they would charge into the water to wash the sand off, looking like shiny black seals in the surf. Then they'd run back up the beach to roll around again, coating their bodies like veal cutlets ready for the frying pan. Samantha laughed and called them the "Shake 'n Bake boys" and took pictures until she felt she had enough.

Marcel steered her over to where Sebastian and Lyon were flying their kite, and they insisted she take the string and fly it herself. Samantha protested that she wasn't very good at flying kites but took it anyway and watched the bright red speck in the sky as she struggled with the string. The wind was very strong, and several other kites looked like they would tangle with hers, so she tried to run down the beach to avoid them.

"Marcel!" she called, laughing. "Those boys keep getting their kites too close to mine!" She kept trying to run away from them.

Marcel jogged along with her. "That's why it's called wind-fighting," he shouted. "They have razor blades attached to their lines!"

"*What*?" Samantha suddenly felt her string go slack and watched as the little red kite spiraled crazily upward, caught by the wind and now free of its earthbound anchor.

"Quick, make a wish," Marcel called to her. "The kite will carry it up to heaven."

Still watching the kite fly away, Samantha stepped backwards into shallow water. She cried out as a sudden piercing pain stabbed the heel of her left foot, and Marcel helped her hobble back up the beach.

"A sea urchin," he said, as he inspected the bottom of her heel. Samantha craned her head to see and discovered several little black spots embedded in her foot. They burned and throbbed like fire, as if tiny hot pokers had been jammed into her skin.

"Are they poisonous?" she asked him. "They hurt like hell!"

"Not really poisonous. The tips of the spines break off inside your skin and hurt a lot, but they're not dangerous." To Samantha's great surprise, he began unzipping his pants.

"What are you doing? I'm injured and suffering here, and you're taking a whiz?"

"I'm fixing your foot," he said, and produced a stream of urine directly onto her burning heel.

"Gross, Marcel! Yuck!" She couldn't believe it and tried to pull her foot away.

"Keep it still!" said Marcel, still splashing her foot. He had a pretty good aim. Other boys on the beach gathered around, many looking like they'd be happy to pee on the American lady's foot, too, and Samantha suddenly imagined herself at the center of an impromptu shower. She jumped up and backed away, laughing.

"It's okay! That's enough! You can stop now!" Marcel zipped up his pants and looked at her, grinning. "Well? How is it now?" Samantha realized with a shock that the pain was nearly gone. She was standing on her injured foot, and it hardly hurt at all!

"It—it feels pretty good," she said wonderingly. Marcel smirked at her. "You can thank me later."

"This will make a great postcard to my mother," said Samantha, and she did thank him on their long walk home, during which her foot only throbbed a little. She told Sebastian and Lyon she was sorry she'd lost their kite, but they said it was all part of the game.

***

The rest of their stay passed quickly. Marcel meant to take her to the south of the island where the good swimming beaches were, but they were so caught up with family and friends in the north that they didn't made it. Samantha never became very good at grating coconuts, but she helped Marcel's sisters make all kinds of Creole delicacies, her favorite being a stew called *blaff*, supposedly named for the sound the fish makes when it hits the boiling soup, but they just used cut-up chunks of fish and sea urchin, not whole fish. Lyon and his friends took her hunting for *crapauds*, forest frogs whose legs were cooked up into "mountain chicken." They had feroce d'avocat, a pulp of avocados, peppers, and manioc flour, and fresh fruit juice every morning: guava, orange, mango, and passionfruit.

Samantha was treated like a princess and lost count of all the people she met. Hibiscus flowers were put in her hair; she drank endless cups of tea; and Daria and Mariette made her another dress for visiting to replace her tank tops and baggy shorts. They taught her how to do her laundry in a bucket of water, which turned out to be a lot harder than it looked, to the amusement of Daphne and several neighbor girls. She wore Aunt Cécile's dress when *Maman* took her to church, which wasn't like any church she'd ever been to; the singing and dancing made a surprising change from the stern sermons she remembered as a child. The bread boy continued making appearances every morning around six, his smiling face popping up in Samantha's window and offering to check her room for bugs. Papa

Devereaux finally chased him away and said he'd send Lyon to go pick up the bread from now on.

Samantha found Martinique to be a place of stark contrasts. In the moment that she was taking in the delicate beauty of jasmine blossoms, she was aghast at all the garbage carelessly tossed on the ground, where roosters and rats rummaged through it. The same kids who would smile endearingly and ask for their pictures to be taken would then turn around and kick a puppy, making the poor thing yelp and run away. The image of the dying snake in the mongoose pit haunted her, but so did the gift of a perfect stranger on a street in Macouba, who handed her a basket of mangoes with only a smile and walked away. Just as she thought she was beginning to get used to Martinique, it was suddenly their last night. They would leave for the airport in the morning.

Marcel, to his surprise, also found his island to be full of contrasts. After 7 months away, the house of his birth now seemed very small and run-down. He couldn't help comparing Samantha with his sisters; in their early 20s they were already spreading out, filling out in the hips and bust from childbearing, and Daria was nearly ready to give birth again. He wondered if they had ever read a book in their lives.

Most difficult for him was his new status as the returning prodigal son, but the constant questions about living in America and of course the much-coveted American girlfriend didn't worry him too much. He would have asked the same questions, too. But now everyone seemed to think he had access to unlimited sources of money and should be sharing it with them. When the requests started in on the second day, he'd started making it clear to everyone that no one was to ask Samantha for money. Thank God she didn't speak French; she would have over-heard some very strange conversations taking place in her presence.

But where did they think he could come up with $50 for neighbor children's school fees, $30 for turnip seeds from Big Town, plus bus fare and a new hoe (the old one had broken), $80 for a trip to Dominica to see an ailing grandparent? He was on a limited stipend at school, and the $200 he'd brought with him had already been given out to his family for all kinds of things. More eye drops for his nephew's chronic eye infections, a new tire for the car they'd borrowed to come to the airport, household supplies, a doctor bill for Grand-mère—the list went on and on, and the money he'd brought hadn't been enough. Indeed, Marcel felt the pull of familism in contrast to individualism. **Familism** is a philosophy in which an individual's decisions and actions are based on the wants and needs of the family or other social group, rather than on the wants and needs of the individual. Marcel feels that he should take responsibility for the economic needs of his extended family, even if it means he will not have the money to take care of his economic needs at college. **Individualism**, on the other hand, is a philosophy in which an individual's decisions and actions are based on his or her own wants and needs, rather than on the wants and needs of the group. The values that Marcel grew up with do not reflect individualism; Marcel prioritizes the needs of his family over his own individual needs and wants.

Now, at the end of their visit, he found himself avoiding people, frustrated that he didn't seem to be able to just hang out anymore. People either wanted to know all about Samantha or they wanted money. Everyone wanted to know when he was going to marry Samantha, but he was a little overwhelmed and hadn't gotten that far. They still had their college careers ahead of them, and he knew Samantha would have to overcome her culture's norm of endogamy if they were to consider marriage. **Endogamy** is the social expectation to marry someone within one's own social group. In some cultures, people are generally expected to marry within their own race, national origin, religion, and social class. Samantha's relationship with Marcel violates the norm of endogamy.

His Christmas package had been a big event; apparently, people had come and gone from the house for days inspecting and admiring the gifts. Maman had worn her pearls for a week solid, and Papa Devereaux had hardly taken off his cap. His brothers had been elevated to rock star status with their baggy 501 jeans, and Lyon had eaten all of his Pez candy in a day and made himself sick. The requests for gifts and money were gaining momentum; people were hinting that they'd like him to send them things from America when he returned (Nike shoes, more marshmallows, even a DVD player). Now he even had someone's uncle from a neighboring village, a man he hardly knew, coming to him for money to buy a new carburetor.

It was exhausting, and Marcel found himself feeling guilty for wanting to get on the plane tomorrow and have some peace and quiet. He had already committed to sending several things from America: reading glasses for Papa, cooking utensils for Mariette and Daria, a pair of jeans for Lyon, a battery-powered light for the bathroom. *Maybe if I don't speak to anyone else until I leave I'll be okay, thought Marcel. I could pretend to lose my voice.*

Of course, that wasn't a good idea given the history he and his dead brother Dule had with sore throats. Which brought Marcel to one last obligation before they left. "Sam," he said as he pulled her away from the kitchen, where she was helping with a dinner of snapper and crab with coconut sauce. "How would you like to go on a little excursion before dinner?"

"An excursion? Where?" she asked, wiping her hands on her skirt. No such thing as a towel existed. She tried not to sound skeptical but she'd been looking forward to a break from the many visits to relatives and friends and meeting people; a couple of hours with the sisters, the snappers, and the kitchen was just what she needed. She knew there would be a lot of people coming over that night, their last night, after dinner.

"Well, my *grand-mère* has been bugging me all week because she wants to take you to see someone. She, uh, she insists that you should meet the Obeahman and get a blessing from him. I've been putting it off all week, but since we're leaving tomorrow ..."

"The Obeahman? You mean the *witch doctor*?"

"Yeah, I guess you could call him that. I tried to tell her you weren't into that kind of thing, but she won't hear it. She thinks terrible things will happen if you don't go and get a blessing." He seemed a little embarrassed. "Is he going to make me eat a chicken heart or something?" Marcel laughed. "Of course not! It's just a little chanting and incense and stuff. It would make my *grand-mère* happy."

"Well, then, let's go! A real witch doctor, huh? Is it okay if I go in this?" Samantha indicated the skirt she was wearing, borrowed from Mariette. He thought it would be fine and went to get *Grand-mère*.

***

Half an hour later Samantha and Marcel sat with *Grand-mère* on a rickety wooden bench outside a little thatched hut deep in the forest. The old lady had her rose-hat back on and her best dress, the one she'd worn when Samantha and Marcel had first arrived. The Obeahman's assistant had seated them on the bench, and the man himself was inside the hut, making preparations. Samantha strained her ears, and periodically she could hear some clanging or ringing and mumbling, and the acrid smell of something burning drifted out the doorway, which was partly covered by a threadbare curtain. At one point the curtain was yanked aside, and a skinny brown arm whipped out, tossing an egg out the door. It landed with a splatter, and a shadowed face peered out from behind the curtain, apparently assessing the results in the dirt. Then it disappeared, and all was quiet.

Samantha turned to *Grand-mère* and asked her about the Obeahman. "What does he do?" The old lady regarded her very seriously. "Obeah go to di edge of de world, and he return wid knowledge. But knowledge by itse'f is danger, ma fille, danger-ous wit'out de knowin', wit'out de wisdom. You nevah know when some-body workin' Obeah on somebody else, you gotta be careful nuh fi eat t'ings from certain peoples. You got to get a bush bath now and den." Only she pronounced it "bush bat," leaving Samantha totally confused.

"*Grand-mère*, Samantha no be wantin' no bush baths," said Marcel.

She ignored him and continued talking to Samantha. "Obeahman use his wisdom to protect you. Obeah very powerful. One time, he want to go de train but him havin' no money. He ax de train man for to ride for free, an' he bring he good luck but de train man, he foolish as a donkey an' he say no." Grand-mère leaned closer and tapped a bony finger on Samantha's knee for emphasis. "Obeahman sat hisself right down on de platform and waited. De train, she won't go. Dey look de engine, dey try and try, but de train refuse to move. Den somebody see Obeah sittin' on de platform and dey say let he on! Let he on! So Obeah get on de train, and she move fast-fast." *Grand-mère* nodded to Samantha, slowly, triumphantly.

The curtain in the doorway twitched, and the assistant, who'd been dozing on a stool, got up and spoke in French to *Grand-mère*. The old lady stood up, smoothed her dress, and approached the doorway. She took her shoes off and entered bare-foot, standing up as straight as her tired old bones would allow.

"She's really something, isn't she?" Samantha whispered to Marcel when the cur-tain fell back into place. He smiled and nodded. "Wait 'til you hear her sing. We're doing some music tonight after dinner. There will be a few people coming over."

Samantha smiled. By now she knew what "a few people" meant—50 or more. It would be fun, and she looked forward to seeing Marcel dance.

Grand-mère emerged from the hut and took Samantha by the hand. Standing in front of the doorway, Samantha slipped her shoes off and stood patiently while *Grand-mère* did her inspection, smoothing her skirt, straightening her hair, brush-ing a piece of a leaf from her shoulder. Finally satisfied, she sent Samantha into the little hut.

She came back out about 10 minutes later, holding something in her hand, and sat down on the bench next to Marcel. "Your turn," she said to him.

Marcel didn't move. *Grand-mère* spoke to him sharply in French, and he answered her quietly. He wasn't going in. He didn't believe in that stuff anymore. *Grand-mère* pleaded with him. It was bad luck to cross Obeahman! You never knew who was making Obeah against you, it was best to get protection! Now that he was a big man from America, people could be jealous, they could wish bad things on him. Go inside and get Obeahman's blessing!

But he wouldn't. He stood, thanked the assistant and gave him the required basket of gifts for Obeahman: a bottle of rum, eggs and mangoes, and a few francs. "Let's go. We'll be late for dinner," he said, and the three of them started on the path back to the village.

"What did you think?" Marcel asked Samantha as they walked. "It was pretty cool. I couldn't understand most of what he was saying, though. He gave me this stone." She opened her hand and showed him. "And I had to whisper my heart's desire to it. Then he did some things to it, I couldn't see very well, but it sat in this little pot while he chanted to it. He had some things in a little pouch that he put in the pot with it, some powder and some bones, I think. Now I have the stone, and I'm supposed to keep it with me. It will bring me my heart's desire."

"And what is your heart's desire, *Mademoiselle*?" She smiled coyly at him. "You think I'm going to tell you? You'll have to find out! So why didn't you go in? Poor *Grand-mère* looks like she sucked a lemon. She wanted you to do it."

He shrugged. "It's just superstition. It's a waste of time."

"Oh. I thought it was cool."

They walked in silence for the rest of the way, Marcel lost in thought.

It was only superstition. But the Obeahman filled Marcel with a nameless dread, which made him angry. He was just a garrulous old man! Sitting in his filthy hut with his rocks and bones and God knows what. Samantha thought he was exotic and entertaining, but she had the luxury of fearlessness and the fearlessness of ignorance. The Obeahman's incantations would never affect her, his wisdom from the edge of the world would just pass over her, leaving her untouched because she can't let it in. Her heart and mind were closed to his power as tightly as a razor clam safely buried in its salty mud. But Marcel, he didn't know how to close himself, how to stay at arm's length from the Obeahman's spell; he did not have the luxury of ignorance. He had refused the Obeahman's blessing out of fear, which he couldn't admit even to himself.

✳✳✳

The last night on the island fell quickly, as it had every night. The bats barely had time to start flickering through the twilight, and it was dark. The tropical nights felt different to Samantha: was the sky larger? Was the air softer? She stared up at the night sky. It didn't seem real, with its sharp, bright half moon and stars glittering like diamond chips scattered across black velvet. Silhouettes of palm trees outlined themselves against the inky black sky, nodding and swaying in the breeze like Marcel's tall, thin brothers with their shaggy dreadlock heads, swaying as they drummed, their faces lit by the light of the fire and several torches and lanterns.

The dinner dishes were long gone, and people from the village had gathered around, clapping their hands and moving to the music, feet subtly rocking, hips swaying gently. The air was smooth and silky and filled with the sound of drums and laughter as people passed around the rum. Someone shouted at Sebastian to sing something. Sebastian, drumbeats flowing constantly out his long, muscular arms, sang loudly, "*Shine-eye girl is a trouble to a man, 'cause she want every-t'ing.*"

Laughter rippled through the crowd. Samantha's hand was tightly gripped by young Daphne's hand. Her eyes were red and swollen from crying all day. She didn't want Samantha to go tomorrow. A lump rising in her own throat, Samantha thought of how welcoming his family and friends had been to her and thought bitterly of her own family, who would have been stiff and uncomfortable with Marcel if she'd taken him home to New Hampshire instead. It would have been dreadful. She could just imagine the lectures on homogamy she'd be subjected to. In Samantha's family, heterogamy was not considered acceptable. **Homogamy** (in mate selection) is the tendency for individuals to select a partner with social and demographic characteristics similar to one's own. For example, in most US marriages, the husband and wife are the same race and are similar in age, educational attainment, religion, social class background, and national origin. **Heterogamy** is the pairing of two individuals who are dissimilar in one or more social or demographic characteristics. The relationship between Samantha and Marcel is an example of heterogamy as they are dissimilar in race, religion, social class background, and national origin.

Marcel leaped to the center of the yard where people had cleared a space, and applause broke out. Samantha's heart quickened; he looked good, with the firelight reflecting off his bare chest and his head held high. He caught her eye and winked.

The music picked up. Tambourines, sticks, and coconut shells joined the drums, and female voices flowed through the rhythms like honey and jasmine. A deep, throaty voice rose above the rest, filling the night air with a mournful glow, the sorrow of parting always on the other side of being together. The husky, beautiful voice rose and fell, riding the melody of the pulsing female voices like a dolphin in the ocean swells, telling of love and luck and life and a thousand other things that blossomed in the hearts of those who listened.

Samantha craned her neck to see where the voice came from and could not contain her surprise when she saw that it was *Grand-mère*. The tiny woman stood straight and proud, the flowered hat perched a little askew on her popcorn-dotted head, and music of haunting beauty poured from her. She was amazing.

Marcel began to move, his limbs loose and flowing in the firelight. He felt good, he felt strong, and the worries of the past few days fell away quickly. How had he thought that it wouldn't be like old times? This was fine, and he felt the goodwill of everyone as they encouraged him with their clapping and swaying. He danced and whirled, filled with *Grand-mère's* singing, and felt the joy rise in him, pulsing and beating and bringing life to his moves.

He danced over to where Sebastian, Lyon, and Loicq were drumming and leaned over, still dancing, to beat on Loicq's drum. Marcel's hands hit the drumhead in rhythm with his dancing, alternating perfectly with his brother's hands. They grinned at each other, speaking their own language of rhythm, and the crowd cheered. Marcel whirled around and leaped over the fire, dancing around it in a circle, and then moving over to a small papaya tree. He danced with the tree as if with a partner, to everyone's amusement, and gave the slender trunk a hard shake. Pirouetting around, he ended up with his back to the tree as a ripe papaya fell right into his hand, cupped behind his back. A roar of approval arose from the crowd, and he tossed the fruit into their midst.

People started tossing him things to keep dancing with, and a hat and a pot made their way out to him, each taking a turn on his head as he danced and moved. He danced on a chair, like Baryshnikov in White Nights; he danced atop a tree stump and a log. An old man's cane was nabbed by some naughty boys and Marcel danced with it, the carved stick appearing to hover in midair as his supple body writhed and twirled around it. He danced back over to the old man and ceremoniously returned the cane to him with a bow. Then he pulled *Maman* out into the center with him and danced with her. She was bursting with pride and rocked gracefully back and forth, clapping her hands as her son pirouetted around her and then bowed all the way down to the ground, as if to a queen.

Then someone grabbed Samantha and pushed her out to Marcel, who took her hand. "*Oh, no, no, I can't do this!*" she whispered to him frantically, trying to pull away. "*I'm not a good dancer, Marcel!*" But he wouldn't let go of her hand—he just kept dancing and smiling at her, whispering back, *"Everyone can dance, Sam. You just got to listen to de music!"*

His brown eyes were twinkling and Samantha grinned, trying to move in rhythm with his steps as the crowd cheered her on. Maman swayed and clapped close by, smiling at her. Samantha started really enjoying herself and caught Marcel's eye. *My God, he is beautiful. I really love this man.*

In retrospect, Marcel would have given anything to prevent what happened next.

As he danced with Samantha in the firelight, as the music and clapping rose higher and higher, the crowd suddenly parted, and a woman stood directly in front of him. A woman he knew.

Time seemed to slow, screeching to an excruciating halt as the young woman slowly lifted her right arm, raising it from her side to rest it naturally, possessively on her stomach. It was hugely swollen in pregnancy, a fact not missed by anyone, and she slowly lifted her other arm and rested it there too, her hands gently cradling her burden, as if about to hand it over to Marcel.

He barely noticed that the music and singing had stopped or heard the murmurs of the crowd as he stared at the young woman. Samantha heard them. *Eee, she bellywoman for Marcel. She gettin' a baby for he.*

He still held Samantha's hand as he spoke one word to the pregnant woman. "Jacinta."

"Marcel." She nodded at the unasked question on his face. And she turned and disappeared into the crowd. Marcel, looking helplessly at Samantha, let go of her hand and disappeared into the crowd after her.

***

Samantha lay awake in bed that night, alone, listening to the tree frogs. She remembered her first night, when she'd thought the screeching of the little frogs had come from some horrifying monsters, but at the moment she'd rather have faced the monsters outside than the horrors of her own mind. *He's gone to see her, the mother of his child.* The thought burned through her with cruel ferocity, over and over, crushing any other lesser explanations: perhaps it isn't his, perhaps she's just a friend ... They were flimsy excuses laid flat by the truth. He was having a baby with Jacinta. She was bearing his child.

She remembered the look on his face as he'd left her in the middle of the dance. Shock, dismay, panic—but because he hadn't known or because Samantha had found out? Had he known but was hoping she wouldn't find out? Was he just never going to tell her about Jacinta and the baby? Could she trust someone who would do such a thing? His father had done it with two other women. For the first time, Samantha wondered if Marcel was really capable of **monogamy**. This is a form of marriage in which an individual may legally be married to only one person at a time. The concept of monogamy is sometimes applied to relationships in which the partners are expected to be sexually faithful to each other; even though Samantha and Marcel are not married, she still expects Marcel to be sexually monogamous and to not be sexually involved with other women.

Was Marcel going to marry Jacinta? A wild thought struck her; she found herself imagining what it would be like to live in a society that practices polygamy. What would it be like to be married to someone who had more than one wife? Could she share Marcel with another woman? On the other hand, what would it be like have more than one husband? For Samantha, polyandry was just as unacceptable ... just as unimaginable ... as polygyny. Samantha paused briefly to consider whether she would feel differently if she had grown up in a society where having more than one spouse was socially acceptable. She wondered if her discomfort with the idea of polygamy was simply the result of her socialization. **Polygamy** is a marriage in which there are more than two spouses. Although polygamy is illegal in the United States, it is both legal and socially acceptable in a number of other societies. **Polyandry** is a form of polygamy in which one wife has two or more husbands. Polyandry is not as common as **polygyny**, which is a form of polygamy in which one husband has two or more wives. Polygyny is more common than polyandry.

Samantha rolled over and buried her face, hot tears stinging her eyes when she found she could still find his scent in the pillow. *He's having a baby, and it's not with me.*

***

On the airplane the next day, careful politeness between them stretched like a yawning chasm. Marcel was lost in some other place, and she couldn't find him. She couldn't bear to look at his face and not see him there, only a distant stranger who seemed to have replaced affection with good manners, so she stared out the window at the infinite nothingness of the clouds. Perhaps if she had looked a little harder she might have seen the fear, pride, and confusion at war in Marcel's eyes, paralyzing him with indecision, but her own pain and hurt camouflaged this when she saw him.

Now Samantha understood the purpose of long trips, as she traveled from one part of the world to another. The cloistered time and space of travel seemed removed from the rest of the world, a hiatus from life, an intermission from reality. Such long-distance travel was a time of transition and contemplation.

Instantaneous travel, like on Star Trek, just wouldn't work, she mused to herself. Even if it could be done physically, it wouldn't work mentally—you'd be totally unprepared for stepping back into your old life because you would have become someone else while you were away, an updated version of yourself. You needed that travel time for your subconscious to adjust, to reframe the perceived past and the imagined future into a present you could cope with. Without that, a person could end up suddenly thrust back in their old life, but forgetting which mailbox was theirs, or how to brush their teeth, or whether they liked their coffee with cream or not. A person could forget that their boyfriend, someone they had loved and trusted and thought they had a future with, was having a baby with someone else. Forever after, Jacinta would be the mother of his child, his firstborn. Her eyes stinging, Samantha wished she could be beamed directly back to her old life, skipping everything in between now and then, to a time when she didn't know this. Because she knew it would never leave her.

***

Chapter 9 Study Questions
THE FAMILY

1. Compare the family **households** in which Marcel and Samantha grew up. What are the differences and similarities?

2. Would you describe Marcel's family as **matriarchal**, **patriarchal**, or **egalitarian**? What about Samantha's family? Explain your answer.

3. Describe an example of **familism** from this chapter. Why is familism stronger in Martinique than in the United States?

4. Why is the **empty nest syndrome** more common in the United States than on Martinique?

5. Do you think that Samantha's attitudes toward **polygamy** would be different if she had grown up in a society where polygamy is socially acceptable? Explain.

The Writing on the Wall

Race and Ethnicity

M ARCEL WIPED THE sweat from his face with a towel and stuffed it back in his gym bag. He'd been dancing for an hour and a half and decided to quit for the night. Normally, he'd go for the full three hours during his evening practice sessions, but tonight his focus just wasn't there, so he thought he might as well go home. These breaks in rehearsal, the two and a half weeks at Christmastime and a week over spring break, interrupted his flow, and it took a while to get it back. It hadn't taken quite so long to get back into the groove in early January as it was now; of course, then he hadn't had quite so much on his mind.

It had been two weeks since returning from Martinique. It was mid-April, and the weather was starting to warm up. The ground was soggy and muddy, and cold rain came every other day. By the time Marcel walked home from the music school or the library, he was usually chilled to the bone, and it seemed to take forever to get warmed up again. The gray, rainy days depressed him, and he missed hanging out with Samantha.

He knew he should say something to her, but he truly didn't know what. What had his father said to his mother with the birth of his two "outside" children? He didn't know. Had his mother been very angry? Maybe she had been. When had she found out—when the children were born, or later? He didn't know that, either. Maybe he should have asked her before leaving Martinique. Maybe it would have helped him talk to Samantha now, but there hadn't been time. Or he hadn't made the time. After talking with Jacinta for two hours, he'd gone and sat by himself, thinking, until very late, and then he'd gone home and fallen into bed exhausted. And they'd had to leave for the airport early the next morning.

He and Jacinta hadn't exactly had a conversation. They had talked at each other, each trying to further their own interests; Marcel by suggesting that the child might not be his and Jacinta by telling him it certainly was and he should stay here on Martinique and marry her.

He couldn't do that. He wouldn't. He didn't want to marry Jacinta, and he couldn't help wondering why she'd waited so long to tell him, if the child really was his. Or, late in pregnancy, had she discovered Marcel's new status and apparent wealth and decided she'd like to be part of that? And the impending birth, regardless of who was the father, would help her get what she wanted? Why else would she wait until there was a big crowd of people, friends, and family who knew him well, not to mention his American girlfriend, and then spring this on him?

"Why didn't you call me?" He had demanded. "You could have at least written me before I came. You've known about this for quite some time."

She didn't know. She didn't have his address or phone number, and how would she pay for such an expensive phone call? She didn't want to burden his family by asking them. *But you didn't mind embarrassing me in front of the whole village and my girlfriend,* he'd retorted. He remembered her eyes filling with tears, and then her angry reply that it was a baby, not an embarrassment. She'd had to leave high school without graduating, but this was their child and she wanted to have it.

And as much as he wanted to believe otherwise, Marcel knew in his heart that she was telling the truth. This was his child. She should have told him before, way before he and Samantha went to Martinique; in fact, he probably wouldn't have gone if he had known. But he'd have had to talk to Jacinta, wouldn't he? Face to face, so he could know if she was telling the truth? But how on earth could he have justified having Samantha pay for their trip (even if it was money from grandparents and frequent flier miles) in order for him to return to Martinique to see an old girlfriend, one who would soon be making him a father?

For a moment, Marcel considered whether it would be best to give up going to school in America and go back to Martinique to marry Jacinta. After all, what were the chances that he and Samantha would have a future together? Marcel knew that Samantha's parents would not support or approve of their relationship because of his race and ethnicity.

The thought of going back to Martinique made his head ache. And he could not, *would* not, give up his life in America, his dream of becoming a great dancer, to stay on Martinique with Jacinta and scrape together a living. Marcel knew that in the United States he would always be considered a member of a minority group and would probably experience prejudice and discrimination. But he would rather be a minority pursuing his dream in the United States than a member of the majority group going nowhere on Martinique. **A minority group** is a category of individuals who share similar physical and/or cultural characteristics whose members tend to have unequal access to wealth, power, and prestige and who are often victims of prejudice and discrimination. Minority groups include those based on race, ethnicity, religion, sex, sexual orientation, age, and disability. A minority group is not necessarily a numerical minority. For example, US women outnumber US men, but women are considered a minority group because they have less access to wealth, power, and prestige. As a Black West Indian, Marcel is considered a minority in the United States. The **majority group** is the dominant group in a society; that is, the group that has greater access to wealth, power, and prestige. In the United States, non-Hispanic Whites are the majority group. On Martinique, Marcel is a member of the majority group, but in the United States, he is considered a minority. **Prejudice** is negative attitudes and feelings toward an entire category of people. Marcel knows that in the United States, many people will have negative attitudes and feelings toward him because he is Black. **Discrimination** is the unequal treatment of individuals because of their group membership. Marcel knows that because he is Black, some Americans may not treat him fairly.

What would he do on Martinique, sell pumpkins? Get a job in Big Town at a shop? He would die, his spirit would wither away, and he would just die. Marcel thought of his sister Daria, who had gotten married when she was 21, a year older than Marcel was now, and was on her second child. Mariette wasn't even married, and her daughter had been accepted and enveloped into the family like any other child. Having children was a natural part of life, something he'd always assumed he would do one day himself. Just not today. This was supposed to happen in some distant time, when he was a successful dancer with a career and a secure future. For most of his friends and family, timing wasn't such an issue; Daria at 21 was living the life she would probably be living at 31 or 41, and being a mother was what she'd always wanted to be. So starting her family young suited her fine.

Maybe Samantha would feel better if he explained things to her this way. He'd started a few times to say something, but those tear-filled hazel eyes had stopped him, and he hadn't actually known what he'd have told her anyway. But the silence between them was becoming unbearable, and he missed how they'd been together. They'd been good, even with their ups and downs, and he wanted that back.

He hoisted the gym bag over his shoulder and was on his way out of the music school when a voice stopped him.

"Jamaica, there you are." It was Professor Cady. "I wanted to catch you before class tomorrow."

"Good evening, Professor."

"Marcel, is everything all right with you? You don't seem quite yourself since you got back from the Caribbean." The diminutive professor stood in the hallway, looking up at him, something approaching concern on her face.

"I'm fine, ma'am. And you?"

"Oh, never mind about me. I'm the same as always. I just wanted to see if there was something going on because your dancing has changed. We can see you dancing, we can see the effort, as if your mind isn't connected with what you're doing. I've seen you get to that place where it's no longer an effort; it all comes flowing out of you like you just can't hold it back. Now you're holding back, you're fighting yourself. You're getting in your own way."

"I'm sorry, Professor."

"You don't have to be sorry, I just want you to know. And if there's anything I can do to help, you have only to ask."

Marcel regarded her, a hundred thoughts wanting to come tumbling out at once. But how rude that would be, to burden her with his problems.

"Thank you, ma'am. I'm sure I just need a little time. You know, to adjust to being back."

"All right, Marcel. I'll see you in class tomorrow."

***

"Hey, Winston," Samantha called to the little man in the doorway of the shelter as she wiped her muddy shoes on the mat. "I see you got a new sweater. It's very nice."

"Miss Samantha! Miss Samantha! I think you're a little late. I think you might be ..."—he checked his watch—"12 minutes late! You're usually only 9. Minutes. Late. Tuesday you were here at 2:03."

"Was I? Well, today I had a hard time finding parking. How are you, Sir Winston?"

"Fine! I. Am. Just. Fine." He cocked his head for a moment, as if listening to something. Or someone. "That's it. That's just it, I have to ... Got to be off. You watch out, Miss Samantha, you watch for the ... for the ... ball bearings! They'll get you every time!" And he scurried off on important secret business, carrying a pink feather duster and waving it in front of him. Samantha knew from experience this was to get the invisible cheerleaders out of his way. They could be a real problem.

She saw Jill Hathaway over at a table helping one of the older residents eat her lunch. She pulled up a chair. "Hi, Jill, hi, Lucy. How are you today?" The old lady just looked at her and kept eating her mashed potatoes; she rarely spoke to anyone. "Hey, Sam." Jill motioned with her chin to the left, and said, "Look who's back with us."

Samantha searched the day room and saw with dismay that Letitia, the young mother, was sitting in the rocking chair by the window again. Her daughter, Shanya Lynn, was sitting on the floor nearby, sniffling and crying, but there was no baby boy.

"No way!" Samantha whispered to Jill. "What happened to her subsidized housing? She was living in an apartment with her sister, wasn't she?" Letitia had left the shelter with her two children shortly after Christmas.

"She had a part-time job, too," said Jill quietly, spreading margarine on a piece of bread for Lucy. "She was working as a cashier at a car wash. She was doing pretty well for a while, but I guess she missed a couple of doctor appointments for Lucius, the little boy. When the case worker went to check and make sure everything was okay, Letitia and her sister were stoned, and Lucius needed medical attention. He's in the hospital, and there's some question about whether she'll get custody of him when he's released. They're talking about making him a ward of the state. She and her sister got kicked out of the subsidized apartment."

"Oh, my God," replied Samantha. "That's so sad. But they're letting her keep her daughter?"

"Yeah, I guess so. I think Lucius has special needs, he has brain damage or something, *and* he's HIV positive."

Samantha got up from the table and approached Letitia and the little girl. "Hi, Shanya, what's the matter?" She could see that the child needed a bath, and had snot coating her upper lip. "Hey, Letitia. How are you?"

The young woman didn't answer, she just rocked the chair a little with her foot and stared out the window, as Samantha had seen her do months before. *Letitia, what happened? You were doing so well!*

Samantha took the little girl by the hand. "Shanya, why don't we go to the bathroom, okay? Can we go get you cleaned up?" She glanced at Letitia, who didn't react. Shanya began to sob when Samantha tried to lead her away.

"Don't worry, honey, Mama's gonna wait right there for you. We'll just go and come right back, okay?" She had to pick Shanya up and carry her, and she cried the whole way to the bathroom. She hadn't been changed in quite a while, so not only did she stink, but in her thrashing to get down as she was carried, Samantha was anointed with the wet, leaking diaper and snot was rubbed into her hair. *Lovely. Now we both need to be hosed down.*

She ran water in the bathtub and stripped the little girl down, calling through the open door to Jill to see if she could find any clean clothes for her. Shanya never stopped crying, thrashing her arms and trying to get out of the tub as Samantha tried to bathe her. Food was caked into her hair and her bottom was sore from diaper rash, making her cry even more.

Half an hour later, Samantha carried the little girl back to her mother and put her on the floor next to the rocking chair. Shanya whined and clutched at Letitia, who looked at her dully, but didn't pick her up.

Samantha was disheveled and breathing hard, with her sleeves rolled up (and damp, like parts of the rest of her clothes) and smelling of dirty diapers. But at least the little girl was clean.

"Well," she said brightly to Letitia, "she's pretty active, isn't she? Kept trying to climb out of the tub! But she's all clean now, and we found some clothes for her." Samantha waited. There was no response from Letitia, so she spoke to the little girl. "How do you like that, Shanya? Now you've got a pretty sweatshirt on, it has little strawberries on it. Do you like—"

"You expectin' some kinda medal or somethin'?" Letitia cut her off. Her eyes were cold. "I beg your pardon?" asked Samantha. "You come in here, you wipe the snot off my baby's face, you get crap on your lily-white hands, and you want some kinda cheerin' section? You all better go find Winston and his dang invisible cheerleaders. Why don't you all just go on home to your nice clean house? Leave us poor folk alone."

Samantha was so shocked she didn't know what to say. She looked down at the child, still whining and looking up at her with suspicious eyes, unforgiving of the big bad bath torture Samantha had just put her through. Without a word she turned and walked away.

She spent the next hour in the kitchen washing up the lunch dishes so she wouldn't have to talk to anyone. Her face was red and tears stung the backs of her eyes. *Jesus, I'm so touchy lately*, she thought to herself. In fact she'd been on an emotional roller coaster ever since coming back from Martinique. She'd spoken to Marcel a few times, but it was difficult trying to talk to him. He seemed like a stranger. *Marcel, where have you gone? Come back to me.*

***

Marcel shoved his hands deep in his coat pockets, trying to stay warm. He crossed the street near Harrison Hall, and as he glanced up to check for traffic, something caught his eye, a flash of color off to the right. He reflexively looked over and stopped dead in his tracks.

It was back. The green spray-paint on the brick wall, the one next to the parking lot, the same wall which had been cleaned up months ago from the first time. The obscene message leaped out at him like a slap in the face.

"STUPID NIGGERS! YOUR ALL WELFARE CHEATS AND DRUG ADDICTS, GET OUT OF AMERICA! KILL THE NIGGERS!"

A slow burn erupted inside him, and his fists clenched inside his pockets. Marcel looked around, as if expecting to find the perpetrator still there, leering at him with the paint can still in his hand. Like he'd just painted a work of art on the wall, instead of defacing it with the worst kind of degrading filth. He wanted the vandal to be there, he wanted at that moment to pound his face in, to let him feel the hate and rage he seemed so intent on unleashing.

Scowling, he headed across the street to Harrison Hall and found messages from Ben and Cliff waiting for him. Michelle already had pictures, and they would meet tomorrow at the cafeteria to discuss this latest **hate crime**. This is an act of violence motivated by prejudice. Hate crimes include intimidation (e.g., threats), destruction/damage of property, physical assault, and murder. The majority of hate crimes in the United States are based on racial prejudice.

***

Standing outside room 306 of Emerson Hall, Marcel paused. How many times had he knocked on this door? How many pleasant evenings had he spent hanging out with her in this room, talking and laughing and making love if Dash wasn't around? Why was it so difficult to knock on the door now? It was a simple thing. Just make a fist, rap on the wood, and she would answer. There she'd be, with her lovely hazel eyes, and a little splash of freckles across her nose. Maybe her hair would be wrapped up in a towel; she was forever washing and conditioning it and using lots of different hair care products on it. Maybe she'd be working on her paper. She'd been doing research all year long at the homeless shelter; she talked about it a lot.

Oh, for God's sake, just knock on the stupid door. And he did.

"Marcel!" said Samantha when she saw him standing there. Was she happy to see him? She seemed to be, but her face was still guarded. She didn't trust him anymore—she wasn't sure what nasty surprises would be unleashed upon her.

"Hey, Sam. I thought you might like to go get some dinner."

She smiled. "Let me get my coat," and left him standing in the hall. Minutes later they were in her car and headed downtown; he had been thinking they could just go to the cafeteria, but she wanted to go to her favorite Italian restaurant.

After twenty minutes of small talk and mozzarella sticks, Marcel couldn't think of a graceful segue, so he just said what he wanted to say. "I'm not going to marry her."

Samantha's face changed. Was that warmth, relief, desire in her eyes? She nodded slowly, breathing out a breath she hadn't realized she'd been holding. "What *are* you going to do?" she asked. "I'm not sure yet. I'm not leaving school. I will try to find a job, something part time, so I can send some money to support the child."

"Oh … When is it supposed to be born?"

"I don't know, a few weeks."

An awkward pause followed. *How had this happened?* thought Samantha. The awkward pause had never been part of their relationship, even in the beginning. Or if it had, it had only been filled with anticipation, having so much to say to each other they hardly knew where to start. Now the things she wanted to say couldn't be said: *I wish you'd never met her. I wish you weren't having a baby.*

As if reading her thoughts, Marcel told her, "I knew her before I met you, you know." It sounded feeble, like he was making excuses. Like he was being defensive, and she couldn't possibly have a right to be upset. But women did get upset about these things; he would just have to weather it.

It wasn't exactly his fault, Samantha thought to herself. It did happen before he'd met her, but he should have been using protection, and she was glad they always had when *they'd* been together. There were worse problems than unexpected pregnancy—he could have been exposed to HIV. With a pang, she realized she knew exactly how many days it had been since they'd last made love: on their second-to-last night on Martinique. Ages ago.

Marcel shifted restlessly in his seat. Time to change the subject. This was going nowhere. "Did you go work at the shelter today?" Tuesday and Thursday afternoons were her usual days, and it was Thursday.

She looked relieved. "Yeah, and you wouldn't believe what happened! Remember that girl Letitia I told you about, the crack addict? She's back at the shelter, minus one of her children. The baby, it turns out, has brain damage or something, from when she was pregnant and stoned. He's in the hospital, and he might become a ward of the state."

"So what happened today?"

"Well, when I got there, her other child, a two-year-old daughter, was crying and filthy. The mother doesn't seem very interested in taking proper care of her, so I carried her into the bathroom and gave her a bath. What a mess! She kicked and screamed and got me all gross. It's a good thing I'd already bathed when you came over." She smiled briefly. "And then when I gave Letitia her daughter back, all clean, with new clothes on and everything, she just snapped at me! She was so mean, I couldn't believe it!"

Marcel was silent.

Samantha continued, running on nervous energy. "For God's sake, I've got a busy schedule, it's not so easy getting out to the shelter even two days a week, and she's just sitting there in her rocking chair all day. She can't be bothered to get off her butt and bathe her own child, and when someone else is nice enough to do it for her, she just gets nasty!"

She looked at him expectantly, nervously. *Why is he looking at me like that?*

Marcel regarded her, his lover, a woman he thought he knew. And he understood with dead certainty that he didn't know her at all. He expected this revelation to come with a painful blow, and maybe that would come later. At the moment, he felt only numbness and a distant sense of outrage, growing stronger the more he thought about it.

"What was she supposed to say? 'T'ank you, Miss Nice Rich Leddy for wipin' the shit off my baby?' Don't you think she knows the whole time, that you don't have to be there, and she does? You get to go home whenever you want, and she doesn't."

Samantha stared at him in shock. "I—I was just trying to *help* her!"

"Were you?" he asked quietly. "What do you get out of it?"

"*What?* What are you talking about?" How dare he! "You think I like getting her kid's snot and shit all over me?"

"I think you like feeling special, helping out the poor Black folk. I think you don't mind getting your research done so you can write all about her and her kids and turn your paper in for a good grade. I think you don't know the first thing about what it's like to be poor. I think you spend more at this restaurant than that woman sees in a month. And you certainly don't know what it feels like to be Black in a society where there's so much racism." **Racism** is the belief that certain groups of people are innately inferior to other groups of people based on their racial classification. Racism serves to justify discrimination against groups that are perceived as inferior.

"You—*you complete jerk!*" She spat at him, horrified to hear her mother's abrasive voice coming out of her but powerless to stop it. "How dare you, after all I've done for you! I've always tried to be generous with my time *and* my money. What the hell is wrong with that? And you've been a primary beneficiary, I might add!"

Marcel stood up and put his coat on. The main course hadn't arrived yet, but he wasn't hungry. "There's a difference between help and self-righteousness, Sam." And he left the restaurant.

***

It took Marcel an hour to get back to campus by bus and walking, and the constant cold drizzle had him chilled and dispirited by the time he reached Harrison Hall. It was too late to go to the dance studio, and he had too much on his mind anyway. The old Marcel wouldn't have had such a problem with Jacinta's pregnancy; okay, it's a bit soon, but not such a big deal. Some of his friends from high school had children already. But now his life was so much more complicated. Both women, Samantha and Jacinta, were now estranged from him, pushed away by his own pride and insecurity. It was an odd turn of events that instead of continuing to take money from the one, he would now be sending money to the other. And he needed to find a job, which would cut back on his rehearsal time; he'd have to wait until after the dance showcase in May. Then he'd work full time for the summer.

The graffiti was still there, its obnoxious message screaming out to him in the rainy night. It seemed incredible to Marcel that someone would hate another just because of his race or ethnicity.

At the moment, Mr. Bigot Racist Vandal, thought Marcel, I wouldn't mind leaving America. But where would I go? I don't belong on Martinique anymore, I'm now the prodigal son. I've got to keep feeding the dreams of those I left behind, and soon I'll be feeding my own child there. It all made him so weary. Marcel couldn't bear the thought of giving up his dream, his life in America. He had already begun the process of **assimilation**. This is the process by which minority groups gradually adopt the cultural patterns of the dominant majority group. Marcel has begun to learn how American college students talk, eat, dress, and socialize, and he is gradually adopting these cultural patterns in his own behavior.

Inside his dorm room his roommate was already asleep, once again a sullen lump in his bed. Trying not to disturb him, Marcel took off his sodden clothes in the dark, and cursed under his breath as some change fell out of his pants pocket and rolled across the floor. A quarter glinted in the pale light from the window as it rolled under Kyle's bed.

Cursing softly, Marcel got down on the floor and reached under the bed, still trying to be quiet. His hand hit something cold and cylindrical, and it rolled across the floor toward him, emerging out from under the bed and coming to rest against his elbow.

The cold fire that had been brewing in Marcel's breast all night finally leaped into flame. He jumped up, clasping the cylinder, and flipped on the light switch.

Kyle propped himself up on one arm, shading his eyes and scowling mightily at Marcel. "Hey, what are you doing? That's my closet!" he said crossly. Marcel had flung the door open and had grabbed Kyle's jacket off the hook.

"Then this must be your coat, is it not?" demanded Marcel, tossing the jacket on Kyle's bed.

"Of course it's my coat, you jerk! Put it back!"

"Looks to me like there's a little paint on it, right there on the sleeve." This got Kyle's attention and he sat all the way up, looking at the jacket.

"Is it possible the paint got on your sleeve from *this*?" Marcel asked him, his voice deadly and his eyes blazing. He held up the can of green spray paint, the one he'd found under Kyle's bed.

Kyle was silent for a moment, looking at the paint can. "You can't prove anything! I can just say you planted it to frame me! I've never seen that coat before or that paint can!"

Marcel, throwing on his robe, opened the dorm room door and looked up and down the hall. A guy named Steve was coming out of the bathroom, Marcel couldn't remember his last name but he'd seen him playing basketball a couple of times. "Yo, Steve!" he called to him, "Can you come here for a minute?"

Steve, a blond-haired, blue-eyed jock, obligingly approached Marcel and Kyle's room and was invited in. "This will just take a second, Steve. What's your last name, anyway?" asked Marcel.

"Hansen. Steve Hansen. What's up?"

"Do you know this guy?" Marcel indicated his roommate, who was still sitting in his bed.

"Yeah, I guess so. You're Kyle Parker, right?"

"And would you say this is Kyle's jacket?" Marcel picked up the jacket from the bed and showed him the label inside the collar. *Kyle Parker* was easily visible on the tag, which his mother had sewn into all of his clothes.

"Yeah, looks like it. It has his name in it."

"Don't listen to him!" cried Kyle. "He's just setting me up!"

"What does this look like to you?" Marcel ignored Kyle and spoke to Steve, showing him the sleeve of the jacket.

"Looks like ... paint. Some kind of spray paint. You know, that's not gonna come off very easily."

"And what does *this* look like to you?" continued Marcel, holding up the can of green spray paint.

Comprehension began to dawn on Steve Hansen's face, and he said, "Well, duh, it's spray paint. Green spray paint!" He now stared at Kyle. "Don't tell me—you've been writing all that racist bullshit?! Hey, man, that is *really* not cool!"

"I didn't do it! He planted that can under my bed! He could have put that paint on my jacket, he's always getting into my stuff!" Kyle's voice was shrill and he clutched at his blankets, as if to protect himself from all these accusations.

Marcel reached for Kyle's hand, the knuckles white as they held the covers in a tight-fisted grip. There was a green smudge on the edge of his right hand.

"Don't touch me! Get away from me!" yelled Kyle, pulling away. "I guess you think I got paint on your hand, too?" Marcel asked quietly, pulling back. He was suddenly reminded of a time not so long ago in the dance studio when he'd had a similar reaction: he hadn't wanted a homosexual to touch him. He was ashamed of harboring a prejudice just as harmful as Kyle's. As if a casual touch from a friend would somehow mark him, like a paint smudge on his skin visible to all.

"You're a major idiot, you know that?" Steve informed Kyle, his face angry.

"Thanks, Steve." Marcel turned to him, handing him the jacket and paint can. "Would you mind hanging onto these for evidence? They'll conveniently disappear if they're left here."

"No problem, man," said Steve. "You just let me know, huh?" He turned to Kyle again as he left the room. "I hope your ass gets kicked out of school!"

Marcel turned to his roommate, his back against the door. "Kyle, what have I ever done to you?"

"You don't belong here! Why don't you just go back to Jamaica or Cuba or wherever the hell you're from!"

"I'm from Martinique. And you know, I'm not even really *from* there. My people were enslaved and brought to Martinique from somewhere in West Africa, I don't even know where. So where shall I go back to? I belong where I am, and I make an *effort* to belong and make a contribution. What's your contribution? Scribbling ignorant statements on cement walls?"

"You can't prove anything," Kyle retorted. "Who's going to believe you? Everyone knows you don't like me!"

"No, everyone knows *you* don't like me. And I think the university might listen to our star witness, Mr. Steve Hansen. So you'd better sit tight while I make a couple of phone calls. Just remember, if you take off, we still have the evidence, and you'll look even more guilty."

***

An hour later there were five people in the dorm room, Kyle and four members of Double Black: Ben, Cliff, Michelle, and Marcel. They hadn't been able to find Raymond on short notice. "Behold, my roommate, the racist vandal." Marcel motioned to Kyle, who was seated on his bed, a hunted look on his face. The other three Double Blacks silently appraised him. Kyle looked fearfully from face to face, finding anger and resentment glittering in their eyes.

False bravado took over. "You don't scare me! You can't do anything to me!"

Cliff raised an eyebrow. "Oh, really? We could beat the living daylights out of you in five minutes flat and throw your worthless carcass right out that window. If we wanted to."

"No, you couldn't! You'd get caught! You'd all be thrown in jail!" Kyle was getting more nervous by the minute.

"Let's talk about who's caught and who's not caught," said Michelle. "Marcel, there's a witness who has the jacket and the spray can, right?" He nodded. She turned back to Kyle. "What's to stop us from going right to the university and turning you in? They're committed to the expulsion and prosecution of the vandal, and as far as I can see, that would be *you*." She jabbed a finger in the air at him for emphasis and Kyle recoiled slightly.

"You can't prove anything! I'll deny everything!"

"Michelle, why don't you get pictures of his hand, and then go over to Steve's and photograph the jacket and the paint can?" suggested Ben.

This was accomplished with more bellyaching from Kyle, who hid his hands at first, but Marcel told him he'd call the police straight away if he didn't cooperate, and then there would be no more discussion. Michelle got the pictures and then went down the hall to see Steve.

"So," said Cliff. "What's to stop us from turning in your sorry butt and letting you swing in the wind?"

"Ah, let's just call the cops right now and be done with it," said Ben, standing up.

"No, wait!" Kyle was just about in tears. "I—I—you don't have to, please don't … call the cops …"

"Why not?" demanded Marcel.

"Because … uh, because, well … I'm sorry." "You're *what*?" asked Cliff. Kyle hung his head, refusing to look at them. "I'm sorry."

"Then why did you do it, *twice*, for crying out loud?" Ben wanted to know.

"My dad … he says … there's too many damn Blacks taking over, they shouldn't be allowed in a good school like this … everyone knows Blacks aren't very smart and now they're taking opportunities away from White students …"

Cliff jumped up, his fists clenched. "Man, that is the worst racist stereotype I ever heard in my life! Let's just pound this cracker right now!"

Kyle threw his arms up in front of his face in fear. "It's true! It's all true! There was a study done, these scientists proved it and everything! The statistics are in the book!"

Ben looked at Kyle in astonishment, and then threw his head back and laughed. "Don't tell me you're talking about *The Bell Curve*!?"

"What is this? What book?" asked Marcel.

"This stupid book analyzing IQ scores and everything, supposedly proving that Blacks have lower IQs than Whites," said Cliff. "It came out several years ago."

Ben pulled his chair closer to Kyle's bed. "Kyle, my man. You ever read any Mark Twain?"

"What? Well, of course I have."

"You remember where he says there's three kinds of lies? There's 'lies, damn lies, and statistics?'"

Kyle, perplexed, shook his head. "Was it in Huckleberry Finn?"

"No, it was not in Huckleberry Finn. The point is that statistics are just numbers. You can make them say anything you want. You want to tell people the sky ain't blue, you throw enough statistics at them and they'll believe it. You pick and choose the right numbers, and they'll say pretty much whatever you want them to say."

"But it's in the book; it was published and everything! My dad has it," protested Kyle, as if publishing and possession made it true.

"You know who helped fund that book?" asked Cliff. "An organization designed specifically to fund research proving that Whites are superior to Blacks. If that book didn't prove what they wanted it to prove, they wouldn't have gotten their funding, now would they?"

Kyle crossed his arms, almost hugging himself, as if to fend off their arguments. "But my dad says it's true ..."

"Well, if it's really true that 'Black people are stoo-pid,'" Ben waggled his head and hung his tongue out of his mouth, "why aren't we all flunking right out of this here institution? You won't have to worry about us takin' any of you White folks' opportunities, will you, 'cause we'll all be packing up and getting out of here tomorrow, right? Once we flunk out of all our classes?" At that moment Michelle returned from Steve's room.

"Michelle, what's your GPA?" asked Ben. "It's 3.75. That was last semester, though; finals are coming up fast. I've gotta get cracking."

"Mr. Radcliff Sutton." Ben picked up a folded-up pocket umbrella and held it like a microphone to Cliff. "The eminent sociology major. What's yours?"

"It's 3.8."

"*Monsieur Devereaux*, first freshman ever to represent the school in the prestigious dance showcase, what's your GPA?" He held the umbrella out to Marcel, who replied, "Mine is 3.6."

"And myself, the modest engineering major, neck and neck with Marcel at 3.59. I'd say we're not too shabby for students at an Ivy League school."

"So, now we want to hear what *his* GPA is," said Cliff, indicating Kyle, "since he's so concerned about numbers."

"None of your business!" Kyle retorted, hugging himself tighter.

"What numbers are we talking about?" asked Michelle.

"This is ridiculous!" Marcel finally burst out. He'd been quiet for a while, brooding. "Let's just turn him over to the police. I don't know what we hope to accomplish by trying to talk to this jerk."

Ben spoke up. "There's plenty to talk about, but I think our friend here, the vandal, should go downstairs and wait."

"You're kicking me out of my own room?" whined Kyle.

"Get your robe on," Marcel pulled a robe from Kyle's closet and tossed it at him. "You're going down to wait in the lobby. If you're not there when we decide we're ready, we'll just call the police and tell them who you are." Marcel marched him out of the room, barefoot and miserable, and parked him on a couch downstairs.

"How long do I have to stay here?" asked Kyle, now sniveling and sniffing. "As long as it takes. And it really doesn't matter to me if you take off—the police will be happy to talk to us and take a look at our evidence."

Marcel left Kyle sitting by himself, looking more like a scolded child than a White supremacist vandal.

***

"So, someone please tell me why we haven't thrown this cracker to the wolves by now!?" demanded Cliff, once they were all together in Marcel's room. They had finally reached Raymond, and he was on his way over. "What more is there to discuss?"

"Is that what we want to do? He'll get kicked out of school and have charges against him," replied Ben thoughtfully.

"Hallelujah! That's the whole point!" said Cliff, pacing back and forth.

"The point is ..." began Michelle, thinking out loud, "the point is to use Double Black to raise awareness about racism, to work on healing the wounds between Black and White. To 'create a new system of essentially human values,' isn't it?"

"So, lots of publicity about getting his butt kicked out of school and pressing charges would raise a *lot* of awareness!" Cliff answered.

"It would, but remember this guy ain't too swift on the uptake," said Ben. "His dad's bible is The Bell Curve, and if he's kicked out of school and sent home, how's that gonna go over back in Rednecksville where he's from? Are they gonna say, 'Jeez Kyle, we're so glad you've been expelled because now you've got us all thinking about racial problems in a positive light?' Or are they likely to say, 'Kyle, what a tough break, those dumb niggers got you kicked out of school. This country is sure going to hell in a hand basket.'"

"Ben's right," said Michelle. "As satisfying as it would be to the Black community to nail this idiot, we're not the ones who need their consciousness raised. And if he does get expelled and prosecuted, the negative shockwaves with his friends and family might do as much harm as the original vandalism."

"I can't believe I'm hearing this!" exploded Cliff. "You all just want to let this guy off the hook? After what he's done?"

Marcel spoke up. "I don't think that's the point. I think Michelle is talking about moving beyond just retaliation; is that right, Michelle? Not to let him off the hook, but to do something that will send a message to both Blacks and Whites that we want peace. Something that will be more constructive than getting him kicked out of school."

Michelle nodded. "We have to ask ourselves, 'Will this further the cause of racial harmony? Or will it just piss off one more ignorant, defensive White person? Someone who will continue spreading hate and poison to his White family and White friends because some whiny niggers got him thrown out of school?'"

"So yet again, dealing with the White-caused problems of racism falls to the Blacks, who just want to live their lives in peace," said Cliff bitterly.

"That's why we're *Double Black*," said Ben. "We can't just be Black and American and be our happy selves and mind our own business. Like it or not, we have to put the most effort into getting beyond racism, because the White majority group will just keep the status quo."

"It is up to us to 'create a new system of essentially human values,'" said Marcel slowly, thinking about Césaire's book. "You got something in mind, Marcel?" Ben asked. "I think I do."

Raymond showed up, and they brought him up to speed on the night's events.

***

Hours later, they were all exhausted. They had gone around and around, quoting Obama, Malcolm X, Albert Einstein, W. E. B. Du Bois, Martin Luther King Jr., Descartes, Socrates, and Hobbes. They argued about White privilege, White supremacy, and White guilt.

They brought up Negritude, Afrocentrism, slavery in Africa and in the New World, and how racism in America was the aftermath of slavery swept under the carpet, a legacy of hatred. They wrestled with the legal, economic, social, and ethical impacts of racism and finally kept coming back to how they could use this situation—Kyle and his racist vandalism—to do the most good in the long run, how it could help lead to **pluralism**. This is a system of group relations in which different racial, cultural, ethnic, or religious groups coexist within the same society and maintain their distinctness, respect for each other, and have equal access to recourses—exactly what Barack Obama has talked about. The members of Double

Black wanted Blacks and Whites on campus to coexist, respect each other, and have equal power and prestige.

Marcel and Ben had eaten a whole bag of marshmallows between them. Notes and wadded-up pieces of paper were everywhere, and they finally had a plan they thought would work.

Marcel went downstairs and found Kyle asleep on the couch, huddled by himself like a lost puppy. He tapped him on the shoulder. "What time is it?" he asked sleepily. "Time for you to meet your fate."

Back in the dorm room, Kyle was told to sit on a chair and then introduced to everyone. It was 4:10 in the morning. Ben Williamson began.

"Kyle Parker, you are accused of making racist statements of the most ignorant and degrading kind in two acts of vandalism on campus this year. You are accused of perpetuating the hatred and hopelessness that has besieged our races for generations, leading to the most heinous of crimes against humanity and forcing decent people to lead lives of poverty and despair. You have two choices: one, you can take your punishment as it currently stands with the laws of this state and the university; or two, you can participate in an education and communication program with the purpose of creating humanistic values. Cliff, will you please outline the terms of the first choice."

"You are to be turned over to the police and the university, along with the evidence and statements from the two witnesses, Marcel Devereaux and Steve Hansen. We have their written statements ready." Cliff held up a manila envelope. "In provision with the university's policy on this kind of racist vandalism, you will be expelled from school and prosecuted to the full extent of the law. We, Double Black, are prepared to carry out a widespread publicity campaign to ensure that these consequences are carried out in a timely manner, namely before school lets out for the summer so the maximum number of people will be informed about your actions."

He handed Kyle a piece of paper. "This is a copy of the first choice." Kyle looked at the paper with its handwriting in neat block letters. "Jeez, it feels like I'm on trial or something."

"You are," said Raymond. "The difference here is that we are accusing you based directly on your actions. But you've already judged us: you've judged all Black people by your statements on the wall."

"The difference here is that we're willing to give you a chance," said Ben. "Marcel, the second choice, please."

"You can avoid the penalties of the first choice by agreeing, in writing, to the second choice: one, that you write up a formal apology for your actions, to the university, the students, and to all people of color, which will be published, without your name, in the school newspaper and two public newspapers. This is due one week from today at midnight. Two, that you clean the graffiti off the wall within 24 hours. Three, that you refrain from any further racist graffiti or racist statements of any kind, publicly or privately. Four, that you read the following books over the summer: *Dreams from My Father: A Story of Race and Inheritance* by Barack Obama; *The Bell Curve Wars*, edited by Steven Fraser (debunking the original book and its statistics); *The History and Geography of Human Genes* (the study that flattened The Bell Curve) by Luigi Luca Cavalli-Sforza; and A. James Arnold's *Modernism & Negritude*. Five, that on the first day of school in September you provide us with a two-page synopsis of each book. And six, that in the next school year you make friends with at least one Black person, to be interviewed by a member of Double Black one year from today.

"If the terms of this second choice are not met to the satisfaction of Double Black or if you refuse to any of its terms, it becomes null and void, and the first choice is automatically instituted. You may contact any member of Double Black if you have questions about option two or need help with its terms; a phone list is provided at the bottom, right underneath where you and all those present sign."

Marcel walked over and handed a hand-lettered copy of the second choice to Kyle, who was wide-eyed and speechless. He looked over the two pieces of paper and finally cleared his throat. "What if, um ... I don't sign?"

Michelle stood up. "Fine, I'll go call the police right now," and she picked up her coat. "Wait! Wait a minute, I was just, you know, asking." Kyle smiled nervously at her, more a grimace than a grin. She remained standing, her coat across her arm.

"We don't have all night," said Cliff. He looked at his watch. "You have 60 seconds to decide."

"Sixty seconds? That's not very long!"

"How long do you think the enslaved Africans were given to decide whether they would get on the ship in chains or get beaten to death on the spot?" Ben asked him.

Kyle looked at him and then looked at the rest of the Double Black members. There was no quarter in any of their faces. They were dead serious about this.

"Anybody got a pen?" he finally asked, his voice cracking.

***

Next door, in Emerson Hall, the lights were out in room 306. It was 2:30 in the morning, and Samantha sat at her desk, using a tiny reading light to work on her term paper, trying not to disturb Dash. But Dash wasn't asleep; she'd been watching her roommate through half-closed eyes. The pain in Samantha's face was as clear as day, illuminated by the occasional tear rolling down her face, angrily wiped away.

Dash slipped out of bed and stood behind her, her hands on Samantha's tense shoulders. "A term paper can't possibly be this upsetting," she whispered. Samantha's shoulders sagged, and more tears came. "I went out with Marcel tonight. We broke up."

"Oh, Sam, I'm sorry," said Dash, and leaned down, encircling her neck with her arms and resting her cheek against Samantha's. "I'm so sorry," she murmured as Samantha wept, holding her tight. Samantha's shoulders shook with grief, feeling the loss acutely, as if she would never feel happy again. Dash caressed her shoulders, speaking softly to her, and then felt Samantha suddenly go rigid as she kissed her ear.

Samantha turned to look at Dash, her eyes wide, full of doubt and confusion. "Don't worry," Dash whispered. "It's okay." And she kissed her full on the mouth. After a few moments of stiff hesitation, Samantha relaxed and stopped resisting.

***

Chapter 10 Study Questions

RACE AND ETHNICITY

1. What is Marcel's **ethnicity**?
2. Where do you think Marcel would experience more **prejudice** and **discrimination**, the United States or Martinique? Explain your answer.
3. Why is the graffiti spray-painted on the brick wall near Harrison Hall considered a **hate crime**?
4. Do you think **racism** is more common in the United States or on Martinique? Why?
5. Give an example of how Marcel has begun **assimilation** into US society.

Chapter 10 Study Questions

CHAPTER 11

On the Uncontrolled Growth of Body Hair

Deviance

Two weeks later, the capricious sun finally came to stay, and the cherry trees outside the residence halls exploded into their spring glory. Sitting on the steps of Harrison Hall, Marcel looked up at their blossoms, pale pink popcorn adorning the branches, and their delicate scent carried with it memories of his island home. He expected a phone call from Martinique anytime now, with mixed feelings of anticipation and dread. Sometimes he thought the whole thing had been a fantasy; the existence of a baby only made real by his being there on the island, and now that he was gone it would have vaporized as a dream at dawn.

He had a clear view of the parking lot wall across the street, now clean of any defacement. The graffiti had been removed as mysteriously as it had come within a day of its appearance. Not so mysterious to Marcel, who now held a copy of one of the downtown newspapers in his hand, folded open to photos of both the original and the most recent graffiti on page 3.

"*Campus Vandal Recants Racist Message*," the headline announced, and Marcel had already read the article three times. It included the university's request for help in identifying the vandal, the anonymous letter of apology to the students, the school, and all people of color. What was most significant to Marcel, and noticed only by him, was that his roommate now spoke to him occasionally; there were no more notes.

Connor trotted up the cement steps and paused as he reached Marcel.

"Marcel, the man himself!"

"Hey, Connor." He shook the outstretched hand. "You just come from rehearsal? How's it going?"

"Pretty good. But I thought you'd be there, tonight being the big night and all."

"I was there this morning from six to nine, and I'll be back for the dress rehearsal at three o'clock. The prof doesn't want me to overdo it, since with the performance tonight that will be about eight hours of dancing today. I came back here to work on my paper for English Comp, but I can't help soakin' up a few rays first."

Connor grinned. "I guess you miss the sun, don't you? Well, good luck tonight, and break a leg!"

"*What*?"

"Haven't you ever heard that?" Connor laughed. "It's just an expression you say to someone who's about to go on stage. It means good luck."

Marcel laughed. "Doesn't sound like very good luck to me! But thank you, I will do my best."

***

In the early hours of the previous night, Samantha had finished the final draft of her sociology paper, the product of many long months at the Miller Street Shelter; working, interviewing, observing, and writing. Jill Hathaway had already looked it over and given a couple of suggestions but had pronounced it good to go. Samantha had read Jill's paper on the effects of homelessness on children, or most of it; her son had the flu that week and she hadn't had much time for sleep or writing. Finals were coming up fast, papers had to be turned in, exams taken, a year of college evaluated by a few crucial letters posted on a bulletin board. Those letters would translate into a GPA, which would ultimately influence their postgraduate careers. The law schools Samantha eventually wanted to apply to would take a long, hard look at those numbers on her transcript, and her chance to make sure they were respectable, even outstanding, was now.

Dash was at the library working on her own paper; it was too weird trying to study in the dorm room together. There hadn't been a repeat of that night two weeks ago, a strange wrinkle in Samantha's reality, and she still wasn't sure how she felt about it. The next morning, waking up in Dash's bed, she'd had to scramble to get to class on time, and she'd been in such a state of confusion she'd forgotten that sociology didn't meet on Tuesday mornings. She told Dash she wanted to continue just being friends for now.

Rereading her term paper, a lump of dissatisfaction sat like a rock on her chest and refused to move. She'd thought finally getting it finished would be a triumphant event calling for a beer at the Crow's Nest or something. She could go dig Dash up at the library and they could celebrate, if it was still open. Well, it was finals week and everything stayed open late.

But the triumph didn't come. This was it, Samantha's masterpiece, the culmination of the school year in sociology, with all the i's dotted and the t's crossed, scholarly works referenced and cross-referenced, methodology meticulously laid out, analyses thoughtfully presented. But as she read it over again, a realization came to her with sickening finality. *Everything she had written was crap.*

It was a 30-page rationalization of her role and the politics and motivation of those in power dealing with the homeless, and it dawned on her that none of her volunteer work had ever been truly altruistic. Her paper was nothing more than the pontification of a "have" on the plight of the "have-nots," and she had no idea what she was talking about. Marcel and Letitia had both tried to tell her this, but she hadn't been listening, too caught up in her vision as a savior of the people, wasting time writing about the symptoms when she didn't understand the cause.

She studied the title page, "Economic and Social Implications of Homeless Shelters: A Case Study," and then wrote "SANCTIMONIOUS DRIVEL" across the title page and dumped the whole thing in the trash can.

After sleeping for a few hours, she got up before first light and quietly slipped out of the room, and after half an hour in the bathroom, she was satisfied with her appearance. Her $200 coat was now beat-up and worn, with scuffs and tears and a big smear of something nasty-looking across one shoulder. Her hair was a mess, tangled and unkempt; she wore no makeup, no jewelry, and no nail polish. She couldn't reproduce Kevin's lack of dental hygiene—he went for weeks without brushing his teeth, but she at least wouldn't brush this morning. She smudged dirt on her face and scratched her fingernails on an old eraser, making them blackened and grubby looking. She had on a pair of ragged shorts over torn, dingy sweat pants, with beat-up sneakers and no socks. She had no purse, no wallet, no car keys, and no identification, and the money in her pocket was only enough for bus fare into town, not round-trip. She would have to scrounge enough for whatever she ate that day and bus fare back to campus.

Samantha walked over to the sociology department, hoping the building would be open early. It was, and she left a note on Professor Rourke's door: *I know this is last-minute, but my paper needs rewriting and will be about 24 hours late. I understand that this will affect my grade. Thank you, Samantha Cahill.* Their term papers were due at five o'clock that afternoon, and Professor Rourke had made it very clear that papers not turned in on time would be marked down half a grade for every 24 hours they were overdue. He only considered three excuses legitimate for tardiness: a death in the family, emergency surgery (on the student), and nuclear holocaust.

Samantha left the building and walked to the bus stop to catch the downtown bus. A woman in a black coat inched quietly away from her as they waited. It was 5:48 a.m.

***

Marcel sat at his desk working on his term paper for English Comp. He sighed, wishing he could talk it over with Samantha; she was good at this kind of thing. But of course, he couldn't do that.

"American Tap Dancing as Individual and Cultural Expression." What an insipid title. He wadded up the page and threw it away. Leaning back in his chair, he folded his hands behind his head and closed his eyes, letting his mind run with ideas.

Savion Glover and his electrifying Broadway performance filled his head. *Claim your history.* Mikhail Baryshnikov and Gregory Hines together in White Nights, a White dancer and a Black dancer. A White man and a Black man. *Claim your freedom.* A little child on a faraway island waited to be born, floating in an ocean of dreams and light. *Claim your future.*

Marcel slipped into a light doze, half-dreaming of secrets and truths, desire and joy and rage. Opening his eyes 10 minutes later, he looked over the scattered array of notes on the desk. He put them away in a drawer, not wanting distraction, and then wrote a new title on a blank sheet of paper: "Heart Beats: The Redemptive Power of Dance." He said it out loud. It sounded strong and solid, reflecting what was in his heart.

He had a good idea what the paper would look like, of what the message would be, but it was still coming, still evolving. He folded up the title page and put it in his pocket so he'd be able to take it out and look at it again as he went out and did what he had to do. Tomorrow he'd write the whole thing, rewriting some of the notes and passages he already had, and he should still be able to turn it in when it was due, the day after tomorrow.

But today was the big day; the dress rehearsal began in an hour, and tonight at 7:30 was the dance showcase. *This is it, the beginning of the rest of my life.* The professor from Juilliard would be in the audience, but Professor Cady had said she wouldn't be pointing her out or introducing her to Marcel until after the show. So he'd be free and unencumbered, not drawn by any particular face in the audience. And he knew Samantha's face wouldn't be there.

✳✳✳

6:36 a.m.: West side of Canterbury Park, downtown. Samantha finds an empty bench and lies down on it as if she's been there all night. It's too uncomfortable after about 10 minutes, so she sits up, watching other homeless people in the park. It's just getting light and there's a chill in the air, winter's last clutches fading in the morning sun. One man with a thick, grayish beard has made a bed out of cardboard and an old blanket; a shopping cart stands near him filled with tattered plastic bags and boxes. Samantha can see the rim of a bicycle wheel in the cart and a battered child's doll with a little pink dress.

Found objects, or the remnants of another life? Did he have a family once, a house, and a cocker spaniel, and a garage and mortgage payments and problems with the plumbing, which he tried to fix himself but then had to call a plumber, at his wife's insistence? Had he come home to find his wife in bed with another man, had he gone on a drinking binge and never recovered, had his family died in a car accident on their way to Grandma's for Christmas? Where did his life begin to unravel, at what point did he lose the threads and find himself unable to pick them up again? Had this come as a shock, an emptiness, a sense of relief?

His deviance began with an act of deviant behavior. When did his world fall apart? When did he actually become a deviant? **Deviance** is the violation of social norms. According to US social norms, people are expected to live in some type of housing. Those who live on the street are violating this social norm. **Deviant behavior** violates social norms. Sleeping on the streets, going unwashed, and eating out of garbage cans are forms of deviant behavior. A **deviant** is a person who is known to violate one or more social norms and is labeled as a deviant. Homeless individuals violate norms and are thus viewed as deviants.

7:21 a.m.: East side of Canterbury Park, downtown. Samantha rummages through a trash can, wondering what people look for and what they find. *Does trash become trash now and forever, once it's in the can? Does the act of removing it and claiming it make it not trash anymore? Or does an object found in the trash remain stigmatized, like a cookie dropped on the floor? Does length of time matter; the longer something remains in a trash can, the more unacceptable it becomes? Perhaps there's a certain skill, a learned trade in sifting through the contents of garbage cans, in leaving an old shoe without a mate but taking a wadded-up donut bag with half a jelly donut left inside. And what is the difference between garbage and trash, anyway? Will others stigmatize me for eating something out of a trash can?* To **stigmatize** is to reject and devalue people with certain physical or social characteristics. Imagine Samantha on her university campus, eating out of garbage cans. This behavior would lead to rejection by her peers and exclusion from the campus social scene. In other words, she would be stigmatized for eating out of a garbage can.

7:50 a.m.: Southeast side of Canterbury Park, downtown. Samantha sees two young men in a small stand of trees engaged in what looks like a drug deal. She keeps moving, her face down, shuffling along the sidewalk, hoping they won't notice that she's just witnessed a crime. She doesn't feel very safe and wonders if this feeling changes once you've lived on the streets and park benches for a while. A **crime** is any behavior that violates a law. Samantha knows the two men standing amid the trees would not appreciate getting caught dealing drugs, an illegal act, and may harass her if they knew she saw them.

Do you feel safer once you know there's no three-bedroom condo waiting for you at the end of the day? Once you've learned how to stick to the well-populated areas and memorized the police beats? Will the police be as quick to respond if a homeless person is in trouble and not a computer analyst on her way home from the gym?

9:04 a.m.: Corner of Haggerty and Linsdale, downtown. Samantha finds a torn cardboard box outside a convenience store and removes one of the flaps. With a pen retrieved from a trash can in the park, she writes in large sprawled-out letters on the cardboard flap, "PLEASE HELP. GOD BLESS." *Now I've made my statement. I've admitted to everyone that I can't take care of myself.*

These four words, "Please Help. God Bless," render me pathetic, an untethered satellite on the fringes of society, circling around and around, captured by its gravitation but unable to land or navigate. I've been cast into orbit by poor education, an inner-city school system with overcrowded classrooms and overworked teachers who never noticed my learning disabilities, by an undiagnosed mental illness passed over by overburdened and understaffed public health clinics, by a bitter divorce and a family who's turned its back on me now that I'm an alcoholic, by an unforgiving economy with too few jobs for people with no skills. These four words at once repel and attract attention of the people passing by, important people with real lives and things to do. But whose doing has gotten me where I am: theirs or mine?

10:17 a.m.: Corner of Linsdale and Scott streets, downtown. Disapproving glances, people turning away from her, and the cold shoulder of a passerby present an informal social control that makes her move toward a storefront. **Informal social control** refers to unofficial attempts to regulate a person's behavior. Samantha sees other people looking at her with disdain as she holds the sign on the street; she feels the disapproving reactions of passersby are their attempt to get her off the street.

However, Samantha has been asked to move from her spot near the convenience store after a short time, and now she sits against the brick wall of a credit union, hoping that people getting money out of the automatic tellers will be inspired to share some. She's hungry and could use an oatmeal-bran-cranberry muffin with low-fat margarine and a cinnamon latte and perhaps some fresh cantaloupe; she'll be lucky if she gets half a donut and a stick of gum.

What motivates people to part with their money? A sense of guilt, a sense of fairness, a sense of altruism? Is giving money away really altruistic? Is giving a bag of clothing to the Salvation Army and not asking for a receipt for tax deduction, is this altruistic? Is altruism the act of giving something without expecting anything in return? But doesn't the giver still get a sense of satisfaction, a good feeling from doing something nice for someone else? Is it altruism only if no one else knows about the act of kindness, it's just kindness for its own sake, sort of an anonymous deposit into some cosmic social account, counterbalancing the evil of the world? Samantha's ponderings on giving money away turn out to be academic; people tend to have only $20 bills when they come from the ATMs, and when she asks one woman for spare change, she answers, "None of my change is spare. I worked for all of it."

The security guard asks her to move on, telling her to get her filthy behind off their sidewalk. Samantha is surprised at her own response to this act of formal social control; she is near tears as she picks up her sign and departs. **Formal social control** is the use of official power and authority to regulate a person's behavior. The security guard uses his official power and authority to get Samantha to leave the area.

12:40 p.m.: Stanton Square, downtown. The lunch rush is on, and Samantha places herself near the heavy foot traffic of the sidewalk cafes and delis. Food and hunger seem a little more compelling to people, and she is given half a sandwich and a bean burrito. They taste heavenly. A woman in a business suit gives her a dollar but refuses to make eye contact. *I am a nonperson, no longer someone you'd have a conversation with. I wouldn't belong in polite company; not only am I unpleasant to look at, but I couldn't possibly have anything worthwhile to say. I'm expected to be ingratiating and overly thankful when I receive something from someone. Thank you and God bless you for your act of kindness—you are a busy and powerful person, yet you've taken a moment to share your wealth and good fortune with me, a humble nonperson on the outside looking in.*

What if I said "Thanks for the sandwich, but I'm a vegetarian. I don't eat roast beef. Please get me egg salad. Thanks for the burrito, but I'd rather have the two dollars. That way I can buy what I want to eat. Beans give me gas, you know. What if I were to violate a taboo as I sit here? For instance, masturbating in public? Would you still give me a burrito?"

What? You think you're entitled to make your own decisions? Oh no, you gave that up, you gave it all up with four little words on your little cardboard sign. We, the beautiful people, we now make the decisions, we now hold the choices in our hands. This is our privilege, our reward for being hard-working, productive members of society. We get to make big decisions like whether to go to Cancun or Acapulco for our honeymoon, what restaurant to eat at, whether we will contribute $1 to the presidential campaign fund on our tax returns. You, a homeless person, you only get to make small decisions. Whether to sleep on a park bench or under a bush. Whether to take a broken umbrella or leave it in the trash bin. Whether to wish you were having clam chowder or fish and chips for lunch. You are now a person of smallness and insignificance.

1:12 p.m.: Beech Street, downtown. Samantha sits cross-legged on the sidewalk with her sign propped against a wall and a plastic cup in front of her. It's from the top of a thermos, found in another trash can. *Are there any benefits to being homeless? I'm obsessed with the security and creature comforts I don't have at the moment, but what if that passes? Would I get to a state where I don't worry so much about how I look, how I smell, how gross rummaging in trash cans is, the lack of hot showers, the uncontrolled growth of body hair …? How long does it take to get to this state? I wouldn't have to pay taxes, go to the dentist, worry about my grades, or stand in line at the bank. No mortgage payments, insurance premiums, or school loans to worry about, no grumbling about the broken fuel pump in my BMW, no worries about my kid's poor performance in school and whether I should take him to a child psychologist. No credit card bills, no aggravating phone calls from family members, no office politics, no computer crashes, no fiddling with four remote controls for the TV and sound equipment, stressing out because you can't remember how to find Netflix.*

Somehow I can't imagine being very content as a homeless person, even without these hassles of the modern world. I think we choose our own stresses, and a change in circumstance affects them but doesn't get rid of them. I guess I'd worry just as much homeless as I would otherwise; I'd just be stressing out about different things. Survival. Food. Shelter. Illness. Avoiding getting beaten up or molested. Snow and ice in the winter, storms in the summer. Any illusions of freedom and absence of responsibility would pale in significance. Problems with the TV remote start to look pretty damn good.

2:28 p.m.: Beech Street, downtown. A man gives Samantha a dollar and then tries to get her to get in his car with him. He wants to take her somewhere: how about a bath and a hot meal? You can come to my apartment (translation: hotel room). Glancing around for help if she needs it, Samantha remains seated on the sidewalk and starts babbling incoherently, acting like an idiot. A little string of drool hangs from her lips. Repulsed, the man leaves and as soon as he is gone, she picks up her sign and cup and walks away, not wanting to be found by him again. What if he comes back with friends or a gun? Best to get lost in the anonymity of the city.

Are we unable to escape our fates, whether it's preying on some helpless homeless woman or sleeping in a filthy alley, in a puddle of your own piss and puke? Does everyone have their own demons, planted early and nurtured by dysfunctional families, which will ultimately manifest themselves in stressful lifestyles? Whether you end up scrounging for a rotten tomato in the garbage or dropping dead of a heart attack at age 45, well fed and wearing a thousand-dollar suit, finishing up a $200 martini lunch in Manhattan, twice divorced and taking antidepressants?

Do these things happen on Martinique? There were people living in deplorable conditions there; Marcel's sister Daria lived in a shack with her husband with no indoor plumbing and no electricity. There were cockroaches in the latrine and rats in the thatched roof. Their personal belongings could have fit into one shopping cart. Their two-room shack didn't look like it would survive the next major hurricane; was the line so tenuous between them and homelessness? But they would never be homeless when the hurricane hit, would they? Even with the loss of everything—the shack, their few possessions—they still wouldn't really be homeless. They'd be incorporated back into the family, into the village. Other people who didn't have much would share what they had with them, they'd get help building another shack, or perhaps they'd live in an extra room behind someone's house; Grand-mère usually stays there, but she can sleep with the grandchildren. We'll throw some extra sweet potatoes in the stew. Come, pull up a chair. Let me hold the baby while you mend your clothes.

Homelessness isn't just losing your home. It's something else.

***

Marcel put his gym bag down on the floor of the dance studio and took his jacket off. Before starting his warmups, he took the piece of paper out of his jacket pocket, the title page, and opened it up to reread it. Then he folded it up and put it back.

His body felt good, strong and supple. Anticipation ran through his veins like some exotic nectar, sending a tingle through his muscles like thousands of tiny electric shocks. Professor Cady had been right; if he hadn't gone home after this morning's session he'd be tired by now, past his peak. Now he was just approaching it, and by 7:30 he'd be ready for anything. *Everything*. Ready to dance like he never had before.

3:35 p.m.: Marcel warms up in the dance studio with Connor, Drew, and several other members of the jazz dance class. He's still wearing his black cotton drawstring pants and no shirt; they're all still wearing their mesh shirts, tights, leotards, carefully torn sweatshirts with the sleeves removed, bandanas, leg warmers, and wrist bands. He doesn't notice.

3:59 p.m.: Marcel glances over at the empty window well for the second time and forces himself to look away. His back and legs tense for a bit as he works out, but then he relaxes and his flow continues, open, reaching, light, and together.

4:23 p.m.: Professor Cady tells him it's time to move to the theater at the other side of the building; several group numbers have finished their dress rehearsal, and it will be his turn soon. "How's everything, Jamaica"? "Got your moves down"? "Yes, Professor, I'm feeling good. Thanks."

***

5:12 p.m.: Samantha is back in her dorm room, still disheveled, feeling tired and grubby, but she's writing notes at her desk. Two pages are already covered, including a title page. Dash Goldman comes bursting into the room and throws her backpack on her bed.

"Hey, kid!" she says to Samantha. "What happened to you? You look like you've been buried and dug up again."

"I *feel* like I've been buried and dug up again. Here, take a look at this." Samantha hands her a piece of paper.

"'Homelessness: A Human Condition,'" Dash read aloud. "'Homeless as a state of being, a psychological loss of connection to other people.'" Dash looked at her.

"This is your sociology paper! Don't tell me you're just writing it now? I thought it was already finished."

"It was. I threw it away." Samantha kept writing.

"You threw it—but it's due at five o'clock, isn't it?"

"Yep, it was."

"And isn't your professor a complete fiend about turning papers in on time? Don't they get marked down by the hour or something?"

"Yep, he is. Yep, they do."

"For God's sake, Sam, just turn in the one you already wrote! What's the matter with it?"

"It was crap. It was just a pretend paper. This is the real one." Samantha kept writing.

Dash stood with her hands on her hips and rolled her eyes. "You must be out of your mind. I came to get you for some dinner. I'm on my way to the cafeteria, but I don't think I want to be seen with you. What did you do, roll in rotting animal carcasses?"

"Yep."

Samantha had thought that Dash would be the last person to disapprove of her hygiene and appearance. But apparently even Dash, the poster-child for self-expression, expects some measure of conformity to standards of cleanliness and self-grooming. **Conformity** is behavior that complies with the norms of a group or society. Even nonconformists such as Dash expect some degree of conformity from others.

"Arrgghhhh! Samantha! Go get cleaned up while I'm eating dinner. The dance showcase is at 7:30, for crying out loud!"

"I can't go."

"Samantha. You're going. I *know* you two are broken up, but this is Marcel's big night. He's been working all year on this. We can't miss it."

"I can't go."

"You're going! And take a shower!" Dash slung her pack over her shoulder and headed back out the door.

Samantha whipped around in her chair as she was closing the door. "Bring me back two cranberry muffins! And a cheese sandwich!"

"Burn those clothes!" Dash slammed the door.

"And some chocolate milk!"

***

5:17 p.m.: Marcel is on stage. He is bathed in red and blue lights, which make his skin glow like a being from another world. There are several people in the audience here for the dress rehearsal, but the Juilliard professor hasn't arrived yet. Hushed whispers echo around the theater, curtains rustle, and sound equipment is checked and tweaked and adjusted. Professor Cady is everywhere, making announcements and pronouncements, fussing and prodding and encouraging, as if the entire show is fueled by her energy. Perhaps it is.

Marcel bounces a little on the balls of his bare feet and then goes to his gym bag, hidden in the wings offstage. He pulls on a pair of old sneakers, which have been specially altered, and they click loudly as he walks back to center stage. Bottle caps have been hammered into their soles.

As he waits for the theater to settle down and the music to begin, Marcel closes his eyes and has a quiet vision of snow falling off a bamboo leaf. He has found a new place; he's looking forward to who he will become and what will happen. He can control only himself at this moment, here and now on stage, and everything else will happen as it happens. The music begins. He has stopped fighting, and he starts to dance.

***

5:18 p.m.: Samantha sits at her desk, thinking about Martinique. She couldn't remember seeing any homeless people there, even though she saw a lot of poverty. Worse than anything she'd ever seen in America, actually. But everyone seemed connected in some way, in some form, with people all around them, and while it certainly didn't guarantee that everyone got along, at least no one was alone. This had even become a little tiring for her while she was there. She found herself missing the sense of privacy she was accustomed to. A couple of times she'd gone into her room to lie on the bed for a little while, just for some peace and quiet, but Mariette or Daphne or *Maman* had always come bustling in.

She wrote in her notebook: "Personal power, shifting ideas of power and responsibility." In walking away from social responsibilities and obligations—taxes, insurance premiums, car payments, family obligations, etc.—was a person reclaiming some of their own personal power by releasing the control these social responsibilities had on them? Was this just an illusion? Was the price paid—being homeless—worth the apparent freedom from responsibility? What did she really know of responsibility, she who was born with a silver spoon in her mouth?

She'd been looking in the wrong places for solutions to the problem of home-lessness, and in her original paper had come up with a list of "if only": if only drug trafficking were under control, there wouldn't be so many homeless people. If only alcoholics could stick with rehab programs; if only everyone got a good education; if only there were widespread family counseling to cut down on domestic violence; if only, if only ...

But she'd missed the underlying cause, the reason for all of it: *if only people felt connected to each other in a fundamental way, they wouldn't have such problems with drugs, alcohol, abuse, and all the rest. These problems arise out of isolation and despair, a backlash against the aching void inside.*

And if she or anyone else were interested in making a difference, in really helping people and helping themselves, they would have to address this fundamental issue. Samantha herself was part of the problem—she'd been expecting gratitude for her efforts at the shelter, cooking and cleaning and taking care of the residents, while ignoring and ostracizing her own family members. And Marcel, someone she cared deeply about.

She left the room to go down the hall to the phone and dialed her dad's number. *Please be there. Please be there.* But only the answering machine picked up, request-ing that she leave her number and a brief message, and they would get back to her as soon as possible. Thank you. *Beeep.*

She cleared her throat. "Hi, Dad, this is Sam. I wanted to let you know, I've decided not to go to law school. I've been thinking about it for a long time, and I don't think becoming an attorney is how I really want to ... how I can be someone

... really helpful. But I wanted to let you know, I think it's great that you're an attorney—it's just not for me.

"And I love you."

***

5:20 p.m.: Marcel's dancing is superb; he can feel it, and Professor Cady and his friends breathe him in as he fills the stage with an innovative combination of tap, jazz, ballet, and something else that can only be described as island soul. The sneakers with their bottle caps fly across the floor, clicking and clacking, pounding and chattering and singing; in his mind, he and his friends are 10 years old, pretending to be great tap dancers after watching White Nights outside the Don't Mind Your Wife bar.

His limbs are infused with a surge of liquid light, and he is Savion Glover. A powerful smile spreads through his chest as the memory "*he looks like me, he looks like me*" chants a beat down his legs, and a rush of rhythm explodes from the scuffed-up sneakers with their impromptu taps. The rhythm of drumbeats flows in his body, pulsing through his chest and arms as the surprised sneakers fly across the dance floor. They are the drums of Broadway, the drums of his brothers around a distant cooking fire as he dances, the forbidden drums of his ancestors as they struggle to keep their spirit and culture alive in a hostile world. His breath comes in short gasps as his feet and body move faster and faster, and beads of sweat scatter like raindrops from the ends of his dreadlocks, creating their own silent symphony as he whirls around. Drumbeats surge through him. The recordings he'd made of his brothers on Martinique, now turned up to full volume, resonate inside him and let his spirit soar. He is a young boy again, full of dreams and desire, running toward a bright future, turning to see who is there with him. The tap sneakers dance out their heartbeat, and Marcel smiles as one bottle cap dislodges itself and skitters across the floor. The change in the sneakers' pattern delights him; it now sounds as if one shoe is asking questions and the other is coyly not answering. He taps out a syncopated conversation, as if composed of shouts and whispers, improvising as he goes, his feet moving faster than his mind. *We shout out who we are while memories whisper in our heads.*

Ancient island memories, transformed by time, tap themselves out in his rhythms. *Dinky-mini, Dinky-mini,* the dance of joy and sorrow, the gathering together to cheer a family who's lost one of their own. *Kumina, Kumina-myal, kumina-myal,* dancing for the light, for the good, a dance to counteract the evil side of Obeah. *Kimbanda-kyas, kimbanda-kyas,* the drums of ritual, the hypnotic conduit of power, the bringing together of light and darkness. The rhythms come faster and faster, creating their own language: kim-ban-da, ku-mi-na, dinky-my-mini, joy, power, time, and sorrow. Dule, my brother, *dinky-dinky-myal-mi*.

The music transforms him, and in two jumps Marcel has kicked off the sneakers to continue barefoot. His body arches and flows, he is made of light and liquid. He is now going on pure emotion, his mind disengaged and flying freely. Thoughts transform themselves into light and color coming out his fingertips; he can practically see them making tracks through the air. His body speaks a language only he knows, but which touches everyone watching—the knowledge of his heart has dissolved into the wisdom of his body. He has become trade winds across an ocean beach; he is splashing with his brothers in a waterfall; hungering after the girls with their bright cotton dresses plastered to their bodies in the warm water; he is the heartbeat of an unborn child. He is Samantha's hair across his pillow; he is a wild horse, a kite, a hawk racing in the summer wind. He is simply Marcel and no one else.

The music finishes with a finale, and Marcel spins like lightning across the floor, coming to a stop in front of Professor Cady, arms curved in front, one leg stretched gracefully out behind, head bowed, chest heaving. The last traces of music dissolve into space, leaving behind a sense of nostalgia, a sense of wonder and loss. Marcel raises his head slowly and meets Professor Cady's gaze.

Not a word is spoken. Esther Cady simply nods to him. A lump of pride has blossomed in her throat beyond which words cannot pass, but her blue eyes are steady as they hold his brown ones.

You are ready.

***

Chapter 11 Study Questions
DEVIANCE

1. Distinguish between the concepts **deviance** and **crime**. How are these concepts similar? How are they different?

2. What examples of **informal social control** does Samantha experience while out on her research expedition as a homeless person?

3. What type of **formal social control** does Samantha experience while doing her research expedition as a homeless person?

4. Is **stigmatization** similar to the concept of formal social control or informal social control? Explain your answer.

5. What example provided in this chapter illustrates how Dash, in many ways a nonconformist, expects **conformity** from Samantha?

The Dancer's Gift

Stratification, Social Class, and Economy

6:02 P.M.: MARCEL returns to his dorm room to shower and change before the dance showcase. He is supposed to be back at the theater no later than 6:40. He won't be eating until after the performance, so that will save him some time, and he can't even think about food now anyway.

Kyle was in the room when Marcel returned from his shower.

"Hey, Kyle. How was your exam?"

"Um. Crappy. Okay, I guess."

Marcel put on a pair of jeans and a clean T-shirt. There was a new pair of spandex exercise pants in his bag, black with a white stripe down the sides. He would be wearing these for the performance with a loose, unbuttoned white shirt. The shirt would come off when he cast off his shoes, halfway through the dance.

"You gotta study for physics tomorrow?" Marcel asked him, putting his shoes on—the ones *Maman* had bought for him when he first came. The sneakers were still specially altered, so he couldn't wear them around.

Kyle nodded, opening his physics notebook.

"Is that your last exam?" Marcel asked him, picking up his jacket.

"No. I still have trig the day after tomorrow."

"Well, good luck," said Marcel. "I am glad that my dance program does not require me to take trig. You must be really smart to understand all that math and stuff." Kyle glanced up at Marcel. "If I don't do well on this exam, there is no chance I will get accepted into the engineering program. If you want something bad enough, you just do it, that's all."

Marcel was awed by Kyle's ability to understand trigonometry. He wondered to himself: *Is Kyle's determination to do well in trig like my determination to do my best in dance class? Does Kyle want to be an engineer because he really loves that kind of work? Or does he just want a well-paying job so he can make lots of money? If Kyle had grown up in a country based on socialism instead of capitalism, would Kyle still want to be an engineer?* **Socialism** is an economic system in which 1) the means of producing goods and services (e.g., natural resources and factories) are publicly owned and controlled by the government; and 2) goods and services are equitably distributed according to the needs of the citizens. Socialist economies emphasize collective well-being rather than individualistic pursuit of profit. **Capitalism** is an economic system in which private individuals or groups invest capital to produce goods and services, for a profit, in a competitive market. Capitalist economies emphasize the individualistic pursuit of profit rather than collective well-being. Marcel wonders if Kyle's determination to become an engineer is based on the capitalistic value for individual profit. The attacks on the World Trade Center on September 11, 2001, were motivated in part by disdain for American capitalism.

6:27 p.m.: The telephone at the end of the hall rings. Marcel hears it but hurries into the stairwell; he's not going to answer it. Someone else picks it up.

"Devereaux!" calls Steve Hansen. "Yo, Marcel! Phone call for you from Martinique." Marcel stops, his hand on the banister. After a moment's hesitation, he sprints back up the stairs and takes the phone from Steve, who is holding it out to him. "Thanks, man," said Marcel, putting the receiver up to his ear. "Hello?"

6:34 p.m.: Marcel walks out the front door of Harrison Hall and crosses the street quickly to cut through the parking lot. He will have to hustle to make it to the music school by 6:40, but a few minutes won't make much difference. His head is in a fog; he doesn't know whether to be relieved, worried, or numb. He just can't afford to think about it right now.

6:36 p.m.: Marcel only hears the screech of brakes—he doesn't see the car until the impact. He'd been looking the wrong way as he'd stepped off the curb into the street.

Disbelieving, Marcel feels a thump and sprawls onto the hood, the car jerking and shuddering with the effort of stopping to avoid him. It was too late. He seems to roll in slow motion across the hood of the car, wondering who on earth was this person who looks just like him being hit by a car, cartwheeling through the air. It couldn't possibly be him; he was on his way to an important engagement. He didn't have time for this.

He could still save himself. He wasn't under the tires. The car is at that moment coming to a complete stop, as it hadn't been going very fast in the first place. His supple body and lightning dancer's reflexes went ahead without him, struggling to right himself, to land on his feet on the other side of the car. But there's not enough time. He was too surprised: by the time he realized he'd be better off to just keep rolling off the hood and fall to the ground, his legs were already poised, a fraction of a second away from hitting the pavement.

And he can't get his left foot positioned in time. His full weight comes down on it sideways as he hurtles toward the street. His whole body seems to hang in mid-air for a second, a horrified "NO!" erupting in his mind as a cracking, popping sound explodes from his left ankle.

And then time suddenly speeds up again as Marcel lies in the street, and the pain in his ankle is nearly as deafening as the shouts of the people nearby and the honking of horns.

6:39 p.m.: Marcel insists that he's okay, he's not hurt, and he struggles to his feet. The driver of the car and two joggers try to get him to remain still.

"I'm okay, really," said Marcel, pulling himself up on the open car door.

"Careful! Don't move!"

"I'm—" Marcel sucks in his breath as he tries to put weight on his left foot. The pain is excruciating; the ankle will not bear any weight. The people around him continue their anxious advice, asking him his name and other irrelevant questions, but he's not listening. *You want to know my name? You can see my name, it's listed in the program for the dance showcase. Solo performance by Marcel Devereaux. But at the moment my name might as well be Bob. Mike. Ted, the guy with the broken ankle. The guy who just stepped in front of a moving vehicle. Jeez, Ted, was that a very good idea? Right before a big dance audition, the biggest performance of your life? Doesn't look like that ankle is in very good shape for dancing, does it?*

6:55 p.m.: Marcel is in the car that hit him, being driven to the emergency room. He insists that he's not hurt badly, and they don't need to call the police or an ambulance. The man in the car has offered to take him to the hospital. Marcel can only think about the huge vacuum a lost dream is leaving inside him, his hope of moving up a few rungs on the social stratification ladder dissolving as his ankle swells. **Social stratification** is a system by which a society ranks categories of people in a hierarchy. Marcel had hoped that by becoming a successful professional dancer, his ranking in society would increase.

"Boy, it's a good thing I'd already slowed down as I approached the intersection," the driver of the car said for the third time. He was a high school football coach, driving across campus that day to see a friend of his, a professor of economics. He was still a little shaken up by the accident.

"One of my students broke his ankle last semester, and he had a cast on for a couple of months. He had to sit the season out, but he was back in shape by this spring," he told Marcel, who doesn't answer. He just looks out the window as they drive, letting the driver ramble on about football and Ace bandages, then retelling the circumstances of the accident over and over. *Doesn't make much difference how it happened, does it? It happened, and I can't take it back. Nothing will ever be the same.*

7:29 p.m.: Samantha, Dash, Daly Brown, and Kevin Bittner are seated in the auditorium of the theater, leafing through the program. Kevin has come back to school after a short stay in the hospital and a week at home. He seems to be doing okay on the antidepressant Cymbalta.

"You didn't bring me a muffin," Samantha pouted to Dash. "You dragged me away from my paper and didn't even bring me a muffin."

"Oh, quit your whining," said Dash, exasperated. "You and your Protestant ethic need a rest anyway. Look, here's Marcel's picture in the program!" *Protestant ethic* is a belief system that emphasizes the importance of hard work and achievement. The Protestant ethic played a key role in the development of capitalism. Samantha's dedication to her paper and Marcel's dedication to dance reflect the Protestant ethic.

Samantha couldn't put it off any longer. The program had sat unopened in her lap, but she finally opened it and began reading. She turned the page and saw him there: *Marcel*. His handsome face was framed by the dreadlocks, his expression unsmiling but thoughtful, his eyes candid, as if he were thinking about dancing.

There was a caption underneath his photo. *"Marcel Devereaux, a native of the Caribbean island of Martinique, brings to us his unique artistic expression in a solo performance called Island Drums. Marcel dedicates his performance to family and friends and asks that we all make an effort to drop the barriers of social class which separate us from each other and reduce the social inequality that exists throughout the world.* **Social class** (also referred to as **socioeconomic status**) is the classification of individuals based on their wealth, educational attainment, and occupational status. In the United States, individuals with high levels of wealth, education, and occupational status belong to the upper class; those with low levels of these phenomena are viewed as being in the lower class; and those with moderate levels are in the middle class. Social inequality refers to differences in wealth, power, and prestige among societies, groups, and individuals. Marcel views social inequality as a social problem and believes in the ideal of social equality.

Samantha, unable to bear looking at his beautiful face for too long, glanced around the auditorium. She was surprised to see a full house, with a large number of well-dressed people, not just students. She hadn't realized the Spring Dance Showcase was such a big event; a number of university patrons had special reserved seats and sat resplendent in tuxedos, fur stoles, and expensive evening gowns. Their conspicuous consumption left no doubt as to their social class—in fact, they were practically broadcasting their prestige. **Conspicuous consumption** is the consumption of goods and services to demonstrate one's wealth to others. Expensive, formal clothing is one form of conspicuous consumption, as well as the luxury cars the patrons arrived in for the showcase. **Prestige** is the social recognition, respect, and esteem associated with a particular status. The university patrons have specially reserved seats for the performance and are given recognition in the program for making large contributions.

Samantha also saw Marjorie Trask, the guidance counselor, and her friend Jill Hathaway. She waved to Jill, who waved back.

7:34 p.m.: A lone figure slips into the auditorium and finds a seat near the back. He glances around nervously; he's not sure if he wants those Double Black people to see him there. Kyle looks at his watch. He'll just stay until Marcel does his thing, and then he'll get back to the dorm to keep studying physics. Hopefully, no one he knows will see him.

In fact, someone did see him—Michelle from Double Black. She nudged Ben Williamson and nodded toward Kyle. Ben saw him and smiled at Michelle. Not for the first time did Ben wonder if they had done the right thing with Kyle; but every time he went over it in his mind, he came to the conclusion that Double Black had been true to its mission.

A tall woman in a cream-colored silk dress fanned herself with her program and looked at her watch. She had arrived an hour ago from Juilliard and would have to drive back after the performance, but she was looking forward to seeing Esther Cady's protégé perform. Her old friend and dance partner had been so enthusiastic about him, a dancer from someplace in the Caribbean, that she had to see him for herself.

7:36 p.m.: Marcel is parked in a wheelchair in the lobby of the emergency room, his left leg straight out on the foot rest, wrapped in an icepack and several bandages. His whole foot throbs and pulses. It feels like it's 10 times its normal size. He doesn't know where the shoe it was on has gone; much later he will find it in his gym bag next to the bottle-cap sneakers, where the driver of the car had thoughtfully stashed it.

He fills out the paperwork on the clipboard given to him by the hospital receptionist. The driver of the car has gone off to fill out a police report; even though it was a minor accident, there was still paperwork to be done. Truth be told, the driver was a little nervous that Marcel would decide to sue him and wants it in writing that the accident wasn't his fault. *It wasn't. It was my own stupidity, my own absentmindedness. I should have looked. I should have been more careful. I should have thought about what would happen ... I didn't consider the consequences.*

8:04 p.m.: Marcel broods in the wheelchair, waiting for someone to take him to X-ray. By now it would be clear to everyone at the music school that something was wrong—the performance would have begun by now, why hadn't he shown up? He couldn't bring himself to call anyone. *Let them wonder. Let them go on without me. Let the Juilliard professor sit there in the audience watching everyone else dance, and not me. Not the "Solo Performance by Marcel Devereaux."*

A little girl, bundled up in a thick sweater and a blanket, sits in a nearby chair staring at him. Scowling, Marcel shifts in the wheelchair so he can look out the window and avoid her inquisitive (and uninvited) gaze. His ankle throbs as he moves his leg.

8:08 p.m.: The lights of the auditorium finally go down, and the music begins. The performance has been delayed, but they finally have to begin. Professor Cady can only hope that Marcel shows up soon; they can rearrange the numbers if necessary and he can go last. *What on earth has happened? He was only going to his dorm and coming right back.*

"Finally!" said Dash as the lights dimmed.

"I'm starving," Samantha whispers to her.

"Shush. We'll go out for pizza afterward."

"I can't, I have to write my paper."

"*Shush!*"

Samantha sits in the darkened auditorium, her heart beating faster as she waits for Marcel to make his appearance. Maybe she can still slip out before he comes on stage. Can she really handle this? But at the same time, she knows wild horses couldn't keep her away. She has to see him.

8:13 p.m.: The little girl in the emergency room lobby is still staring at Marcel, making him more irritated. "Mommy, why does that man have yarn for hair?" the little girl asked in a loud voice. Marcel gritted his teeth.

"Hush, honey, that's not very polite," said the woman sitting next to her. She glanced at Marcel apologetically: kids, you know how curious they are. The woman wasn't very old, maybe in her mid-30s, but she looked exhausted, with dark circles under her eyes. She leaned back, closing her eyes and sighing wearily, as if the weight of the world rested on her shoulders. The little girl kept staring at Marcel.

He looked out the window again, his reflection cast back to him with the night sky blocking the glass. His dreadlocks created a wild mane, cascading down to his shoulders, drawing looks on a regular basis. Go ahead, keep staring at me. I'm a freak, and I don't really belong here anyway. I thought I was a dancer, but now I'm not so sure.

8:15 p.m.: To Marcel's dismay, the girl becomes talkative. "I just had a birthday party. I'm eight years old."

Marcel kept looking out the window, although it was too dark to see anything outside, and pretended not to hear her. There was only his glum reflection to keep him company. Little girl, can't you see I'm busy? *There's no room for anyone else in this bad mood of mine. It takes all my attention to properly feel sorry for myself.*

And sorry he was. He had hoped for **social mobility**. This is a change in an individual's position within a society. If Marcel became a famous dancer on the New York stage, his position would change from a lower-class foreign student to a successful member of a higher social class. His dream of being a great dancer wasn't just about dance—it was about going somewhere, being someone. He was the first one in his family to really achieve some kind of intergenerational mobility and intra-generational mobility. **Intergenerational mobility** is the upward or downward change in the social class position of children in relation to their parents. Marcel had hoped to achieve a higher social class position than that of his parents. Intra-generational mobility is a change in social class position during a person's lifetime. Marcel had hoped to improve his social class position by pursuing a career in dance.

"How old are you?" *Oh man, she just will not let up!* He finally turned back to look at her. He was surprised to hear that she was that old; he would have guessed five or six. She looked small and fragile, an effect heightened by the bulky sweater and blanket, and her face was pale and white.

"I'm 20," Marcel told her. She had a complexion of alabaster, almost translu-cent, as if there were no blood in her skin. But there was; a tiny blue vein pulsed in a hollow temple, the kind you'd see on an old person. Her eyes were large and vivid blue. They looked haunted and out of place in a thin face with no baby fat. There were no roses in her cheeks, no color to her lips. Her wispy hair was covered by a knit cap.

"What did you get for your birthday?" he asked.

"I got a sweater and a watercolor set, and a Rainbow Brite, and three books," she answered, pausing to catch her breath, as if this little speech had sucked the wind right out of her. In fact, she did seem to deflate for a moment, leaning back and closing her eyes briefly; fragile, fringed petals closing over porcelain eyes. Then she opened them again and said, "I'm Katie. Do you like books?"

"I like to dance. I'm Marcel."

Katie glanced at his foot, bundled up in bandages and towels, dampened by the ice packs. "What's the matter with your foot?"

"I broke my ankle."

"Oh. Does it hurt?"

"A little. I got a shot."

She rested, a brief respite from the rigors of conversation. When she opened her eyes again, she said, "I have acute lymphocytic leukemia. I need a bone marrow transplant. We can't find the right tissue type," she said matter-of-factly, as if she were describing her hair color or what she wanted for lunch.

Marcel stared at her. *Eight years old and she sounds like a medical encyclopedia. Are there any shots for that kind of pain? The kind deep in the marrow of your bones?*

Glancing over at the child's mother, he saw that she was watching him. He recognized her hopeless, despairing expression, and he understood: *this child will not live long enough for any bone marrow transplants.*

An orderly appeared with a wheelchair, and he leaned down to pick the little girl up. "Hi, Katie! How's my best girl?"

"Hi, Frank!" She wrapped her arms around his neck as he gathered her up; they were like little sticks inside the fluffy sweater. "I want a CBC and chemistry profile, stat! And don't forget the electrolytes."

Katie's mother had suddenly come to life, fussing and tucking the blanket around her in the wheelchair. Katie's little white face peered out from the blanket and cap like a dormouse in a hole, guarded by a watchful and ferocious lioness; no one would harm a hair on that child's head while she was around. But the desperation of the mother's actions belied the truth—no amount of vigilance or courage would stop this insidious danger, this unseen enemy draining the lifeblood from her child. Frank rolled the wheelchair down the hall, the mama lioness hovering close by, looking for an enemy she could see.

8:29 p.m.: Another orderly shows up to take Marcel to X-ray.

Marcel saw a pay phone down the corridor as they turned the corner, his swollen, sodden left foot pointing the way like some kind of war club at the leading edge of battle. He hoped no one would crash into it as they cruised, as the orderly was going kind of fast. Marcel swiveled around in the chair to look at the guy's name card.

"Uh, Reginald, Reggie? Can we stop at the pay phone? I need to make a phone call. I don't want my friends to worry." Reg, as he liked to be called, parked him under the phone and told him he'd be back in a minute. Marcel took the phone off the hook and began dialing.

8:42 p.m.: The curtains close after an especially clever dance number; six guys at a construction site. They're wearing clunky work boots, tool belts, and hard hats, with skin-tight shiny spandex pants and, of course, no shirts. Connor and Drew, sweating, hold hands and bow as the crowd applauds.

There's a delay before the next performance, and a spotlight illuminates a small form marching to center stage in front of the curtain. "That's Professor Cady, Marcel's dance instructor," Samantha leaned over and whispered to Dash.

"Ladies and gentlemen," announced Esther Cady, majestic in a glittery blue sequined tunic and black silk pants, "I regret to inform you there will be a change in the program. Marcel Devereaux will not be performing tonight." And she left the stage.

A murmur rippled through the audience. Many people were there just to see him, and of course there was one woman who had come all the way from Juilliard.

9:33 p.m.: Marcel is waiting for his X-rays to be developed, and his wheelchair is parked in the corridor outside Radiology. He has more time to reflect on his bad luck and his sudden cessation of social mobility; he had come from a solid proletariat background, and he knew his family saw him as their hope. The **proletariat** is the working class in society composed of those who do not own the means of production (factories, department stores, etc.) and who sell their labor for wages. On Martinique, Marcel was a worker who owned nothing and always worked for others. As a successful dancer, he could own his own studio and hire others.

The elevator at the end of the hall opens and a hospital bed is wheeled out, approaching Marcel. He recognizes Frank the orderly and Katie's mother, the mama lioness. They walk on either side of the bed as an IV bottle swings gently from a pole at the head. The prone figure in the bed is nearly buried in pillows and blankets.

Marcel leaned over and inspected a little supply cart against the wall next to him. There were cotton balls, gloves, and a few instruments, including several different sizes of scissors. He quickly made his selection as the bed approached.

"Excuse me," he said, catching the mother's attention. "Excuse me, is Katie awake? Can I talk to her?"

The bed rolled to a stop in front of him, and he worked the wheelchair forward, trying to keep his outstretched left leg out of the way.

Katie's doll face peered out at him with her cornflower blue eyes, and her small hands rested like wilted flowers on the covers. Her face had a luminous quality to it, as if she were not quite in this dimension. Marcel took one of her limp hands in his. "Hi, Katie, remember me? I'm Marcel, the dancer."

She smiled. "'Course I remember you. How's your foot?"

"It's okay. They think it might be just sprained."

"That's good." She sounded very sleepy. "You gonna be dancing again soon, huh?"

"Yes. So will you. You take it easy now, okay?"

"'Kay, Marcel. Bye." The luminous eyes closed again, and the bed continued its journey down the corridor to wherever they took dying children for desperate eleventh-hour miracles. Katie opened her eyes and looked down at her hand, in which was clutched a single fuzzy dreadlock.

***

Samantha didn't get her paper finished until late that afternoon, staying up most of the night after the dance showcase. Dash had invited Daly and Kevin over for pizza when they'd returned, since she couldn't get Samantha to leave her paper, and the cold pizza in boxes scattered on the floor had sustained her throughout the day as she worked.

Finally, it was finished, printed out, and two copies made. She hurried over to Professor Rourke's office to turn in one copy, just about 24 hours late. Well, with luck she might receive an A minus, and she was glad she'd done what she'd done. Her only regret was that she hadn't seen Marcel dance last night. Where was he? What had happened? She hurried back to the residence halls and headed up the steps of Harrison Hall.

It took a few minutes for Marcel to answer the knock at the door. He was still learning how to manipulate the crutches without falling. He opened the door. "Marcel!" All the things she wanted to say seemed to have vaporized, and she stared dumbly at the cast on his foot and the crutches.

"Samantha," he said quietly. "It's good to see you."

"Marcel, what happened to you? Is your leg broken?"

"I sprained my ankle. It was a stupid accident. I didn't get to perform at the showcase last night."

"I know. Professor Cady came out on stage and made an announcement halfway through the show."

Marcel was silent for a moment, surprised. "You were there?"

"Of course I was there."

They looked at each other for a minute.

Why does she have to look at me like that with those hazel eyes? With those cute freckles underneath?

God, he's still gorgeous, even on crutches.

"Can I come in?" Samantha finally asked, breaking the silence.

"Oh, yeah, sure, come on in," Marcel replied, laboriously shifting himself out of the way and back over to the bed, where he sat down with a sigh. Samantha watched him with a pang, his usual powerful grace and effortless, artful movement shot down in mid-air. It was like watching a soaring eagle crumple to the ground.

"How long do you have to keep the cast on?" she asked.

"A couple of weeks. Then they're going to check it out again and see if it needs surgery. There are some torn ligaments."

"But you'll be able to dance again?"

He smiled at the concern on her face. "Yes, I'll dance again. Just not very soon."

She pondered this, Marcel going for a long time without dancing. His leg would be stiff and weak, whenever it healed up, and it would take a lot of work to get it in shape again. She glanced at his face and saw that he knew all this. But he seemed to be okay with it.

Once again, with no good segue leaping to mind, Marcel just came out with it.

"Sam, the baby died. It was born dead yesterday."

Her eyes opened wide. *The baby died? It's dead? What does this mean? What does one say to this?*

"Oh, Marcel. I'm sorry. I'm so sorry."

He nodded. "It wasn't meant to be."

What did he mean? The baby, or us?

"Was it a boy or a girl?"

"I don't know. I didn't ask."

For some reason, that made a difference to Samantha. It was somehow incomplete, not to know if the child had been a boy or a girl. How could you not find out a thing like that?

But for Marcel it was easier to accept; it was somehow less of a loss if he didn't know. It was not meant to happen.

Samantha realized she was still holding a paper bag she'd brought over. "I uh, brought you something." Marcel opened it up and pulled out a bag of marshmallows. He looked up at her and grinned. "How did you know I've run out? I have to finish my term paper and I'd never make it without these. Thanks."

"My term paper's in there." Samantha nodded at the bag, and Marcel pulled out a neatly bound copy of her paper.

"'Homelessness: A Human Condition, by Samantha Burns Cahill,'" he read.

"Well, you helped me write it, so I thought you should read it."

"I did?"

Samantha stood and paced the floor. "You know, I was angry with you for a long time after you broke up with me. I thought you were wrong. I thought you were trying to hurt my feelings when you questioned my motives for working at the shelter."

"Sam, I'm sorry—"

"No, no, you were right. You made me think about things I'd been avoiding, and once I started really listening, I discovered ... a lot of things. I saw that my paper and my study were complete trash, so I dumped it and started over. Yesterday."

"What! You wrote this whole thing in a *day*?" Samantha grinned. "Well, not exactly. Dash fished it out of the trash and gave it back, thinking I'd need at least some of it in the rewrite, and I did. But the basic idea had to be redone. It's much better now."

Marcel looked at the paper in his hands. "Well, I look forward to reading it."

"It's not just that, either," Samantha continued. "When I was ... out doing research for this, the new paper, I had some time to think. I was thinking about homeless people and what that would be like, but I also thought about you. And me, and how angry I was with you. I ... uh ... looked down inside myself, and I was horrified to discover that what makes me tick is just an oversensitive bundle of defensive reactions. ... I realized that I've spent too much of my life trying to protect myself from other people. I'm always afraid they'll hurt me. I was hurt when I found out about ... you know, Jacinta and the baby. But I've been asking myself the wrong question all along. I shouldn't be so concerned with 'will other people hurt me'—because they will, it's inevitable—but 'can I trust myself to handle it when they do?' You were just telling me what you needed to tell me, and I couldn't hear it.

"And I *can* handle it. It's no good living in fear your whole life." Marcel just looked at her, stunned. He really hadn't expected this. She leaned over and kissed him on the cheek. "I hope you enjoy the paper, and I hope your foot heals up soon."

Marcel reached out and took her forearm as she pulled away, and she looked at him quizzically. To her surprise, his eyes were glistening.

"Samantha, you are a brave lady," he told her, his grip on her arm strong and sweet.

"I am?"

His warm brown eyes held hers as he spoke, his voice full of emotion. "You are not afraid to look where others won't. You go where other people are not wanted. You care for someone else's child when they don't appreciate it. You just do it because it's the right thing to do. You live a courageous life, Samantha."

Samantha's throat closed up, and she didn't think she could speak. She didn't really feel courageous, but somehow, when Marcel said it, she felt differently. He understood her as no one else did.

Finally, the words came. "I guess you'll let me know what you think—" she gestured at the paper in his hand, "when I come back tomorrow?"

Marcel smiled his dazzling smile. "I'll be here."

Samantha lingered in the doorway for a moment, her face a study of emotion, wanting to say a thousand things, but finally she departed.

Marcel stared into space for some unknown amount of time, letting the thoughts settle out before turning to the term paper in his hands.

He opened it up and found a quote inside the title page: *"This is how we save the world. Individually, one friend at a time, or together by changing the context in which we find ourselves which will change us all."*

THE END

ABOUT THE AUTHORS

D R. MEREDITH KENNEDY's lifelong quest of crossing boundaries and unconventional learning styles made her jump at the chance to write this story. She has lived on Caribbean islands, in several African countries, in New Zealand, and Belize. She has developed college-level student programs focusing on experiential learning, making her relate deeply to Marcel and Samantha and their journey. Trained as a veterinarian, Dr. Kennedy has also worked with World Learning, Inc., as an academic director for 10 years. She holds a master's degree in music.

Marty Zusman, Professor Emeritus of Sociology, Indiana University Northwest, has focused his career on teaching Introduction to Sociology. Dr. Zusman is the winner of the prestigious Sylvia E. Bowman Teaching Excellence Award given to the most outstanding teacher in the entire Indiana University system.

Tracie E. Gardner, Esq., Teaching Assistant Professor, East Carolina University, has taught Introduction to Sociology for more than 23 years. She earned both her MA and BA from East Carolina University before moving to California, where she taught for California State University and several community colleges and worked as a research associate on several local, state, and nationwide studies. She earned her JD from Southwestern Law School in Los Angeles in 2013, then returned to her roots in North Carolina, where she teaches at East Carolina University and handles court-appointed cases for indigent juveniles. An avid storyteller in her classes, *The*

Dancer's Gift fits perfectly into her teaching style by applying sociological concepts to "real life."

Dr. David Knox, Professor of Sociology, East Carolina University, has used *The Dancer's Gift* in his marriage and family classes to engage students via the relationship between Samantha (a sociology major) and Marcel (the dancer). The fact that the novel deals with the divorce of Samantha's parents, Marcel and Samantha's interracial relationship, their LGBTQ friends, career differences, etc., is perfect for sociology courses beyond Introduction to Sociology.

CPSIA information can be obtained
at www.ICGtesting.com
Printed in the USA
FSHW011841230719
60322FS

9 781516 598045